MORE STORIES BY CANADIAN WOMEN

14.

MORE STORIES BY CANADIAN WOMEN

Edited by Rosemary Sullivan

Toronto
OXFORD UNIVERSITY PRESS
1987

CANADIAN CATALOGUING IN PUBLICATION DATA
Main entry under title:
More stories by Canadian women

ISBN 0-19-540636-2

1. Short stories, Canadian (English)—Women
authors.*   2. Canadian fiction (English)—Women
authors.*   3. Canadian fiction (English)—20th
century.*   I. Sullivan, Rosemary.

PS8321.S85 1987   C813′.01′089287   C87-094706-0
PR9197.33.W65M67 1987

Printed in Canada by
Webcom Limited

Contents

Introduction

When Oxford University Press invited me in 1983 to put together an anthology of stories by Canadian women, we had in mind a book that would provide a serious historical survey of writing by women in the genre. It was an exciting project—to see, for the first time between covers, writing by Canadian women that spanned a hundred years. There were discoveries: the wonderful wit and sophistication of Sara Jeannette Duncan's stories in *The Pool in the Desert* (out of print since 1903); the encounter with a whole body of women writers in the 1860s and 1870s who began as professional journalists and then turned to fiction. It became clear that there is a rich tradition of writing by women in this country that began more than a century ago. *Stories by Canadian Women* also included many contemporary women who have established powerful reputations in short fiction, from Ethel Wilson and Margaret Laurence to Mavis Gallant, Alice Munro, and Marie-Claire Blais (who wrote a new story specifically for the anthology).

But I was always uncomfortable that constraints of space led to a slighting of new writers. The test of a tradition is its cumulative energy. The historical narrative of achievement in the first volume was open-ended. Where was all this energy leading? Without making excessive claims for the anthologist, one can see that, from one perspective, editing an anthology involves an act of recognition, a retrospective ordering of the territory to see what has been done. But it should also be a reconnaissance mission, in which some effort is made to see what lies ahead, to locate where the tradition is leading. *More Stories by Canadian Women* is my effort to identify those writers who have surfaced in the last two decades, who have been, as it were, trained and turned loose by the generations of remarkable women writers who have preceded them.

Writing always includes a retrospective dialogue with one's predecessors. The great Latin American writer Victoria Ocampo, writing in 1936, lamented that women writers had neither the necessary training, the freedom, nor the tradition that would allow them to break out of their silence, and she wondered: ''What can be accomplished by genius alone without these three things; can it produce anything of value?'' Half a century later, women are no longer constrained by the temptations and ambiguous relief of silence. There are now too many examples of what can be done. In fact, it's better than that. Having broken through the silence of centuries, women can begin at the beginning by claiming subjects men have long exhausted; and they are driven by a sense of the historical imperative that must fuel great writing: the human story must no longer be seen as his/story; it must be rounded out to include the perspective of those who have always been dismissed as suspect witnesses.

I am pleased to say that *Stories by Canadian Women* was greeted with enthusiasm and, seemingly, relief. It found its place as a book people had been waiting for. However, one thing puzzled me. Some reviewers confessed to a restlessness with the idea of *segregating* women into separate books or bookshelves. They were uncomfortable with borders or distinctions. I admit puzzlement because I have never understood this discomfort. I remember when I first broached the idea of offering a course in women's writing at the University of Toronto. One of my colleagues reared in indignation, saying he wanted to give a course called 'Great Men Writers'. I pointed out that that course was already on the books; it was the only one we taught. But the reason for offering a collection of women's writing is not only that sometimes, if a voice is going to be heard, it needs its own stage. Nor is it simply to trace the tremendous strides women writers have taken in a changing social context. Rather, it is because I feel there is such a thing as a tradition of women's literature, correlative if not co-extensive with men's writing, paradoxically interdependent and independent. Virginia Woolf, whose importance as a critic is growing now that we can see her uniqueness against the andro-centric backdrop of Modernism, has eloquently reminded us: "Masterpieces are not single and solitary births; they are the outcome of many years of thinking in common, of thinking by the body of the people, so that the experience of the mass is behind the single voice." She continues in *A Room of One's Own*, "Jane Austen should have laid a wreath upon the grave of Fanny Burney." She was speaking specifically of women writers.

The importance of collecting women's writing is to me obvious. The great work of art is produced only when it has been silently prepared for many years. The writer needs to locate her tradition with confidence, to have the assurance of writing out of an imaginative continuum that stretches over generational barriers.

One of the exciting things to note among modern women writers is how a dialogue is now occurring over time. Jean Rhys can dig up Rochester from the pages of *Jane Eyre* and ask him questions that would never have occurred to Charlotte Brontë. Janette Turner Hospital can advise T.S. Eliot that she knows his hyacinth girl, and can confidently reframe the nascent sexuality sublimated in his vision. Women, and not only women writers, can identify the tradition that has slowly, painfully been telling their story.

Virginia Wolf tentatively posed issues for women writers that are still the focus of confusion. Is there a female syntax? an exclusively female experience? My own bias is that the politics of gender should have more to do with the pragmatic aspects of writing, whether women's writing gets published, whether they are free to choose any subject or any use of language, than with the imposition of ideological constraints on women's writing—as if there were such a thing as indigenously female writing. The women in this volume are confronting the archetypal human themes: love and hate, progeny, sexuality, the power politics of relationships, in a variety of genres from science fiction to realism and surrealist detective fiction. There are voices here that would have been in the first volume had there been space, and voices that have come to our attention since that time. Together they represent a variety of linguistic and regional backgrounds that is peculiarly Canadian. But what is most striking is their confidence. Clearly the presumptive assumption by male writers that they represented the tradition has been broken. Women writers are no longer merely colonials or eccentrics. They have assumed the writer's mission—always and everywhere to extend the limits of the real, to fracture and reinvent language so that it is capable of carrying our unique experience. They have taken up the only commitment we can demand from the writer: to chart a centrifugal course against the reductive forces that would have us live anonymous, acquiescent lives.

In editing this book I would like again to thank my editor, Richard Teleky. Often the work done by the general editor of a press goes unrecognized. At Oxford, Teleky has done a great deal for Canadian literature, in English and French, by men and women. He was the one who initiated this project, perceiving the need for a collection of short fiction that could provide a historical view of women's writing in Canada. And he saw the necessity for a complementary volume to acknowledge the explosion of short fiction by women that has occurred in the last two decades. For this I am grateful. There are still, of course, important writers, both well known and new, absent here. The ambition of *More Stories by Canadian Women* has been to provide only a hazy cartography of the new fictional territory inhabited by women. Many other editors—thankfully—will continue to fill in the details.

ACKNOWLEDGEMENTS

CLAUDETTE CHARBONNEAU-TISSOT. 'The Hot House' appeared originally as 'La Serre chaude'. English translation copyright Michael Bullock, reprinted by permission. MARIAN ENGEL. 'Anita's Dance' from *The Tattooed Woman* by Marian Engel. Copyright © The Estate of Marian Engel, 1985. Reprinted by permission of Penguin Books Canada Limited. MARGARET GIBSON. 'The Butterfly Ward' from *The Butterfly Ward* reprinted by permission of Oberon Press. PHYLLIS GOTLIEB. 'A Grain of Manhood' from *Son of the Morning and Other Stories* copyright © 1959, by Ziff-Davis Publishing Company. Reprinted by permission of the author and the author's agent, Virginia Kidd. KATHERINE GOVIER. 'Responding to Pain' from *Fables of Brunswick Avenue* by Katherine Govier. Copyright © Katherine Govier, 1985. Reprinted by permission of Penguin Books Canada Limited. ELISABETH HARVOR. 'Our Lady of All the Distances' from *Women and Children* reprinted by permission of Oberon Press. JANETTE TURNER HOSPITAL. 'You Gave Me Hyacinths' from *Dislocations* by Janette Turner Hospital. Used by permission of the Canadian Publishers, McClelland and Stewart Limited, Toronto. ISABEL HUGGAN. 'Into the Green Stillness' from *The Elizabeth Stories* reprinted by permission of Oberon Press. JANICE KULYK KEEFER. 'Mrs Putnam at the Planetarium' from *The Paris-Napoli Express* reprinted by permission of Oberon Press. BHARATI MUKHERJEE. 'The Lady from Lucknow' from *Darkness* by Bharati Mukherjee. Copyright © Bharati Mukherjee, 1985. Reprinted by permission of Penguin Books Canada Limited. MADELEINE OUELLETTE-MICHALSKA. 'The Cat' appeared originally as 'Le Chat'. Reprinted by permission of Madeleine Ouellette-Michalska and her agent Louise Myette. English translation copyright © Luise von Flotow-Evans, reprinted by permission. MONIQUE PROULX. 'Feint of Heart' from *Intimate Strangers: New Stories from Quebec* edited by Matt Cohen and Wayne Grady. Copyright © 1985 by Monique Proulx. English translation copyright © Sheila Fischman, 1986. Reprinted by permission of Penguin Books Canada Limited and Québec/Amérique. ROBYN SARAH. 'The Pond, Phase One' copyright © Robyn Sarah, reprinted by permission of the author. CAROL SHIELDS. 'Mrs Turner Cutting the Grass' from *Various Miracles* by Carol Shields. Reprinted by permission of Stoddart Publishing Co. Limited, Toronto, Canada. JANE URQUHART. 'Italian Postcard' from *Storm Glass*. Copyright © Jane Urquhart, 1987. Published by the Porcupine's Quill, Inc. Used by permission. HELEN WEINZWEIG. 'Causations' by Helen Weinzweig from *Small Wonders* edited by Robert Weaver. Copyright © 1982 by Canadian Broadcasting Corporation. Reprinted by permission. ADELE WISEMAN. 'On Wings of Tongue' reprinted by permission of the author.

Every effort has been made to determine copyright owners. In the case of any omissions, the publishers will be pleased to make suitable acknowledgements in future editions.

CLAUDETTE CHARBONNEAU-TISSOT

The Hot House

Everything was green in this room, the armchairs, the tables, the carpet, and all these troublesome plants which, if the session didn't soon come to an end, were going to assail us with their climbing stems that would twine themselves round our ankles, our wrists and compel us to continue this difficult lesson until death ensued.

Perhaps he had brought me to this hot-house precisely because he believed that here it would be easier to act upon me as he acted, in this same place, upon the fragile seedlings of the exotic and delicate plants he cultivated.

I was beginning to suffocate in this overheated room. I asked him if I could open one of the windows that looked out on the garden, which was even greener and even more encumbered with leaves and flowers than the room.

He replied that none of them opened. And he immersed himself once more in this game that I was no longer able to follow, being too preoccupied with this moisture-laden atmosphere that made the sweat break out in beads on my forehead.

Although I knew that nothing was supposed to interrupt the game, I suddenly rose and asked him if it was possible to move into another room or put off the end of this game until later.

He nodded agreement.

Without even knowing which of the two proposals he had agreed to, I made my way to the door. But I couldn't open it.

Perhaps it was the moisture on my hand that made it slip on the door-knob. I felt as if I was going to faint or even die, drowned in this room in which the air was systematically changing into water.

I looked round at the gaming table. They hadn't moved, as if they had turned to stone as soon as I rose. K was still holding a mah-jong piece in his left hand, and in his right a cup of the tea that stood simmering on the tiny hot-plate which only increased the unbearable heat of this room.

I told him I couldn't open the door.

He asked me if I wanted some more tea.

I began to lose patience and told him I wanted to leave.

As if he hadn't heard, he told me it was still very hot.

This time I shouted that I wanted to leave.

He put down his cup, crossed his hands and, as if I wasn't there, he concentrated on the pieces in front of him. His forehead was dry and his breathing normal, like that of the other players. Perhaps they belonged to some amphibian species, so that they had no way of understanding the state of suffocation I was in.

I went up to K and begged him, in a low voice, to open this door on whose knob my hand slipped because it was wet.

He discarded the green dragon.

I turned round and was about to go back to the door when I saw, at the bottom of my cup, among the leaves, a whitish deposit which was not sugar and which must have contributed to the strangeness of the taste of this exotic tea, the particular variety of which K told me he chose himself each time.

I showed him the cup and asked him what that was at the bottom.

'Tea,' he replied with a smile. 'Didn't you drink tea just now? Perhaps you would like a little more to warm up what's left at the bottom of your cup?'

I didn't answer and put the cup down on the table.

A continuous buzzing started in my head as if it had suddenly been invaded by a swarm of bees. Little by little, these insects began to dance before my eyes until my vision was completely blurred. I dropped onto the rattan sofa and plunged into green water full of pondweed and lotuses.

When I returned to the surface, I was somewhere else, stretched out on a rush mat in a room with no other vegetation than that on the wallpaper, where tiny birds rested their thin claws on the interlaced branches of jasmine.

I rose with difficulty and immediately made for the door, which opened easily. I found myself on one of the landings of a tenement house which not only had nothing oriental about it but was not even situated in the Chinese quarter.

Once in the street, I walked as far as the nearest intersection, where I hoped that the names of the streets would enable me to draw the co-ordinates that would give me my exact position. But the two street names were unknown to me and therefore no help in finding my way in this district which, while it resembled the districts familiar to me in its buildings, its traffic, its posters, and its pedestrians, seemed to me, through the mere fact that I didn't know where I was, almost as strange as if it had been a district of Shanghai.

I boarded the first bus that stopped at this intersection. The conductor told me I was going in the right direction to make the connection that would take me home.

I sat down on the first seat, near the door.

It was hot.

Little by little, my eyelids grew heavy and I couldn't fight sleep.

I don't know how long the journey took. I woke with a start when the conductor told me I had arrived.

I got up, still completely stupefied, and hurried out of the vehicle, which immediately closed its door and drove off.

The sun had gone a long way down.

I looked around me. There was no other bus line than the one I had just got off and I recognized nothing in this new place, not even the street names.

Perhaps the conductor hadn't understood my question. Or perhaps I hadn't even asked him my way home. My mind was still confused by all these insect larvae K had caused to hatch in me when he introduced the swarm of bees into it, and I didn't even try to clarify the situation.

I started to walk, at random, hoping that one day I would find a clue capable of transforming the alien universe in which I was walking with no other aim than to escape from this particular place, into a familiar universe in which every step would take me somewhere.

And this happened, when night had already fallen and I had been walking for a very long time. There it was, almost identical to everything I had been seeing for hours, since they were the same advertisements for cigarettes, soft drinks, and gasoline, similar groceries offering the same canned goods, the same tobacco, but this time there was that little difference in the arrangement of each of these things, in this or that detail, which meant that this was no longer just any old place but this particular place, which I recognized and could situate in relation to others.

From that point on, I was able to find my way back to my apartment.

When I got there, I immediately stretched out and went back to sleep, drawn by something heavy inside me which not merely relieved me of all worry and all curiosity regarding what had happened to me, but also dragged me down into sleep like a stone tied round my neck. I did not resist this force.

When I woke next day I had an ice-cold shower to rouse me from this torpor that I had been unable to shake off since the afternoon on which, as I had been doing for some time, I went to K for a mah-jong lesson.

After trying in vain to fill in on my own the gap of two days in my memory, I decided to go back to K to try and find the missing parts.

I picked up my handbag and was getting ready to go out when I suddenly saw, in its usual place, my mah-jong set, which had been on K's table at the moment I lost consciousness.

Someone else had brought it here, unless I had done so myself without realizing it, as I had perhaps also done with my car, which I found in its usual place.

I did sometimes confuse reality and dream and vice versa, imagining I had done something I had only dreamed and imagining I had dreamed something I had really done.

At times I even went so far as to create breaches in reality in order to insert in them a fragment of dream capable of breaking the monotony of everyday life.

It was a game.

But I had been doing this for such a long time that it had become almost automatic, so that now I sometimes allowed myself to be deceived by it.

Perhaps this had happened once again.

I pushed all these riddles to the back of my mind and headed for the town centre.

I parked the car quite a way from K's home, outside the Chinese quarter, and made the rest of the journey on foot so as to give myself time to prepare for this meeting, not knowing yet whether I ought to talk to K about my fainting fit, the memory blank that followed and my dangerous mania for confusing dream and reality, just for fun, or whether, on the contrary, I ought to act as if nothing had happened, as if I had simply come to continue the interrupted lesson, and wait for him to start talking about these things, or whether again I ought to assail him with questions the moment the door opened, asking him what he had put in the tea I had drunk, what had happened to me after that and how the mah-jong set and the car had got back to their places.

I reached K's house and chose the second solution, even if it meant reverting later to the first or the second.

I rang the bell.

K's servant opened the door. He wore the enigmatic smile that never left him, almost as if it was a theatrical mask glued to his skin, a mask, incidentally, of which there must have been several replicas, since even K sometimes used to wear it, without my ever being able to determine why he was wearing it on that particular occasion, because he was just as likely to adopt this smile when he said hello to me as when he reproached me with a bad move in the game or questioned me about my travels or my journalistic activities.

The servant asked me to wait in a tiny parlour I had never been in before, a kind of miniature museum in which were gathered bronze chimeras, tea bowls of fine porcelain, jade phoenixes, ink and wash drawings of mountain landscapes and pagodas. Some of the items seemed to be very old.

I didn't hear him coming in his embroidered silk slippers of very faded pink. He had that smile which narrowed his eyes more than usual and suddenly it seemed to me that all this too was part of a dream, unless K was quite simply a wax figure come to take his place in this collection of fossils.

As if nothing had happened, he took me into the green room where, although it was neither the day nor the time, the two other players were sitting (perhaps they were only robots whom K shut up in a cupboard and only took out when he needed someone to play with) and the tea was already on the hot-plate.

The two old men rose and greeted me together, bowing slowly, very low.

K invited me to sit down and served me a cup of that tea which, this time, I had decided not to drink, not wanting to be caught twice in the same trap and not wanting to miss anything of what was about to happen. I put the cup down on the table, close to the hot-plate, while he filled their cups and then his own, nodding his head slowly up and down and retaining that smile which now seemed to me slightly mocking, although to tell the truth I couldn't spot any detail that differentiated it significantly from his usual smile.

After putting down the teapot and taking a sip of tea, K lifted the lid of the mah-jong set that I had put on the table, opened the drawers one by one and began to take out the tiles, the underside of which was made of bamboo and the upper part of ivory and on which were painted, according to the function of each piece, a figure, a character, or a number.

Each of his gestures seemed to form part of an unfailing ritual, so that it appeared to me now completely senseless to imagine that, three days ago, something could have interrupted the sequence of his gestures, impossible to believe that K would have allowed anything to disturb the established procedure of the scene which he reproduced faithfully every time I came for a session of instruction.

For a long time now I had ceased to be able to distinguish K from the archetypal image I had of the oriental master and I had often imagined that, when the lesson was over, K changed into bronze and remained like that until my return, unless that other old man whom I had once met as I was leaving the house, and who looked so much like K that you would think he was cast in the same mould, as did the other two old men by the way, unless this other old man came to take my place in the game and all four went on playing until I came back, without ever getting hungry or tired, content to play and drink this ambrosia tasting of tea that seemed never to run dry at the bottom of the tea-pot.

The sun came in through the windows and although it was neither cool nor dry I did not feel I was suffocating and there were no beads of sweat on my forehead.

We played for a long time and K made no allusion to the previous lesson and I did not dare refer to it, almost convinced, now, that I had dreamed it all and had mistaken my dream for reality.

When K replaced the bamboo and ivory tiles in the box, he told me he had to go away for a while and would not be able to see me. But a man would get in touch with me and would continue the mah-jong sessions with me, so that I shouldn't lose the skill I had acquired with so much hard work.

The servant was already there. K and his look-alikes rose and bowed deeply to me. The servant took the set from the table and put it in my hands.

And I found myself outside, at the door of the house, knowing almost nothing more than a few hours earlier, when I stood in front of this door in the same way I was standing now, with the mah-jong set under my arm, so that, for a moment, I had the impression that I hadn't yet entered K's house today, and I imagined I was still free to choose between the three solutions: whether to talk about my fainting, about nothing at all or about being kidnapped. To convince myself that this was only an illusion, a trick of my mind, I knocked at K's door again. A few moments later K's servant opened it and, before I had time to say a word, told me that K had had to go away for a while and that he wouldn't be able to see me.

But I knew that K hadn't had time to leave and certainly couldn't have gone out without my noticing, since I hadn't left his doorstep, unless he had gone out through the back door, which opened onto an alley filled with garbage, which would have been surprising, so that either he must be inside and didn't want to see me (perhaps he had already changed into bronze) or, but I hesitated to believe this, this was the first and not the second time I had knocked at his door that day.

I couldn't bring myself to turn around and go home, so I told K's servant that I thought I had left a mah-jong piece behind when I was there just now, the green dragon to be exact.

The mask came off his face for the first time, for the fraction of a second. He remained silent for a moment, then he said he would go and see if the piece was still lying on the table.

He went off and I immediately took a few steps in order to glance into the miniature museum, where most of the rare objects seemed to have been replaced by plastic replicas on whose bases, if I had not been afraid of the servant's return, I felt sure I should have found labels saying MADE IN JAPAN.

I barely had time to go back to the door when he reappeared. Automatically, I looked at his feet. I imagined it was embroidered silk slippers that made them as silent as K's, but instead of slippers I saw under the fabric covering his legs the thick crepe soles of shoes in a current style.

He told me he hadn't found the missing piece.

He took the mah-jong set from my hands, put it on the table, lifted the wooden lid and opened one of the drawers. There was the green dragon, between the red one and the white.

He said perhaps it was another piece that was missing.

He immediately opened all the drawers.

No piece was missing.

I stammered excuses.

He had recovered his mask. He returned the set to me and I went out, embarrassed.

A strange sensation came over me and my mind was filled with a chaotic mingling of the atmosphere of Malraux's books and images of the Blue Lotus opium dens.

To this was added the picture of K, when he was still in England, sitting at a mah-jong table where the stake consisted of this house whose threshold I had just left.

I tried to imagine this other scene, unable to remember whether it also formed part of what L, before introducing me to K, had told me about him, or whether it too was something I had made up. So I tried to imagine the scene, which must have taken place in England, or perhaps in China, in which the two Chinese who always made up the party during my practical mah-jong lessons, when they were completely ruined, had become the stake in a game of mah-jong which K had won.

And I had often wondered, as I entered that room in K's house in which I had taken my first mah-jong lessons, where the only furniture was four gaming-tables, chairs and an immense glass-fronted cupboard containing a mah-jong collection, whether all these sets had not been acquired in the same manner, that is to say when the opponent, ruined, had nothing else to wager but his mah-jong set and his soul.

Suddenly, I felt I might perhaps have gone too far in my imaginings. I had lost all notion of the boundary between reality and dream and I no longer knew in which of these universes I was now swimming.

So I decided to stop imagining scenes and set about verifying certain facts capable of clarifying my situation.

I drove towards the unfamiliar district in which I had woken up the previous evening completely disoriented.

But I was no longer too sure whether I hoped to find those unknown streets and that tenement house on the second floor of which there was a room whose only furniture was the rush mat on which I had woken up; I was no longer sure whether I hoped to find those elements which would prove that something had really happened, or whether, on the contrary, I hoped not to find any trace of this room and of that nightmare walk, which on the one hand would prove that I had not been the victim of a kidnapping but which, on the other, would prove that I was the victim of a mental disorder which was perhaps worse than everything that might really have happened to me during those two missing days.

Suddenly, as I turned a corner, it seemed to me that I had passed this spot, although there was no precise sign to justify this impression, although I could find no detail, not even the name of the street, because even though I remembered having looked at several of the street names as I walked along, I couldn't recall any of them, although I couldn't identify a single detail that would have enabled me to find my way in this maze, through which I was now certain that I had walked the previous evening.

I set off down this street, but I soon felt that I was lost again and I decided to return to the exact spot that had aroused vague memories in me.

From this starting-point, I decided to pursue my search on foot.

And I started walking, guided solely by this impression.

When I moved into another street, the vague impression that I had been here before left me; I turned around and tried walking in a different direction, until this impression returned.

After more than an hour of this trial and error I felt exhausted and went into a Greek restaurant.

I hadn't even had time to order anything when I saw, through the greasy window of the restaurant, the tenement house I had been looking for all this time.

I immediately got up and rushed into the street, toward this house in front of which I had stopped as though by instinct, as if it had been prearranged that I should reach the requisite degree of exhaustion after walking the distance that brought me here.

I went into the tenement house, climbed to the second floor and found the door behind which I knew there was a room with walls whose paper had a pattern calculated to give anyone who was coming round from the effects of a drug stretched out in the middle of a room and looking through half-closed eyes, the impression that he had turned into a statue in a Japanese garden, whereas in reality there was neither cactus, nor shell, nor plaster pagoda with upturned roof on this wallpaper invaded by dry branches that would certainly break if you leaned on them or catch fire if you dropped a spark from a cigarette on them.

I turned the doorknob, but without result. My hand was so damp that it slipped on the metal sphere. I tried again, in vain.

Suddenly there were noises and laughter on the other side of the door.

I could have gone and hid under the stairs and waited until one of those inside decided to come out.

But that might have taken a long time.

So I decided to knock without further hesitation.

The door opened almost at once to reveal a woman outlined against a wall covered with a metallic paper bearing a geometrical pattern, strips of which still lay around the floor among paint pots, brushes, and rolls of adhesive paper.

For the second time, perhaps the third, the woman asked me what I wanted.

I replied that I thought I had been to this apartment the day before and had left behind a piece from a game.

She turned to the man who was with her and asked him if he had seen what I was looking for.

He asked me to describe the piece and I described the green dragon, although I knew perfectly well it was in its place in the wooden mah-jong box, which was in the car.

As I looked with them I told them I preferred this modern wallpaper to the oriental wallpaper that had covered the walls the day before.

I expected them to talk about this wallpaper or even to deny that the wallpaper underneath had an oriental pattern. Then I would have had no means of checking that they were wrong except to pull off a piece of the new wallpaper, which they must have taken a great deal of trouble putting on in order to make sure that each line of the pattern on one edge met the same line on the other edge.

But instead of talking about the wallpaper the woman asked me if I knew the people who had lived in this apartment before them.

This question took me by surprise and I answered no.

At this they stopped and looked at me in astonishment.

The man asked me what I was doing in this apartment the day before, which by the way has been empty for several days, if I didn't know the previous owners.

I said someone had made an appointment to meet me here to return the game, which belonged to me and from which I had discovered later that a piece was missing.

They had become suspicious and I preferred to apologize and leave.

I left this house, which did indeed exist; and even if I hadn't got to see it, I knew that in one of the rooms of this house there really was, under a metallic wallpaper whose paste was not yet dry, another wallpaper covered with exotic vegetation that would soon wither and whose birds would shortly die from lack of air, water, and light.

I took the first taxi that came by and had it drive me to the place where I had left the car.

But the car wouldn't start. It was almost night already and I hadn't eaten anything yet and was exhausted. I took an amphetamine, as I did almost every morning when it looked like being a bad day, when the coffee had a bad taste, the last scraping of rouge caked on my cheek, the typewriter refused to print a letter. Then I walked to the nearest garage, where they towed in the car, which wouldn't be ready till the next day.

I took another taxi and went home.

The door to the apartment was ajar.

I pushed it slowly, switched on the light and looked around cautiously before entering.

There was no one there, but someone had been there and had rummaged through the apartment, though without taking anything.

I phoned L and asked him to come over.

As soon as he arrived I told him these fragments of story which I was unable to link together.

I had the feeling now that during the two days I couldn't remember someone had attached an invisible chain to my ankle, perhaps even it was a tendril of one of those climbing plants that were invading the green room in which I had lost consciousness, so that I now felt tied tight to this extraordinary story of which, in fact, I knew almost nothing.

As if it were a puzzle in which he had not merely to place but also to find the scattered pieces, L questioned me about my meetings with K, and the way I had spent my time during the last few days, not neglecting any area of my life and hoping that one of my replies would yield a clue, a trail. But we got very little out of them.

Then he made some phone calls, one of which disclosed that K had recently lost several buildings at mah-jong, among them his house in Chinatown.

This was one more piece of the puzzle, but we didn't know what to do with it or where to place it.

We put the whole thing off until tomorrow.

L stayed with me that night.

Suddenly a bell rang and I wondered where it came from, since there was no burglar alarm, no telephone, not even a door in the vast field in which I was breathlessly running among stalks of maize.

L shook me violently and dragged me out of this dream, from which I emerged as out of breath as if I had really been running, which supported the theory I had often defended in arguments with L, according to which dreams were a form of metempsychosis, of passing over into a world just as real and physical as the one in which we were at present.

L said it would be better if I were the one to answer the telephone.

L put his ear close to mine. I lifted the receiver and gave my name to the man at the other end, whose own name I couldn't catch, his voice was so nasal and his accent so strong. I had to ask him to repeat what he had said several times before I understood that it was the man K had told me about, who was to continue my mah-jong lessons. I was about to make some excuse, when he told me the lessons would continue to be in K's house and that we could have our first meeting that same day.

I thought at first I hadn't heard right, but I was too embarrassed to ask him to repeat it a third time and L nodded his head to tell me to accept.

I answered that I would go.

I hung up.

Something wasn't clear and I was frightened of going back to that house.

L said that he would go with me and keep an eye on me, from a distance.

It was only when I was on the doorstep of K's former house and had rung the bell that I realized I didn't have my mah-jong set with me. I had left it in the car, in the garage. The man who had phoned me certainly had one of his own, or he would choose one from the glass-fronted cupboard, unless K had taken them all with him. In fact this detail didn't matter much, because I had come here not so much to play as to see the man who had made the appointment and try to cast some light on the mystery of the last few days.

A Chinese in western dress opened the door a crack. He wasn't smiling and I was suddenly sure I had misunderstood the telephone message, so that it wasn't the man who had called me a few hours earlier who was in the house, but the one who had beaten K at mah-jong and with whom I had nothing to do.

However, before I could turn around and start running, as in my early morning dream, he asked me my name and as soon as I had given it he put on the same mask as K's servant, opened the door wide and said I was expected.

It seemed to me now that if I crossed this threshold and let the Chinese close the heavy red door behind me, I should never be able to turn back again and would enter not the time machine, but the space machine, so that I would soon be catapulted into a strange world where I should be the only one with white skin and eyes that were not slanting and where everyone would spend his time playing this game of which I should soon become the principal stake.

I turned my head slightly and looked to see if L was at his post behind the window of the restaurant, where I saw Chinese lanterns made of crystal paper covered with hieroglyphs and edged with a long red fringe that swayed in the puff of air from the fans. L wasn't there.

I turned towards the Chinese, who was waiting for me to go in, but without bowing like K's servant, who used to double up as I passed till his torso was almost at right angles to his legs. It was too late to turn back and I went in. The Chinese led me to the far end of the house. At each step his stiff shoes creaked. He showed me into the green room and asked me to wait a few seconds.

The arrangement of the room was unchanged and the gaming table, the green rattan sofa, the hot-plate and the tea bowls were still there; but there was something different in the air, which was no longer saturated with moisture and in which there floated a vague odour of decomposition. I soon noticed that the troublesome entangled plants were beginning to wither, although I hadn't noticed anything of the sort the previous day or the day before that.

I heard a creaking sound and I knew that the Chinese had come back. He was accompanied by another Chinese, quite young and dressed like him in western clothes though rather more elegantly.

He greeted me with a nod and introduced himself. He said a few words about K, who had had to go away for a while on business and who had entrusted him with the task of continuing my lessons in Chinese dominoes.

We were about to sit down, when he pointed out to me that I hadn't brought my mah-jong set.

I was on the point of replying that I had left it in my car, but then I would have had to explain that my car had broken down, that it was at the garage, which might have taken a long time and would certainly not have been of the slightest interest to this man. So I simply answered that I had left it at home.

He signed with his hand to the other Chinese and the latter went out.

Then he crossed his hands on the little table and remained silent.

His eyes were resting on me and soon I didn't know how to look.

Without thinking, I asked him if he had been here long.

I immediately realized how clumsy and even dangerous my question had been, because now that he had told me that K would be away from this house for some time, whereas I knew very well that he had lost it gambling (but perhaps L's information was wrong, or perhaps K had meanwhile won the house back), I suspected this man of being an imposter, although I couldn't think why he should have taken the trouble to lure me here or what he hoped to gain by it.

Before S had replied to my question, the servant came in with a black mah-jong box, which he must have polished before bringing it, because it was so shiny that otherwise it would have shown fingerprints.

After putting the box down on the table, he sat down on my right. Then the fourth player arrived and without being introduced or any exchange of words sat down in his turn.

S began to take the pieces from their tiny drawers.

Suddenly, when I was no longer expecting an answer, S said that he had been here for some years and that he was K's son.

Then I tried to imagine K copulating in his encumbering garments and his embroidered silk slippers that were like a second skin to him. I couldn't. Perhaps he had had recourse to artificial insemination.

We started to play.

From time to time, S asked me a question about the game in progress or about the way K had taught me to play. Then he asked me whether K sometimes, when the game was over, invited me to have a meal with him or took me into the garden.

He must have noticed my astonishment at these questions, because he told me his father hadn't said much to him about what he was supposed to do apart from getting me to play mah-jong.

When I told him that my meetings with K had always been limited to playing mah-jong and that as soon as the game was over I had always left, he seemed surprised. Then, with a knowing smile, he said that of course it would have been surprising if a woman like me had taken any other interest in the company of a man as old as his father apart from an educational one.

We had continued to play, but I saw that they were beginning to get impatient. Without moving their heads, they sometimes cast strange glances at each other. This, together with the ambiguous nature of the preceding remarks, gradually made me feel uneasy. Beads of sweat began to form on my forehead (although, this time, there was no tea on the switched-off hot-plate) and before I was overcome by a feeling of suffocation, I decided, although it was sacrilege to interrupt the game and in spite of their mute disapproval, to go and wash in cold water.

I rose and left the room, followed by their heavy looks.

As I passed the room which K had dedicated to mah-jong I couldn't help lightly pushing the door, which was ajar. The mah-jong boxes were no longer in the huge glass-fronted cupboard but scattered all over the floor and on the gaming-tables, where the bamboo part had been detached from the ivory part of each piece with the aid of hammers and chisels, which were still lying there.

I heard the creak of shoes, far away, and I hurried to the bath-room, where I locked myself in.

I remained for a few seconds leaning against the door, holding my breath.

The creak of shoes drew near, stopped, then moved away.

Then I splashed my face.

The towel was on the floor.

I dried my hands and went out.

As I passed the mah-jong room I noticed that the door had been shut.

When I entered the hot-house room the three men were by the window, talking in low voices in their language. I no longer felt like going on with the game and hoped they would say as much. But they came back to the table and we went on playing.

At a certain moment I wanted to take a tissue from my handbag and I noticed that it had been closed with the press button, which I never used.

When the game was finished, S offered to see me home.

I was on the point of saying that L was waiting for me (unless he had got tired of waiting or had imagined that I had been swallowed up forever once I had crossed the threshold of this house), but I changed my mind and told him I had my car and was going to do some shopping before going home. When I was on the point of leaving, he told me (but it was more of an order than an invitation) to come back next day, at the same time, and that I had played very badly today and still had a lot to learn.

He didn't wait for my answer and shut the door.

I immediately looked for L behind the window of the Chinese restaurant where he had said he would wait for me.

He wasn't there.

So I walked in the direction of the car in which, feeling tired, he had perhaps sought refuge from the smell of the food that was being cooked around here.

The door wasn't locked. I sat down on the set and waited for him, barely a few seconds. He had stopped under an arcade to look, from a distance, at a group of slit-eyed men playing mahjong in a courtyard.

We left that district and went for dinner in a quiet spot where we talked about my visit to K and the events of the last few days.

When we came out, a few hours later, the car was no longer where we had left it. We looked for it and, as we couldn't find it, L called up the police, who found it three-quarters of an hour later in a back street a few blocks away. The trunk and the glove compartment had been turned upside down and the seats ripped open.

The police made out a report asserting theft and vandalism, ignoring the points that did not agree with such a conclusion.

I would have liked to tell them that something else was involved, that we were mixed up in some strange business, that my apartment had been ransacked, but L lowered his eyes and gave me an imperceptible sign not to do so.

When it was all finished, we went to L's place.

It was only after I had been over the facts several times that I remembered telling S, who wanted to take me home, that I had my car. So it probably wasn't L's car they had wanted to search but mine.

I wanted to go to the garage where I had left it and where they must certainly have finished the repairs, which in any case was of no importance, since what I wanted at the moment was not to start the car up but to open up with a knife its seats covered in a common brocade, to search through the trunk and the glove compartment to see if they didn't contain something unusual.

L said that the people who were looking for this thing, to which we couldn't yet give a name, were probably waiting for this action on my part which would lead them to the object they were after, assuming that this object really was in my car. He was probably right.

He suggested that I should go back to my apartment, while he went to the garage and searched the car.

I put the key in the lock and opened the door. The apartment had been ransacked once more. I immediately telephoned L, but he had already left. I was going to hang up when I heard the creaking of footsteps behind me.

The man with the noisy shoes was there and so was S, who took the receiver, listened and then, hearing nothing but the dialling tone, hung up.

He asked me where I had put what K had entrusted to me.

I said K hadn't entrusted anything to me.

He remained silent for a moment then, changing his mask and the subject, he said they happened to be passing and had come to play a game of mah-jong.

Then he asked me where my set was.

Immediately, in a flash, I saw the mah-jong set on the front seat of the car. I had forgotten all about it when I made a mental inventory of what was in the car.

S repeated his question, this time firmly.

I stammered that it must be here, in the kitchen or perhaps in the bedroom.

Without having to check my statement, since they had already searched the apartment, he told me that before I arrived they had wanted to play but hadn't found the set.

Without thinking, I said that anyway the game was usually played by four.

He started laughing, but at the same time his hand came down like a sabre on my left arm.

I found myself on the floor, my head buzzing. The numbness of the shock wore off almost at once and was replaced by pain.

Assuming a falsely contrite air, S apologized and bent down to help me up, but instead of taking me by my undamaged arm he grasped my bruised arm, I cried out, but he didn't let go until I was standing up.

He asked me again where the mah-jong set was.

This time I saw no reason to persist in defending this set which, in reality, didn't have as much value for me as it seemed to have for them.

I told them where it was.

They left immediately and at this moment, if it hadn't been for the pain in my arm, I could have believed the whole thing had been merely a figment of my imagination.

The telephone rang and when I heard L's voice I suddenly realized that I had sent S and the other Chinese to the garage while L might still have been there.

L said he hadn't found anything unusual in the car but that he had brought back everything he could, including the mah-jong set.

I realized that as soon as they saw that the car had already been searched and that the mah-jong set was no longer there they were bound to come back. I told L, without giving him any explanations, to wrap up the mah-jong set and go to our usual meeting place, where I would join him as soon as I could.

I rang off at once, took my handbag and quickly opened the door behind which, unknown to me, the Chinese with the squeaky shoes was acting the watch-dog.

Without his having any need to take out a firearm, a knife or a sabre, the mere persuasion of the look that filtered out from beneath his folded lids made me back away into the apartment without daring to utter a cry or even a word of protestation.

He told me to sit down and I knew without any explanations from him that we were waiting for S, who was not long in returning, his eyes even narrower than usual in his anger.

The watch-dog spoke a few monosyllables to S, whose face seemed immediately to relax.

S turned to the third player and spoke a few words to him in his singsong voice. The third player immediately left the apartment.

S sat down in the green velvet easy chair and we stayed like that, waiting, though I didn't know what for. S now had his disquieting smile.

Suddenly, after more than ten minutes of silence and immobility, the phone rang.

The sweat began to run down my forehead as S rose and went to the telephone.

He lifted the receiver and after a few seconds of silence he uttered two or three sounds in his language and slammed it down again.

Again anger rendered his eyes almost invisible under his lowered lids. He came up to me and asked me where L was.

His question took me by surprise and I remained open-mouthed.

Then he said the Chinese watch-dog was at L's apartment and L wasn't there.

I concluded that the watch-dog hadn't heard the meeting place.

For the second time, S asked me where L was.

I couldn't take my eyes off his hand and I was afraid it would leap out and smash down on me again.

But I answered that I didn't know where L was.

S began to sway his head from left to right and from right to left, clicking his tongue in his mouth.

I closed my eyes and told myself it was time to wake up, to return to reality, to come out from this dream in which I was no longer taking any pleasure.

Suddenly there was an explosion inside me; I staggered and fell to the floor.

I opened my eyes and saw S's hand returning to his thigh.

I had made a mistake. The thing was not to return to reality but to get away from it before it was too late.

In spite of the violent pain in my arms, I closed my eyes and tried to go backwards in time, to flee this place, these beings, to get out of my body, to leave nothing there but an empty carcass, an abandoned hulk.

But S's hand was sufficiently long and hard to seek me out in this tunnel into which I was slipping with difficulty.

The hand leapt into action and reached me on the floor.

This time, the target was my face and I felt pieces of broken teeth inside my mouth.

Everything was going too fast now and I couldn't even manage to close my eyes, I was so afraid that S's hand would leap out again.

The telephone began to ring.

S said it must be L.

I wanted to get up and rush to that telephone, even though I wouldn't have known whether I ought to shout to L to come to my aid or, on the contrary, to run away and escape from these diabolical beings.

But I was incapable of getting up and S, who had gone over to the phone, was pressing the receiver as though better to feel the vibrations of the bell.

After a certain time, S lifted the receiver but without putting it to his ear.

From where I lay, I could hear L's voice over the phone.

Suddenly, realizing that they had forgotten to gag me, I began to shout L's name.

After a few seconds, S rang off.

I knew he was going to come over and start hitting me again, but his face was relaxed and he told me I had done exactly what he expected of me and that now L was bound to come.

Aided by the watch-dog, S stretched me out on the velvet chesterfield at the far end of the room facing the door.

S switched off a few lights while the watch-dog went to the kitchen and made tea.

When he came back, S took the cup in his hands and brought it to my mouth, in which I scarcely felt the scalding of this liquid as it flowed down my throat mingled with blood.

I would have liked to push the cup away, but I couldn't raise my arms or move my head from the cushion where S had placed it.

Little by little I felt the sweat return to my skin and I felt as though the liquid was running into my lungs instead of into my oesophagus. I began to cough painfully as if I were drowning in glaucous water full of pondweed and lotuses, into which I was gradually sinking but through which I nevertheless continued to see the watch-dog and S, who moved away from me, in slow-motion, then disappeared.

I felt no more pain now and I had the impression that I had really become an abandoned hulk. Perhaps I had succeeded in re-entering my dream, perhaps now I was safe.

I remained like this, fixed in this sweet eternity where there was nothing to do but stay stretched out, in pieces, on this green velvet chesterfield bathed in the soft light from the tortoise-shell lamp.

Dull thuds at the door slipped into this eternity without breaking its continuity. Then I saw the door slowly open to reveal L, who was carrying under his arm a packet wrapped in brown paper.

When he saw me he stopped moving and I thought that he too was going to be fixed in this position forever.

But he soon started running slowly towards me, as in an underwater ballet; then he bent over me as S appeared behind him, raised his hand and struck L on the nape of the neck, so that he slowly collapsed on top of me and then slid down onto the floor.

S and the watch-dog took the brown parcel and ripped the paper from the mah-jong set that I had bought some time ago at an auction, not knowing that it contained a magnetic charm capable of attracting these yellow men, who switched on all the lights before taking out each of the pieces.

They spread out a large sheet of copying paper on which they put the pieces one by one before splitting them open like oysters, separating the bamboo part from the ivory part. From each piece came a white, crystalline powder which they at once slipped carefully into an envelope of the same paper.

Only the green dragon contained no powder. S took from it a tiny scroll of thin paper on which were written characters as incomprehensible as the monosyllables they exchanged.

When they had finished collecting the powder from the pieces, they sealed the envelope containing the powder and the other envelope in which they had put the tiles as they split them open. S put the tiny scroll in a small metal cylinder, which he slipped into the inside pocket of his jacket. Then they rose and left.

L and I were left alone, at the bottom of that warm, transparent water from which L emerged first but in which I remained for a long time after him, as in a dream, away from pain.

I was taken to hospital, where they made me pass quickly from the green, fluid, luminous water to a black, deep water into which I sank heavily.

I was rising to the surface but still only half-way up when I had the feeling I was being mummified and wrapped in bandages. Soon I felt that I was a prisoner in a sarcophagus which I should never get out of.

When I came completely to the surface, my two arms were covered in plaster and a metal rod protruded from one of them.

A taut strip of webbing held my chin down so that I had to keep my mouth open.

The room was empty and I couldn't reach the bell that had been pinned to my bedcovers, but a little too high up.

I tried to call, but the strip of webbing holding down my jaw prevented me from forming any words. I uttered a few whimpering sounds, but without result.

There was nothing I could do but wait for someone to come.

But when the door finally opened, I regretted having hoped for this moment.

It was a slant-eyed man, in western dress, whose face seemed familiar even though I didn't recognize him. It was only as I saw him coming slowly towards me in his crepe-soled shoes that I recognized K's servant.

When he reached the bed, he bowed double in greeting, then straightened up.

Then he placed K's personal mah-jong set on the bed, or an exact replica, a very beautiful set of purplish-blue wood like rosewood, on which were painted tiny flowers in whose corollas miniscule birds seemed to be sleeping, unless they were dead, like those greedy bumble-bees that gorge themselves on pollen till they can't fly and then die on the ground.

The servant said that K was sending me this present because of the trouble he had caused me.

He said goodbye and left, without another word.

I looked with terror at this rosewood box full of dead birds, as if it were a deadly poison. I started to scream and tried to huddle up as close as possible to the head of the bed.

A nurse came in and, seeing me in this agitated state, at once called for help.

She took the box inside which, in each little drawer, there were no doubt hollow bamboo and ivory tiles inside which there were perhaps other little dead birds; she took the box and put it down on the bedside table.

She didn't seem to be contaminated by the contact as I had been by contact with the other set I had bought at the auction. But perhaps that was a long-term process, as it had actually been with me.

Suddenly the idea of breaking the spell by giving the mah-jong set to this stranger occurred to me and I tried to make her understand that she could take the box, that I was giving it to her, that I was making her a present of it.

But she couldn't make head or tail of my inarticulate groans and to put an end to my agitation she took a syringe from the little tray she had been brought. I tried to push it away because I didn't want to plunge again into glaucous water full of pondweed and dead fish.

But it was a wasted effort. The air began to grow heavy and the room was soon changed into a hot-house and then into an aquarium.

When I was completely submerged, they went out and left me alone again.

But while I was under water, S's men came in and carried me far away from the universe that was familiar to me.

And I sometimes wonder if they haven't shut me up alive in one of the bamboo and ivory pieces of a gigantic mah-jong, with which some yellow gods are playing as they slowly sip a tea-flavoured ambrosia.

And when I hear someone crying out at night, I wonder if it isn't L who has been shut up in the next piece.

Translated by Michael Bullock

MARIAN ENGEL

Anita's Dance

It was a morning fit to convert any pessimist, and a Sunday to boot. Anita spent part of it in the garden virtuously weeding; then she poured enough coffee to float an army into her special mug and brought it out into the garden. Instead of reading, she sat stretching her neck to the sun and thinking how lucky she was; nothing to do but please herself all day. From time to time friends lectured her about being selfish and set in her ways, an old maid. And it was true she was sometimes lonely. She had, however, no reason to feel sorry for herself when she compared her life to theirs. She had a house, a garden, a car, a piano. A good job. A greedy, bad-tempered cat. Two eyes, a nose, and ten fingers, all in good working order. What did she have to feel sorry about? And was happiness selfish?

She mused over her library book. She had never really wanted to get married, except for a brief and embarrassing episode when she was at university. A boy she was very fond of had wanted her to drop her scholarship, marry him and put him through law school. Her fondness had ceased abruptly when he argued that, being male, he had more right to an education than she had. Winning the argument had hurt a lot.

Those days were over, she thought, and if she was wrong, she had no daughter to tell her so in exemplary form. I have my house, she thought, my garden with delphiniums and daisies and poppies. My piano, on which I have taught myself to play the simplest and saddest waltzes of Chopin. I have company in the form of a bad-tempered cat. What is more, I have a date with Clive this afternoon. I feel good with Clive. The something that is between us is nothing; there is no self-consciousness. We swim towards each other as if the water were our element. All's right with the world.

She had wanted to study literature but on practical grounds had chosen economics instead. She still, however, attempted to keep up with good books and now she was reading a novel by a man in England called Berger, who was supposed to be both good and avant garde. She opened it now, and put on her sun-glasses.

It was good: his main characters were small souls, which showed a sort of left-wing point of view, but she liked the way he got into both their heads at once and managed to stay there, so she could feel both the room they were in and the beating of their rather constricted hearts.

It took place in a small employment agency; both characters, the owner and his clerk, were weighing large changes in their private lives while appearing to deal with clients. The owner, a fiftyish man who had always lived with his sister, was considering independence: marriage even.

She looked up and smiled at the sun. That was funny. She read on.

A woman came into the agency to look for a housekeeping job. A largish, comfortable, middle-aged woman. The proprietor had an instant vision of the comfort she could provide for him: a well-kept house—not too well-kept, Canadian and mowed in the lawn departments, just a sort of comfy English house, fish and chips for tea, a kettle on the hob.

'I could live with that,' Anita said to herself. 'What I couldn't live with, not ever, is a set-up like this plus a job, plus three children and entertaining for a junior executive now portly and senior. No wonder I'm the way I am.'

She frowned at the book, closed it, and put it down. It had revealed to her a seam of domesticity she had been avoiding recognizing: it was cosy, and it was basically English working class, and basically (except for a mob of children) what she had come from.

She had never wanted her mother's life, one of flying elbows and fits of bad temper and aspirations that were a muddle of impulses. Her mother had never seemed to be able to think anything through, she was always anaemic from childbearing and exhausted from scrubbing; crying out 'You girls . . .' Get this, fetch that, turn off the soup, scrub the sink, do the dishes, iron that. When she was an old woman they had bought her an automatic washing machine with a window in the door and found her sitting on the basement steps watching it like television. 'I was

remembering the day Lanie got her hair caught in the wringer,'
she said.

Anita shuddered: that dream of cosy domesticity was a male
dream; she'd been living in a man's world too long. The real thing
she'd lived through and it was what had made her so happy to
get a scholarship to university. Never mind that she'd had to
char and work in a grocery store to put herself through.

She stretched lazily. The cat was scowling at her through the
kitchen window; he didn't like her to be happy. Too bad for him.
She was going to enjoy this day. Clive and she weren't meeting
until two and she didn't even have to change.

She heard scuffling footsteps on the gravel, the footsteps of her
brother Jack. 'Oh damn,' she thought. 'He's found me.'

'Hi Nita, how's tricks?'

'Where did you come from, Jack?'

He was big and he was stupid, something of a bad dream: the
one who hadn't succeeded. 'Oh well, you know,' he said, plunking
himself down on the chaise longue so it clicked and shivered. 'I
was wondering if you had any jobs for me, like.'

'Broke again, eh? Want some coffee?'

'Sure.'

She slammed the kitchen door as she went in. The cat gave her
a satisfied look, pleased that her moment of glory was over. She
poured Jack a coffee, creamed and sugared it, and stumbled as
she went out, staining her white summer pants. 'Here,' she thrust
it at him.

He sat up like a patient in bed and began not so much to drink
as to inhale it. He looked badly hung over. 'What have you been
doing lately?' she asked.

'I been doing . . . well, littla this, littla that. Delivering leaflets.
You know.'

She knew. He was no good, Jack, and that was that.

'I keep up with the work around here myself,' she said. 'I don't
really have anything for you to do.'

'There must be something, the way you lie around reading all
the time.'

She refused to rise to the bait.

'Lanie's poorly,' he said. 'I was there yesterday.'

He must be making the rounds again, she thought, borrowing
from all of us.

'She's got cancer,' he said, almost with satisfaction: the voice
of the child at school announcing family bad news for current

events class. 'She looks awful, and she can hardly move.'

'She's doing all right,' Anita said.

'Gotta get worse before you get better, eh? I don't think she'll get better. Ross is scared out of his wits. You should take the kids.'

'I can't. I go out to work, remember?'

'I remember,' he said and continued to stare at her, trying to put her in the wrong before he asked her for money.

'I wrote to Rosie but she's just had an operation. Kit's on the sick list too. Bill won't open the door to me. In the old days, a family stuck together.'

'Maybe we still do,' she said evenly, furious with him. 'Look, I have to go out and see a man about a dog. If ten dollars would do you, I could see you on your way.'

'Drop me off somewhere?'

It wasn't the clothes he was wearing, it was the condition he was in: tousled and dirty. 'Ten bucks and a subway ticket. That's it, Jack.'

'You always were a tight old broad.'

She went inside again, slamming the door, and pounded to the front of the house so hard that the petals shivered off the poppies she had set in a bowl in the front hall. She dashed upstairs and changed into another pair of trousers. As she went down again she made sure the front door was locked, then the back. 'Here,' she said, handing him ten dollars and a ticket. 'You can stay and finish your coffee. I have to be off.' She put her library book in her purse and strode off without looking behind her.

She was meeting Clive at the end of the subway line and they were going out in the country to browse through antique shops. That way he wouldn't have to drive downtown to her place first. That way, she thought grimly, he avoided Jack, thank God.

She had known him for only a few months and hadn't taken him seriously at first. An ordinary man with an ordinary job, he had seemed: indeed there was nothing special about him except the fact that they got on together, very well indeed. They were still in the wonderful time stage, however, and she wondered vaguely if that would change. He was divorced, and he had made it plain he wanted to set up housekeeping with someone again. She didn't know whether she wanted to live with anyone else: it had been so long since she hadn't had the morning paper and the morning clock and the morning coffee to herself that she was afraid she would resent an intruder.

She saw him swing into the parking lot and smiled to herself.

An intruder! He got out of the car and came towards her, a smile on his face. He had a wide, rather shy smile, a funny walk. 'Hi,' she said, and ran towards him. 'Marvellous day.'

'Wonderful.' He put her into the car like the gentleman he was, said, 'Belt up, now,' and headed north.

Ordinarily, this act of merely strapping herself in beside him made her happy, but today it was different. Jack niggled and danced in her mind. Being mean to Jack made her feel like the mean, ignorant child she no doubt had been, that Jack still was.

'What's the matter?' Clive said. 'You're twitchy.'

'I'm mean-tempered today,' she said. 'As bad as Martha the cat. My brother Jack turned up. The no-good one.'

'You have one of those, have you? Most people do. I always used to wonder why they felt sorry for me being an only child. How much did you give him?'

So that was on her face too. He read her well. 'I was having such a good time.' she said, 'reading in the garden. Then in stomped Jack, and I still feel shattered.'

'Whom were you reading?'

'John Berger.'

'I'm always amazed at your taste: hardly anyone's heard of him. Look, about your brother, you'd better tell me about him and get it off your mind. No use having a day in the country if we're not in good spirits. Was he mother's blue-eyed boy?'

Suddenly she heard her mother yell, 'You girls, Nita, Rosie, look after that Jackie and make sure he don't fall in the well.' She hunched herself and said, 'First, you have to understand we were small-town people and not what you'd call well off.' She had used the genteel phrase for so long it didn't surprise her any more.

'Born with a plastic spoon?'

'Tin. My father was a sergeant in the army.'

'Powerful influence?'

'When he was there. There were four girls, then Jackie and Bill. Jackie tore the wings off flies and drowned our kitten in the rain barrel: we hated him. I'm sure he was disturbed or something, but I don't bleed for him; he was an awful kid and he's an awful man.'

'I was a social worker in my first incarnation,' he said, profile to the wind against a blue and scudding sky. 'No good at it, but I met a lot of them, awful boys who never grew up. I suppose they radicalized a lot of big sisters in their day. How often has he been inside?'

'I suppose three or four times: petty theft, drunkenness, nothing big or skilful. We were no help to him, you know. He needed a lot of attention from adults, not sisters who'd rather be doing something else.'

'Don't flog yourself, for heaven's sake. There are bad apples, and handing them the barrel doesn't help. Where is he now?'

'In my backyard on the chaise, I suppose. I gave him ten bucks and a subway ticket. But there's no real hope he's gone yet.'

Clive looked down at her and slowed the car down. 'I think,' he said, 'that we'd better go back . . .'

'Clive, I don't want to spoil your day in the country.'

'You're more important than a day in the country and you're miserable. And that oaf is probably inside drinking the liquor cabinet: you can't win with those guys, Nita.'

'I locked the doors.'

'He's probably got Martha to open up for him by now; come on.'

He turned the car and drove very fast down the half-empty Sunday highway into town. They were home in twenty minutes.

They went in the front door and found Jack reclining with his work boots on the white corduroy sofa. He was drinking Nita's precious duty-free French cognac from her last trip to Europe from a kitchen glass.

'Jack!' she roared.

'Snob,' he said with an impish smile. 'So you caught me, you and your fine feller here. Nice coat he's got on. You're coming up and up and up in the world, aren't you, girl? Ma would be proud of you.' But he swung his boots off the chesterfield.

'I think you'd better go,' Clive said. 'You're bothering Anita.'

'Do you think so, Mr Pretty-boy? What are you doing hanging around our Nita? Don't you know she's our Educated Woman, too good for a man? Why, all she cares about is white velvet and books and doilies. She don't even go to visit the sick and the dying, she . . .' He spoke in a stage Irishman's accent. Anita's blood began to rise and she could hear children in the background chanting, 'Nita's a nitwit, Nita's a nobody . . .'

'Jack,' she said. 'Get out.'

'And why would I want to get out, with a fine house to come to and a fine sister to look after me?'

'You should go,' said Clive, being reasonable, trying, being also, Anita thought, very sweet and middle class, 'because your sister has asked you to go.'

'Oh, I never did nothing Nita told me. It was Rosie had the good left hook. Nita was nothing, all skin and bone and no bust. No wonder she never got married or nothing. But then you wouldn't be so foolish, mister, would you, as not to open a package before you put it on the shelf?' His mouth turned down and he leered at Clive. He stood up and prepared to raise the bottle to his lips.

On the one hand, Anita wanted to laugh because he was being a self-defeating grotesque, asking for punishment, exile, anything: he had always been like that. But she was also very, very angry. She could hear all the fourteen-year-old boys in the world whispering, 'Nita Nobody, got no tits . . .' and the rest of it, which was worse. The rest of us reclaimed ourselves, she thought, as Mother wanted us to. We got out of misery and brutality. We stopped swearing, read books, got at least a smattering of education: cleaned up the family act.

Jack took a swig from the bottle. Clive balled his fists. Nita looked at the two of them and sized them: Clive was taller, but Clive was nervous. Clive had never had to punch anyone out.

Jack put the bottle down. Nita took his measure and lashed out, one two, one two, and bang bang bang on his falling head with her fists. Jack went down like a lamb.

Nita sat down on the sofa and started to cry. Clive sat down beside her and put his arm around her. Jack came to.

'Nita, you shouldn't have ought to have done that. Nita, you damn well broke me false teeth.'

'Get out, Jack,' she said. 'Get flaming well out of this house and don't come back. If you don't or if you ever come back, I'll flaming well . . . I'll call your probation officer.'

Jack stood up, holding his head, trying again. 'Nita, you're a hard woman. You should know,' he said to Clive, 'this is the kind of woman you're after: she's got no heart, she's all hollow.'

'Shut up, Jack, and go and tell your government psychiatrist you're persecuted by your sister,' Nita said. 'Get out. Get on with you. Go home and tell your mother she wants you.'

He went.

Anita sat trying to pull herself together. In the scuffle she had lost more than a lamp: the brandy bottle oozed on the carpet, the glass was broken. She sat up and sighed. She looked at Clive.

'Well,' she said. 'Now you know.'

Clive got up and reappeared with a cloth. He began sponging the brandy out of the carpet. 'Look,' he said, 'there's something I should tell you, but I want to know first how you did that?'

'What?'

'That wonderful kayo; I've never seen anything like it.'

'I wasn't born a lady and a scholar,' she said. 'I was born on the outskirts of Camp Borden, a longer time ago than you were, I have to come clean and tell you that. I was one of six children. Circumstances were not good. But in addition to being a sergeant, my father was a fighter, and when he got a beer or two into him he'd spar with anyone he could find. We saved my mother a lot.'

Clive disappeared for a moment again. She picked up the fallen glass, looked at herself in the mirror, smoothed down her hair. Thought desperately: now he knows. It's over.

Clive reappeared with a tray and glasses. 'It's our turn for a drink. There's something I said I would tell you, and I will. The real reason my wife and I got divorced was boredom. We never got quite so low as Graham Greene, who had a tooth out once when he couldn't stand it any more. But we got bored in a terrible way; we got so bored we felt we needed some kind of violence; we knew it wasn't for us, but we started to pick fights because we drove each other crazy. All our friends celebrated when they heard we were getting a divorce. Perfection drives everybody up the wall.'

She managed to look up at him and smile.

'So drink up, love. I don't care what happens between us; I know it won't bore me. But if we ever do take up living together and things get all sedate and cosy, would you . . .'

'I'd do anything for you,' she heard herself say, not believing she had said it, but hearing it anyway.

'Well, I'm not really that way, but . . . well, hell, Nita: you're magnificent in the boxing ring.'

Much later he said, after tangling with her, 'It wasn't that I wanted violence: I wanted a feeling that I was alive, that you were alive, that even our hair was growing.'

She smiled at her professor again and rubbed her bruised hands together.

MARGARET GIBSON

The Butterfly Ward

Sometimes it can be beautiful inside this space. Most people, people who can ride on buses and streetcars and eat doughnuts for breakfast if and when they want and don't have to dial 0 on their phones to make a call would think that statement crazy. Maybe it is a bit crazy. Even phone calls cannot be simple here, everything twisted into complications but I am getting used to it now.

I have been here a month now on the neurological ward of a big hospital in Toronto. The biggest, I am told, with new wings that gleam and old ones that make me feel like a nun hiding in a bombed-out convent. I come from Kitchener, that is my home, but they sent me here. They, whoever *they* may be, said that the doctor working here on my case, Dr Carter, is the best neurologist in Ontario, maybe even all of Canada. The mysterious and secret *they* who have so neatly pigeon-holed my life. I wonder if I was supposed to be impressed with this news as my mother packed my suitcase and told me of all the wonderful little boutiques in Toronto, slipping in the famous name among the dried coloured flowers of the boutiques. My father stood in the doorway with his pipe in a reassuring mouth. I was not impressed. I had seen so many doctors for the secrets that dwelt inside my nebula that I was not. If a year or two ago they had told me of the famous Dr Carter in this huge city hospital in Toronto—then, then I might have been impressed. Not now. I am a cynic, old and tangled in the opal of my mind. I was twenty-one last April, it is the end of May now. I came to this place—NEUROLOGICAL WARD, it was like that in bold letters, on the 28th of April and it is now May 30th. Yes, sometimes it is quite beautiful. I lie in my bed at night and creep into my nebula and watch fire and white matter like fine mists drifting past, I float with the clouds. There is no fire in there, my imagination has placed it thus so it can drift with the white mists. I have always loved beautiful things.

They have come to poke and pin Mrs Watson. She moans, no, no she cannot drink another quart of water and no more needles. Now, now they murmur softly. I am supposed to be asleep but I watch from the fine mists of my nebula, so beautiful and secret in there. I know this game and how to grit your teeth and pretend it doesn't matter that ten times in one night you are pinned with needles like a butterfly to a board or that you must drink a quart of water each time until it is like a poisonous liquid, a gas bloating up your stomach. Now, now the two nurses murmur softly, only two more to go, with their pins and poisonous liquid. One jabs her in the hip with the long, slender needle, pinned again, the other holds out the quart of water to her in a plastic jug. No, Mrs Watson whimpers, I feel sick to my stomach. Now, now they murmur. The pinned butterfly drinks the poisonous liquid, the two collectors of butterfly wings stand beside her board to make sure she drinks it all. They go. The pinned butterfly flutters and gasps and is free for another two hours. I know this game and how to play it. I have been the butterfly three times. The injections keep the liquid from pouring out, from escaping the body otherwise the doctors could not get a clear picture of the bloated nebula. Brain, to strangers to this place. I know this game.

Mrs Watson flutters and gasps trying her twisted wings. 'It's all right, Mrs Watson,' I murmur now from outside my nebula. I am lying in bed on the neurological ward and I must say to this woman that it is all right. She is forty but looks nearly sixty. I am twenty-one but look eighteen. I must say to this woman that it is all right. She has never been pinned on the butterfly board before nor drenched inside with the poisonous liquid bloating her stomach. She has only been here five days.

'Is that you, Kira?'

'Yes,' I answer softly. My mother is fond of Russian books and her greatest desire is to go to Russia someday and see the Kremlin and its turrets gleaming in the sun in white snow, thus the name Kira, which is Russian. At my conception visions of Russia and bells and snow going on forever and ever and the Kremlin shining in the sun were mingled with the sperm that made me, Kira. They lay in her womb ready for the sperm that would make me a Russian. Waiting, simply waiting unbeknownst to my father. The sperm came and the womb filled with Russia mingled with the

sperm and received its new comrade, Kira. I have forgotten what
it means but something very lovely I am sure. Mrs Watson whispers in the darkness, 'You are such a nice girl, Kira, so young.
What are you doing here? Are you crazy?'

'No,' I say.

'They sent me here from a mental hospital. An O.H. I don't
belong here, I didn't belong in that other place either. They said I
cried all the time and got angry and threw things but I didn't!
Liars, all of them! I don't do those things, you can see that for
yourself. I thought the mental hospital was bad but this is worse.
I'd rather have a shock treatment any time—zzz—burns out the
brain. Does that scare you that I'm from a crazy joint?'

I can see her grey hair frizzled in the darkness like the zzz sound.
'No,' I answer because it doesn't, nothing much does anymore.

'Then why are you here?' Her voice is curious, grasping for a
reason she can borrow.

'I have fits sometimes and no-one knows why. The pills for
epilepsy don't work for me. Maybe I'm a new breed of epileptic, I
don't know.'

'They said I had fits and threw things and hurt people but I
never did. Everyone lies, don't you forget it ever, everyone lies
so they can get just what they want from you. They lie.' Her teeth
look purple in the dark and tiny night lights.

'What do they want from you?' I ask.

Mrs Watson leans toward me from her bed, turning her head
closer to me, her breath smells of the poisonous liquid. 'Money,'
she whispers fiercely, 'money! I've written my lawyers over and
over again to let me out of the crazy house, to tell them how it is
all a lie and a sham to get my money, but I know my lawyers
never got those letters, never saw the truth. Otherwise I'd be out
of there, out of here. The doctors at the crazy house opened them
all and laughed and took more money from my estate, ripping
my letters to bits, destroying vital information. Just take, take from
my estate, laughing while they do it.' Mrs Watson's fierce whispers
are filled with hate. I say nothing. I have never known a crazy
person before, I am not sure of her map. 'I heard you been here a
month, right?'

'Yes.'

'They . . . the staff, do they do this thing with needles and water
often? I feel like I could throw up all over this bed but I can't.'

'That's because of the needles.'

'Well, do they do this often?'

What can I say? I have been pinned on the butterfly board three times and tomorrow comes the bigger board, the worst one. I do not want to tell her about what will happen tomorrow morning. They have pinned me to the butterfly board so often because the famous Dr Carter can find nothing. Maybe she will be lucky and they will find something in her nebula. 'No,' I finally answer, 'not often.'

'How often?'

A nurse with a flashlight beams it into our corner of the small ward. 'Kira, let Mrs Watson get some sleep, her next injection is in less than two hours. You know we like our patients to rest, sleep between injections.' The flashlight beam is gone and she with it. For a moment we do not speak. In fact I don't want to talk to Mrs Watson and her secret estate any longer. I have decided that I do not like her with her fierce whisper and teeth showing purple in the dark and her breath and her frizzy-zzz grey hair.

'How often?' she repeats.

Now I am mechanical in my answer but I will not tell her about tomorrow, I have decided that, I will not tell her. If she were my friend I would tell her but she is not. 'If they find what they're looking for in the picture of your brain maybe just once, maybe you will be lucky. If they don't find it they will do it again. Maybe three times.'

'Ahh God, you had it done three times?'

'Yes.'

'Ahhh God!' she moans. 'What happens in the morning, they told me I can't have any breakfast, what happens in the morning Kira?'

'They weigh you . . .' I say and let my voice trail off into a pretend sleep. Maybe I will really fall asleep.

'And then?' I do not answer, I breathe deeply as one does in sleep. 'And then?' Her hand, thin and veined and wretched-looking is pulling at the sleeve of my nightgown like an old bird's talon. I do not move or speak. 'And then?' Her voice is frantic, demanding. I say nothing, I am breathing deeply. She releases the sleeve of my blue cotton nightgown. I hear her whisper hatefully, 'Bitch! You little bitch! Let me tell you something, sleeping brat, sleeping little brat, I am the only sane person left in this whole damn world, little brat!' I am glad that I did not tell her what will happen in the morning, she is no friend of mine, she hates me because my veins do not bulge and I have never been to a crazy hospital. I belong to no private club. I am awake for her next injection, I hear the butterfly gasp and flutter and then I am asleep. The pill they gave me at nine o'clock has finally worked, my nebula turned dark with sleep. Drifting in the mists until morning.

It is a quarter to eight in the morning. Everyone in the small ward is awake, there are six beds in this room counting mine. Three on one side, three on the other. I am lying on my side waiting for my breakfast, pretending I do not hear Mrs Watson's demand and question over and over, 'And then?' I eat my milky scrambled eggs and cold toast and drink the coffee which is good and hot this morning. I brush my long hair then lean back against the two pillows with a lighted cigarette in one hand, my coffee cup in the other. Today I have no tests, I can smoke and drink coffee and watch the television my parents rented for me. The third day I was here a girl from some other part of the neurological wing in a wheelchair came into this small ward and screamed at me, 'Where did you get the TV! Who from?'

'From my parents,' I answered.

'Christ are you stupid!'

A nurse called her by her name, Linda, I think, and she wheeled herself out of the room giving me a hateful glance. I didn't know what she was talking about and I hated Toronto with its huge hospitals and the famous Dr Carter. I felt like crying. I asked a nurse to tell Dr Carter that I wanted to go home. The Cogitator came. 'This is just because you are unused to hospital routine. You've never been hospitalized before have you, Kira?'

'Only for a day and a night occasionally.'

The Cogitator, a woman called Dr Wells, patted my hand and told me that I would get used to it. She told me to call her Karen. Dr Karen Wells. She is in her late thirties and has nice legs and wears eyeshadow. She patted my hand that day and said, 'You'll get used to it.' She is chief Cogitator for Dr Carter. One sees Dr Carter only during the great pinning day or as he flies through the ward, white coat flapping, nodding to his charges, a group of new Dr Carters trailing behind him from bed to bed. He talks about you at your bedside as if you had merged with the pillow and the new Dr Carters fumble and ask and answer questions with reddening faces. Perhaps they sense their smallness, know already that they will never be a great and famous Dr Carter, only small Dr Carters. There is room for Greatness in only one on this ward.

They have weighed Mrs Watson. 'Gained nine pounds,' she says aloud to everyone in the small ward. 'Feel like I could burst open,' she says to Miss Smith who has Parkinson's disease. 'What do you think of that? After my money, all of them.' Miss Smith does not answer, only the tremors in her arms seem to weigh the related message and respond to it. Her face frozen in rigidity reveals nothing. 'Nine pounds on their vile water in one night,' she says again. The first time I gained ten pounds. Oh, how my nebula must have showed up clear and bright and bloated on their pictures! I ignore her. She pulls at my sleeve, I will not talk to her. 'Brat! Bitch!' she whispers even in daylight to me. I drink my coffee. If she were my friend. . . . She is not. At ten o'clock The Pinners with a touch of mania to them come and take Mrs Watson away. She is going to the big butterfly board but she does not know it. Not yet. 'I don't get angry or cry, ask that brat Kira! She knows. Thinks she's too good to talk to me. Ask her, that brat knows the truth!' Truth? She is asking The Pinners as they walk her from the small ward, 'What's going to happen? What's going to happen?' Her voice is plaintive. The Pinners do not answer, saying only, 'There, there,' and they are gone.

She said I knew the truth. I used to think I knew all there was to know about truth. I am slender and pleasant looking with long auburn hair and I graduated from high school with honours, in the top fifteen. That was a truth, the diploma and the cleverness. I went to the graduation dance with Adam, who was tall with husky shoulders and sky-blue eyes and soft brown hair, who had been telling me for the last year how much he loved me and that we should consummate our love. He wore a navy blue suit and a pale blue tie and I wore a long pink gown with a scoop neck and we danced all night together and drank a tepid fruit punch from a huge crystal bowl. Our love was never consummated. That was another truth. Adam finally gave up telling me how much he loved me, mouth aching from the word and left me. I didn't care too much.

I went to work in The Home for Retarded Children, that was a different kind of truth. There were mongoloids there and water-head babies and the simply retarded, retarded beyond grasp or pain. Flies buzzed in the spring and summer in the playground where the children who were mobile went out to play. They constantly fell and cut and bruised themselves, the flies knew this and followed them, a dark buzzing cloud ready to light on the open wounds. The buzzing cloud followed them back into the Home when play period was over. Even after their wounds had been cleaned and bandaged a few flies still hovered with tenacity near the children's beds. Limbs of rubber, the waterheads. Some of them were quite beautiful, limbs of rubber, toes touching forehead. I felt no disgust or pity. I did feel compassion but more than that I felt necessary. That was another truth. 'Why do you work in a place that's so depressing and pays so poorly? You're so smart, get a better job,' everyone said to me. 'Go to university with your fine brain,' my mother said. They didn't know that I would simply be a numeral at university, perhaps a clever numeral but a numeral all the same. I could think of no other job that would make me feel as necessary. I tried to discuss this with my mother, this truth. I thought that she of all people having held Russia in her womb would understand. I was being a good proletarian working for the collective for a small amount of money per week. My mother had pointed out to me again and again since childhood the Mennonites when they came into town in their horse-drawn wagons, travelling with ease among cars and buses and pedestrians. 'Look how selfless they are.' She said it over and over again as we bought fruit and vegetables from the somberly dressed Mennonites. Mother, who should have understood but did not said, 'You should go to university. It's a very fine thing you are doing working at the Home but Kira you can't go on like that forever. Save your money and then you and I and your father, if he wants to, will go and see Russia next year and the next year you will go to university. It would be a shame to waste such a good brain. Study—study child psychology if you want. But don't waste that brain of yours Kira.'

'Russia?'

'Yes, the most beautiful country in the world. People for the people, green forests, all that snow, the Kremlin in the winter . . .' She did not understand that there in Kitchener, Ontario, I was being a good proletarian. But I was doing it out of selfish reasons like a spy. It made me feel necessary.

I got a small apartment with a girl who was a beautician when I was nineteen. I filled the apartment with plants and flowers of all colours and sizes and watered them carefully and put plant pills in their soil before going to work at the Home. The beautician sat under the hairdryer each night for at least two hours, filing and polishing her nails as she sat there. Her hair was as brittle as dried twigs and the colour of straw in the sun. I was happy. That was a truth. It was when I was just twenty that I moved into the nebula, or that is to say it moved in on me. I would have a seizure and remember nothing afterward. 'A convulsion, kind of,' my roommate with the twig hair told the doctor. I had never thought about the brain, at least not my brain, despite my working in the Home—much less the nebula that had moved in on me. But that realization was only to come later, of the nebula. That was the newest truth, the next truth. I had e.e.g. after e.e.g. and still nothing, minor tests and finally this huge hospital in Toronto with the famous Dr Carter. 'The best in Ontario, maybe in Canada,' my mother had said. I was not impressed. My nebula. As I said, it can be beautiful inside this space.

I am dressed in pale blue brushed denim jeans and a blue cotton top. I sit propped up on my bed watching television and drinking coffee, no tests for me today. They came for Mrs Watson at ten o'clock, it is now ten-twenty, I know that for certain because the Phil Donahue Show is just beginning. Mrs Watson with her secret fortune is now pinned on the biggest butterfly board of them all. There is no anaesthesia for the dying butterfly. Yes, she will feel that this is dying. No anaesthesia, nothing can interfere with the test. She lies on the sterile table, hands clenched by her sides. Dr Carter will tell her to unclench her hands. Two long needles, one on either side of her face have been driven through her jawbone. Pinned. Dr Carter will tell her to lie perfectly still, the butterfly will lie pinned like that, still and dead for half an hour. Dr Carter and others will peer into her bloated brain but only Dr Carter will matter.

The first time I was the butterfly on the giant board, the pain of it—the sheer, smooth glass covering the butterfly board, from wing tip to wing tip, that first time it took The Pinners three tries before the giant pins settled properly into my jawbone. I thought perhaps my jawbone like my fits was different and unexplainable. The last two times however I was pinned in a neater fashion. I did not move, not the first, second or third time. I did not cry. I threw up afterward each time, ten pounds of poisonous liquid down the toilet. The first time I sat beside the toilet after, sweating and holding my head in my hands, my long hair stank of vomit and my mother waited for me anxiously outside the washroom. We had been sitting in the cafeteria after the pinned butterfly had risen from the board and suddenly I knew I was going to be violently ill. Mother, kind and gentle, wanted to come with me. 'No, alone,' I managed to say.

'Kira, please.' I made it just in time to the washroom. It was there, I think, in that tidy, stinking cubicle that I perceived my brain as a nebula and it was then too that I knew what was in it and what they would never find. At first it was just an idea, a play toy in the long hours of white boredom, but as the tests went on and on, thrice the butterfly, my pain the smooth glass shield, it was no longer a toy. It is my escape. I am not a Mrs Watson, but when the night comes or I think I cannot bear another commercial for Brillo Pads or Mr Clean or when I have another e.e.g., I crouch in the mists of my nebula where it is beautiful and everything is calm, safer somehow in that beautiful misty space. 'You'll get used to it,' and Dr Karen Wells had patted my hand. It seems so very long ago now. This hospital in the big, shining car city, so many cars here, with streets of sparkling light at night, this city of Toronto where there are no Mennonites, just the famous Dr Carter who has become the next truth and with him the nebula. Is it the final truth? I am something of a novelty. They probe and pin and stick and pill and nothing changes, nothing works. I was always so ordinary before, simply Kira, a bright comrade born in an alien land but I adjusted, and my life read like a dull book, a simple map.

I think of my mother at home. Is she standing in front of the somberly dressed Mennonites buying their fruit and vegetables and marvelling at their selflessness? Soon I will get a letter from my father and he will write an amusing piece of poetry in it and tell me the latest news of everyone I have known and everyone he knows. He never runs out of words to fill sheets of paper with for my letters, the words brim over the pages like the tears in his eyes when I left. Tall, quiet Father, pipe in his reassuring mouth, gentle, tears in his eyes when I left for this huge monument to science and flesh. Mother finds it difficult to fill a single sheet of paper with words and yet it is she who comes here when I am pinned to the giant board, three times she has come; it is Father who cannot force himself to be witness. To what, I wonder? The Pinning, the aftermath of The Pinning of course. Tears brimmed up in his eyes when I left. Is it because of Russia, the land of the worker, the harsh land, the proletarian land, that my mother can come and bear witness like a good and sturdy comrade and my father cannot?

It is eleven o'clock, the Phil Donahue Show takes a commercial break. The Pinning has been over for ten minutes for Mrs Watson. Is she vomiting now? Weeping? Cursing the laughing doctors who opened her letters to her lawyers? I only vomited. Dr Carter himself said I was a very stoic person. Dr Karen Wells, chief Cogitator, beamed at me and so did the lesser Cogitators at these words for me, all for me, from the famous Dr Carter. Three times on the butterfly board and I have yet to weep. Is it that I am stoic or simply that I have the secret of my nebula and tell no-one. You see I have deduced what is wrong with my brain. Why don't I tell them? It would all be so simple. Would they think me high-strung giving in to stress? I'm not though, I am a sturdy comrade. I crouch in the mists of the nebula.

Mrs Watson has to be helped back to her bed, she is weeping and moaning, fingers tentatively exploring her aching, burning jawbone without actually touching it, sketching the pain of it in the air. 'I want all my personal belongings! I'm leaving your Dachau!' she screams. The nurses try to calm her down. 'There, there,' they say. It is their code word. 'Nazis!' she screams and begins to tear apart her bed. Pillows fall to the floor, a sheet tears, the night table topples over with a crash and the splinter of the glass ashtray. Pinned again. The slender, efficient needle plunges into her leg muscle. She sleeps. One nurse sighs and then turns to me smiling, 'How are you today, Kira?'

'I'm all right, a little bored I guess.'

'You can go down to the cafeteria or to the gift shop and buy some magazines, there's nothing scheduled for you today.' She means to be kind to this novelty, Kira-stoic.

'I probably will after lunch,' I reply. Two aides are straightening up the mess of Mrs Watson's bombed-out bed, removing the ripped sheet. Mrs Watson rolls like a piece of clay as they pull it out from under her, oblivious, her mind in a place of Not. Not anything, darkness is not even there. What strength in those thin bird-claw hands!

The next day is simple. I have another electroencephalograph. The needles are placed all over my scalp, little pin pricks, no pain. Blink. Stop. Deep breath. Stop. Fast shallow breathing. Stop. Deep, slow breathing. Stop. Blink rapidly. Stop. How used to all this I have become. Dr Wells patted my hand, 'You will get used to it.' Later after the e.e.g. is over I take a brief walk around the hospital block. It is now June. The June air is sweet and cool, a slight breeze caresses my hair and scalp where minutes ago it was covered with the little pin pricks of needles. I do not stay outside long. Soon I am back in the small ward watching the Mike Douglas Show. I drink a ginger ale and smoke. There is a comedian on and everyone in the TV audience laughs, even I laugh a little. It is June second, the beginning of my second month here. The nurse comes and gives Miss Smith a new pill to try, as if anything on earth could stop the small volcano in her arms and fingertips or smooth out the rigidity of her shoulder and face. I am given new pills to try out, grey with black little dots on them. I swallow the three round pills and soon my mind begins to feel heavy. My nebula fills with fat rain clouds. I sleep.

It is June the fifth. I received a long letter from my father today with an amusing poem in it and he ends by saying that he knows that what the doctors are doing is right and that soon his Kira will be healthy and home.

I am to be pinned to the giant butterfly board again this morning, hands flat on the board, no flutter of wings. I could tell them quite simply that the thing that causes my fits is not a thing that a pill can cure. The amoeba. Yes, that is what it is. I knew that after my first pinning to the great board. It is nourishing itself on what they call my brain, enveloping the minute organisms held there. It floats in my nebula. It does not matter how many quarts of water or needles they give me at night to bloat my brain, everyone knows that an amoeba changes shape and because it is so changeable the famous Dr Carter will never catch it on his bloated-brain scans. Why do I not tell them this? They would not put me in a crazy house like Mrs Watson, who now wanders in a daze on a new drug, sometimes bumping into walls and furniture. No, not good stoic Comrade Kira. High strung and nervous under all the strain of it they would say kindly. Dr Karen Wells would simply pat my hand as she did on my third day here when she first told me I'd get used to it. Why don't I tell them that it is the amoeba eating away that is causing me to faint, have fits and forget? Why not?

I am walking to the elevators with The Pinners now, in a few more minutes I will be the butterfly, wing tip to wing tip pinned on the giant board. They will look and find nothing, the famous Dr Carter will shake his head in confusion. I feel no shiver in the pit of my stomach as I have on other Pinning Days—this will be my fourth time on the giant board. Yes, I am getting used to it. I will lie pinned there as still as the dead butterflies in a collector's box, lovingly, carefully pinned. I will lie like that for half an hour and then my wing tips will flutter faintly and I will rise, the secret of the amoeba held within my lovely, fluttering wing tips, fluttering softly in the large Pinning Room. Everyone will smile. Poor butterfly. Yes, I am getting used to it. Perhaps that is the final truth of them all, the last.

PHYLLIS GOTLIEB

A Grain of Manhood

She was lying formless; the contour of her body was lost except for the white ring of pain that worked its way downward every so often like a wedding ring over a swollen knuckle. All her other miseries were encompassed by this masterpiece of nature, a force at one with lightning and thunder, the hurricane, the great reach of the four-thousand-year-old sequoia.

In the intervals she was a person again, and she turned her eyes to James, who was standing at the window watching white peaks rising out of the shadow of night. She asked for the first time, 'James, what will you do when this is over?'

'I don't know.' He spoke through the window to the sky. In spite of the unexpected hurry to the hospital he was wearing his dark suit, pressed and fresh, and a tie knotted with painful neatness.

'Why do you always call me James?' he asked suddenly. 'Why not Jim or some other kind of short thing?'

She would have said, Why not, it's your name, but she was too miserable for even the feeblest humour. 'I don't know. You always looked like a James to me. Hair parted neatly, folded handkerchief in pocket, buckled briefcase.' And on Earth perhaps a bowler hat and tight-furled umbrella. 'It seemed suitable.'

'You mean stodgy and prissy.'

'No, James, just suitable. It's right for you, and I've always liked you as you are.'

But he kept his lips compressed and his eyes on the white peaks.

The hospital lay in the crater's plain circled by the mountains of Axmith's Territory II. Not a person in the whole of the Community who did not know them, and all he had ever wanted was to dissolve among them like a grain of salt without much more colour or savour. She liked him as he was—and what she had done to him!

'You never did explain—' he began.

'Oh, James, let it go!' She tensed on the bed and then tried to make herself limp and slide under the coil of pain. 'You wouldn't let me, all those awful months. Now I don't want to.'

Light reflected back on his face from the mountains of Axtu, and for a moment it showed open and vulnerable. She set her hands warily over the frenetic writhing in her belly and said with bitterness, 'A virgin birth would have seemed more reasonable to you.'

He said in the precise way she claimed she had never hated, 'There are at least three people on Axtu beside us who know I am sterile.'

Shut up! Shut up! You married me because there was a good job for a married man out here! Shut up! 'And of course no one could want me but you, James, you're pretty sure of that.' Perhaps not. She stared at the pale green ceiling, green walls, palely enameled nighttable, water-pitcher, callow-coloured with the uncertain light reflected from the western wall of the pumice crater. All things sullen, solid, a hard shine to them. In her mind colours flickered, shifting pure prism-hues, only paled and whitened by pain, till she opened her eyes to the nothingness of reality.

She said, 'What's there to explain? The old story . . .'

He opened his mouth and closed it. Then he said, 'When *that* is born—'

'I'll go away, if you like. You'll never have to see me or it again.'

'Don't be foolish. It can't be hidden now. Damn it, why couldn't you have gotten rid of it, like any other woman?'

'Why couldn't you have had children, like any other man?' she said softly. It drew the blood to his face. Could she ever have pretended to love this man, who used so much nastiness to cover his vulnerability? With an effort she kept her voice gentle. 'When we found we couldn't have children, I couldn't help being restless . . . all the money we'd saved with my working, and I hadn't seen my people for three years . . .' The time-old tale of alien grain. No use saving money for the child, and she used it to visit Earth.

But she had forgotten that life on Earth was what she had married to get away from. There was nothing for her, and all she had was the return fare to Axtu, and she started back.

But the shipwreck changed it.

She shared the life raft with the mutilated body of an old woman who had taught her the Italian hemstitch a few hours before; it took three days till the boat homed on a safe planet and landed battered and useless on the rocky shores of a lake. The equipment seemed crushed. The radio had told her that the air and water were usable, but now it was silent, and she had no idea whether it was still sending the automatic SOS, nor how to repair it or use it.

She crawled outside at last, poising on jagged rocks that bruised her feet, and looked out over the grey expanse of the lake, flat and sunless.

Nothing worse than the hell I've always lived in. She grinned in despair and went back into the boat to salvage food.

The lake was in a craterlike depression, a stony saucer of water, and she was unable to see beyond the rim. When the boat landed she had been asleep and had not seen the planet's face—a grim tumbling sleep with the consciousness of the blanket-wrapped body beside her, the vacuum of loneliness in an old woman who had died without her descendants around her. There was only one other blanket. She stuffed it into a canvas bag with some concentrates and a canteen and slung it over her shoulder. There was not much to eat. Even if there were her survival would be only a matter of inertia.

She stared around once more. There was no sign of movement, not a wind carrying gull-cries, scuttling run of lizard, or oozing of any alien life she might have imagined. The air and water might be all right, but the planet gave no sign of being any more generous than that.

There was a tinge of chill to the grey air; she wiped sweating palms on her skirt and began to climb the rim. Once her foot dislodged a stone; it rolled downward for a few feet, and that was the first sound she heard beyond the beating of her own heart.

She climbed, and before she reached the top she began to hear something more: the trill of a pipe so faint and uncertain it might have been the singing of blood in her brain. But it grew and paced her as she stumbled on; it traced the whorl of her ear.

Light grew overhead, palely, and then burst into a burning sun; the sky became blue, as if she had risen out of a cloud. The points of the rocks dulled, the ground softened. She was walking on clipped green turf.

She stopped, took off her shoes, and stood with her toes pressed in the grass, dropping the canvas bag from her shoulder. The piper was walking beside her, fingering the stops. His scales were blue, green, amber, and silver; colours writhed on him like the lights on a peacock's neck.

The unfluid walls of plaster and fiberboard faced her, and the falsely soothing colours of metal-frame tables. 'That was Kol-anddro,' she said. 'I didn't have to explain anything to him. He knew already.'

'The way I never did,' said James, and added half under his breath, '—and never will.'

She remembered the months of nights she had lived alone with the half-formed creature in her, screaming in nightmare that it was clawing and ripping its way out through the frail membranes of protection that were all she had been able to give it—or maintain against it. . . .

The former face of the planet had crumbled like a clay mask. Here there were heavy-leaved trees; grass grew damp and cool beneath them. But in the sunshine the strange people who lived here had raised gaudy paper pavilions of pure colour. They came at the sound of the pipe and gathered around her. She would have said that they were dressed, but they were wearing only the fur, scales, or bat-wings their curious nature had given them, and there were no two alike.

They were humanoid, but flat-nosed and narrow-jawed; it was hard to find the form beneath the skin. Some of the feathered and crested ones looked like the eighteenth-century romantic's idea of the Noble Savage, but she was able to find neither nobility nor evil in their faces.

The scaled man beside her said, 'This is Nev; I'm Kolanddro, and you see these are my people. You came from the wrecked boat.'

'I did. How could you have learned my language?'

'I translate alien tongues. I'm the Interpreter.' That explained it to him, perhaps.

He lowered his shining lids with the effect of a smile. 'You'll understand it later.'

'I see. You people are telepathic.'

'No. *I'm* telepathic. That's why I'm the Interpreter.'

'And I don't have to tell you that my name's Lela Gordon, and I'm from Earth, etc.'

'Nor ask to see anyone more important than me, because no one will understand you.'

She smiled, then sighed. 'It doesn't seem very easy to leave here. Can you help me?'

But he had turned to speak to someone, and she looked around at the Nevids who had approached her. They returned her interest with a kind of inoffensive curiosity, and when they had seen enough left to go about their business. Kolanddro brought her a bowl of fruit and fresh bread.

'We don't make this kind of thing with our grain, but we baked it when it became evident that you would be with us.'

'Are you clairvoyant too?'

He made a glittering gesture. 'I have great range. There's little I can't do here.' He blinked. 'No, I can't repair your boat. We haven't many hard metals—and we don't need them.' He pointed out a winged man who resembled the Spirit of Communication which for centuries had graced the telephone book. 'We have Messengers.' He tapped his head. 'We have Interpreters.' Recognizing the panic rising in her he said anxiously, 'Please eat. You won't come to harm here.'

She said, 'I believe you . . . but the strangeness . . . is overpowering.' But she calmed herself enough to eat her meal under the tossing shade. The bread was rather heavy, but good enough for having had the recipe drawn from a fleeting picture in a sleeping mind.

Kolanddro blinked and asked, 'What is lemon soufflé?'

'Something I'm glad I didn't dream of while I was sleeping,' said Lela. She added very gently, 'I really don't like having my mind read.'

'While you are staying here you will have to get used to it.'

But I don't want to stay here. She was uneasy with the strangeness, the sense of having already become completely integrated into the life of the planet in an hour's time. She thought of the old woman dead in the boat who might have been happy to spend the last years of her age under this sun, and brushed crumbs from her skirt.

'I think I'd better stay near the boat in case the signal's working.'

He stared at her with his black-and-green eyes. 'You'll never reach the boat without my help,' he touched the pipe, 'and if you go you won't come back, or even remember all this. There'll be no more food or shelter for you.'

She said slowly, 'Open Sesame?'

'The connotation's unclear. . . . I see, an old story (perhaps you'll tell it to me sometime?)—yes, something like that.'

'Kolanddro . . .' she spoke to his still shadow on the grass; '. . . are you an illusion?'

'You will have to decide that for yourself.'

The chill that crimped her skin was not an illusion, at least not more so than the whole cosmos of matter. Where in relation to this place were the grey lake and the overcast sky?

'There's nothing to be afraid of. Believe me.' He ran a pearl nail around the rind of a yellow fruit and halved it. 'But if you stay here you must live as one of us. We like privacy and we don't let anyone leave us who'll endanger it.'

'It's beautiful here,' she said reluctantly.

'It is. And we know what kind of things aliens will bring us. We've had experiences with them.' He stood up. 'I'm busy now, but most people like to rest in the heat of the afternoon. I think you will be glad of a rest; you may have my house.' He pointed out a particularly vivid pavilion of crimson and purple. He swallowed the rest of the fruit, spat our four green pips into the palm of his hand, and cast them to the winds.

'Four more zimb trees,' he said.

'You had already forgotten me by then,' said James.

'James, I thought you would have been glad to forget me. . . . They wouldn't have taken your job away from you here just because your wife was lost in space.'

'That wasn't why I married you.'

'If there was another reason it was because feeling so trodden on yourself you had to have someone to hurt in return.'

'Don't, Lela. I never meant to hurt you.'

But she was thinking of the last few months of sullen meals, crushing silence, and loneliness. *What in hell are we going to do with a little bastard who looks as if he'd escaped from a prism, no matter how appealing he may be aesthetically? How can we keep him here? Where can we hide him?*

The colour flows on you like the broken light of a prism.

'All you people,' she said to Kolanddro, 'have the same form basically—I think—but no two of you are alike on the surface. That seems impossible.'

'Not when our germ plasm is almost infinitely tractable.'

'What do you mean?'

'We can take in any form of intelligent alien life. The children become pure Nevids within three generations.'

'How?'

'All psychokinetic faculties on Nev don't rest in the Interpreters—although I will say,' he added complacently, 'that most of the intelligence does. All Nevid parents have a choice in deciding before the child is born what form it will take—externally, not in the vital organs.'

'And the child has no choice in the matter?'

'No. His happiness depends on how well he lives with the shape we give him.'

'And if he doesn't?'

'He'll have an unhappy but interesting life.'

She shivered. 'I don't think I'd like that for my children.'

He waved his arm at the Colony and the multicoloured flow of the strange people and the wind-rippled walls of their houses. 'A quarter of these people are descended from aliens. We've found for every alien an Interpreter who could bring him into the life of the planet. I don't think any of them have been unhappy.'

'I can't believe I could ever be a part of your life.'

'I'm no more part of the life here than you are. The Interpreter is born, not made by the longings of his parents, and he comes no more often than'—he searched her mind for the parallel—'the true genius on your planet. Man or woman, he gives up private life.'

'Your laws are cruel.'

'Only as cruel or weak as the people who live by them. Do I seem that way to you?'

She never really knew the shapes of their souls or the range of their emotions, and only had rare glimpses of the mines and orchards, weavers and gold-beaters, that produced what she used and ate. Sometimes she thought she had glimpses of city spires beyond the forests, and though she knew that the Colonies often shifted with the seasons, there was no change as long as she was with them, and she never found out what they traded for with coins or feathers, or if they sacrificed the living on stone altars, or the names of their strange gods.

She woke late one morning after a restless night; she was queasy and aching, and was struck with the sudden fear that she was going to have a child. She made breakfast, and when Kolanddro came in and stood silently looking at her, her teeth began to chatter. He only smiled, and loosening a strand of her hair laid it across his green-white palm, where it lay very black, as if he were matching samples of material.

'I can't go through with this,' she whispered.

'You've accepted the conditions . . .' He became hesitant and faltering for the first time since she had known him. '. . . I have had to accept them.' But she turned away. What had he had to give up?

Late afternoon when the sun was falling toward the west, a woman dropped down from the sky. She did not come directly into the encampment where the cooking-fires were going, but folded her wings and waited at the edge of the clearing, searching in the shifting coloured frieze her people made of their most commonplace actions.

Kolanddro noticed her and moved forward; Lela turned from her task to watch them as they spoke, soundless shadows in a green shade. Something in their attitudes made her very still, though her halting command of the language would not have allowed her to understand them even if she had heard their voices.

The Nevid woman pointed toward the west; her downy hands flickered and her head lifted urgently to his calm face.

Then she turned away and came into the clearing where there was a late gold patch of sunlight lingering; she stopped and stood with her head bent down, almost as if to thrust it under her wing. Soundless and motionless she waited for the desire for flight to thicken her wings with blood. When the great delicate membranes opened she rose against the sun in a blaze of heraldic red, diminished, and was gone.

But Lela soared with her in imagination over thickets and rolling hills, perhaps past stone towers and shimmering rivers, half-blinded by the deep light that warmed the clear air, and without pleasure in the flight.

A voice murmured in her ear that the meat was scorching, and she felt both foolish and sick; she recognized Kolanddro's sacrifice to the laws of Nev. When she looked again, she saw that he was gone. He came out of the pavilion a few minutes later; he was wearing an obsidian dagger.

It was not until after supper that she saw the stranger emerge along the forest trail from the same direction the woman had come. He was a crested and feathered man as splendid of his type as Kolanddro; Kolanddro washed his face and hands in a basin and went out to meet him.

They faced each other in a pantomime of tense hieratic gesture; Kolanddro spoke, unfastening his belt with the dagger and laying it on the ground. He moved his hands in a wide gesture, as if to erase whatever angers were between them, and they turned and separated.

Lela sat waiting for him in the pavilion. The sun had almost set and the evening air had thickened to sweet dusk heavy with the smells of flowers and fruit. Indoors was the heart of a rose. The simple dress the Nevids had made for her slid over her body in rich folds; the sky was mauve and pearl flowing with the last of the sun.

Kolanddro came in, his mind so full of his own affairs it was quite blind to hers. He murmured, 'That was a long journey for nothing.'

'I think he'll make it again,' she said. 'I'm going back.'

He stared at her. She went on falteringly, 'I know it will be a lot of trouble to put things right—but they will be right. . . . I thought I could be a moral person simply by accepting the inevitable. Now I no longer believe it's inevitable.'

'If you leave we can't take you back—you understand?'

'I understand—the kind of law that lets you risk death fighting a rival even when you're the most important member of the Community.'

He said, 'A superman on your world would have to live by the same laws as the rest.'

'I agree. I don't think your laws are unjust, or even inflexible—but they aren't sensitive.' The word conjured James, with his capacities for loneliness and self-laceration and suddenly time, even a lifetime, seemed very short. 'They've gotten stunted along the way, and on Earth they're always reaching, like a tree, for the ultimate justice—not only in law-courts, but in relations between persons. . . . This justice, it's a clumsy, top-heavy thing, full of stupid mistakes and dead ends—but it grows.'

'If people on Earth are much like you they must make themselves terribly miserable for nothing.'

'They do. Will you let me go?'

'No one may ever find you out there.'

'I have enough food for a while, and there's water.'

'My son?'

'I think you'll have other sons. Please.'

'What can you and your husband make of him on Earth?'

She winced. 'Perhaps someone who can love both Earth and Nev.'

'No. He won't know anything of Nev.' He watched her gravely a moment, and she waited. He said, 'When everything is quiet I'll take you back to the boat. I'll break the law, for you.'

When the night was dark and quiet I took off the dress the Nevids had made for me and put on the one I came in. Render unto Caesar. *We went down along the smooth grass and the colours shimmered on him even in the dark. All I could think of, feeling so foolish and sick, was that he was going to kill that splendidly feathered man, or be killed, and there was nothing to say, because I'd told him what I thought of his laws.*

'But we don't fight to the death.'

'Thank you.'

'Our law would never allow anyone to leave as cold and unprotected as you are doing. I must bring you food and clothing.'

'No . . . they'd make me feel worse.' But there was one thing I wanted from him. I knew he guessed it, but I said it anyway.

'Kolanddro. Don't make me forget Nev.'

I found my canvas bag. It was weatherproof, but the shoes were rotted from nights of dew and days of hot sun.

He put his pipe to his mouth, and I had one glance of his fingers glittering on the stops and then the stones

cut her feet. She stood on the sharp edges like the transformed mermaid who walked on knives of pain as long as she had legs. She thought she could hear a last thin echo of the pipe, but it faded into the hollow lapping of the waters on the shore under the night wind.

There was no clear memory of how long she waited on the shore, days and nights. She ate concentrates when hunger became painful, and drank water when her tongue rattled in her throat, and nightmares chattered around her. She wondered that the baby lived, but it clung fiercely to the fetal stalk and thrived, walled away from her terrors.

She could hardly move when a loud bleep sounded in the boat at last, and she crawled into the terrible place on hands and knees to pick away at the wreckage and find the source, and push the switch that told them she was there. When the rescue ship lifted, she was in a bunk tossing with fever; she never saw the face of the planet.

'Lela.'

She was fastened in one clench of force. 'Please call the nurse now, James,' she whispered. He pressed the buzzer.

'You came back, even when you could have died out there—'

'James, I could fall downstairs on my head anytime, or pull a hangnail and get septicemia; it's a chance. But I don't care now. I just want to die.'

'Don't talk like that! I want you to live and be happy. With me, whatever happens! I love you, Lela. . . .'

Bu the mist was rising before her eyes, red as the blood in the wings of the Nev woman against the sun.

She opened her eyes once out of the chaos of pain and sound; a rubber-gloved hand was holding a shining thing by the heels, a baby gleaming with the detritus of amniotic fluid. She sank back.

He was a complete and perfect replica of James, down to the last neat lock of dark hair on his forehead. A stranger in the world, he lay beside her; his arms and legs trembled, his face crumpled, his pink hands moved aimlessly with unconscious grace.

'I can't understand it,' James said, '. . . but he is beautiful. Lela, I have to tell you this now; I thought I could get away with it, but I can't. I knew I was sterile before we were married.'

'I guessed it,' she said. 'That was really why I went away. I was going to leave you. But it doesn't matter now.'

'But you did come back.'

'Yes. I didn't expect much.' The months gone, the long slow growth of a child in her, the woman's right she had wanted so deeply—eclipsed in bitterness and recrimination. She smiled without joy. 'The tie that binds.'

But he said quietly, without arrogance, 'No. This depends on us.'

She bent to smell the newness of the child's flesh, and to feel the hands on her face. 'All right, James.'

The white sun of Axtu was very clear and warm in the room. She moved her clean drained body under the sheets, grateful enough to have her breasts ripening with milk, the baby in her arm, and James beside her with the faint pulsing of hope between them.

KATHERINE GOVIER

Responding to Pain

'You should have got an ambulance for this, lady.' The taxi-driver was a whiner, and he didn't know the one-way streets so it took them forever to get to the hopsital. Sara sat beside Jackie in the back seat, propping her up with an arm around her small shoulder. The unconscious woman couldn't weigh more than one hundred pounds, still, Sara had had to get one of the stoned film-makers to help carry her friend out of the house.

At the hospital she answered the questions. Age, twenty-six; occupation, proof-reader. Jackie would have felt poorly represented by her job title. Sara added a slash and 'poet.' She produced Jackie's medical insurance (expired) from the purse she'd picked up in her room. No evidence of foul play, history of drug abuse extensive. Details unknown. Sara went to the waiting room and sat for two hours watching the clock. Finally a doctor came out.

'Are you her next of kin?'

'Her parents live in Halifax.'

'They should be notified. And it would help if you could find out what she took. She's still deeply comatose. She's not responding to anything.'

It was after one o'clock in the morning. The night before Sara had begun calling Jackie at seven. The telephone rang and rang: Sara could picture the small, neat room where it sat. The noise would seem like a violence in the silence. Jackie had not turned up for their regular jogging at six. That was not surprising, but they'd had a date for dinner after. The dinner date wasn't something you'd just forget about, not for Sara. When there was no answer by eight o'clock, Sara had gone down to the fish and chip place and had eaten slowly, thinking over the things she'd been planning to tell Jackie that night. The number of phone calls she'd had at the office this morning over the show on Saturday and the tension in her back from crooking her neck around the receiver. The way the producer had looked at her in story meetings when she had made a suggestion: God, you'd have thought she was speaking Russian. By nine o'clock she was home again, and Jackie still did not answer her telephone.

Sara listened to the ringing and tried to think. When had she last seen Jackie? Noon on Sunday was the last time she'd spoken to her, and that was over the telephone. She hated the telephone, impotent snaky black thing in her hand, a pretence at communication. Who would know where Jackie had been for a day and a half? She called Jackie's landlady. The landlady was having a party to celebrate the completion of her company's first film.

'I haven't seen her all day,' she shouted. 'But the light's been on in her room since last night. I've heard the phone ringing so I assume she spent the night out somewhere.'

The night out. Sara put down the receiver. With the man she talked about. Sara's heart began to pound. She started calling around—people who might have seen her or who knew who this man was. Joanne wasn't home. Don wasn't home. Don's boss wasn't home. Ellen had her answering service on. Someone knew the man's name but not his number. Twenty calls later, Sara threw the telephone against the wall. It began to beep. At eleven o'clock she left her house in a taxi and went to Jackie's place. She had decided to look in her room to see what coat she'd been wearing and then go to the police.

Outside the brick front she asked the driver to wait. She opened the front door without knocking, knowing it would be unlocked as always.

The landlady's guests stood in curls of smoke staring past one another's shoulders. She heard an Elvis Costello record and talk about rushes. Taking the stairs, Sara turned her back on the party. She was nervous: her breath was short as she climbed to the second floor where Jackie stayed, a second class member of a non-family. Suddenly the landlady was there, darting past her, apologizing, and saying she should have checked the room herself. Duty struggling to replace drink on her face, the landlady ran across the second floor landing ahead of Sara and opened the door to Jackie's room.

Autumn had come to the room that day. All the small prizes of Jackie's world—the flowered shawls, old buttons, curling postcards—the minute, sentimental trinkets she captured in junk stores along Queen Street and placed in faultless formation on the walls and ledges had been knocked to the floor. Jackie was hardly visible where she lay on the bed, crumpled in the midst of her coats and dresses, her feet curled under her and her head dropping sideways. She looked like a newspaper blown against a fence.

'Oh, look, she's only sleeping.' The landlady's face relaxed into an idiotic grin.

Sara stepped in front of her and reached for her friend.

A long straw of spittle was hanging from Jackie's mouth and had made a pool on the spread. Her head rolled when Sara tried to sit her up. Her eyes, when Sara lifted the lids, were star blue and black, the seeing part vacant as space. The irrelevance of eyes without consciousness impressed her. Sara's relief, the smile that had started up on her face at the sight of Jackie, was fading. But she wasn't afraid yet: Jackie's body was warm, very warm, and she was breathing. The warmth was what she clung to.

After listening to the doctor, Sara took another cab back to the house where Jackie rented her room. The party was quieter now. Several guests had settled in for the night in the living room. Sifting through the detritus in her friend's room, Sara found an empty bottle of prescription pills. She called Jackie's parents and then a cab to go back to the hospital with the bottle. She gave it to the doctor, but he did not seem hopeful. Jackie was still not responding, and chances of her recovering were becoming slim. There was nothing to do but wait. One more taxi and Sara was home.

It was nearly four in the morning. Sara lay awake in bed. Jackie had not turned up for jogging, and now she was gone. Maybe dead. She had begun dying hours ago, as Sara had run their regular jogging course in the cemetery. It had been Jackie's favourite place, of course, and she had no doubt appreciated the irony of the fact that Sara would be there, pushing herself toward some obscure goal as usual, while she tore her room apart and swallowed a bottle of pills.

It was a very exact loss, the loss of Jackie. It was as if she had been vacuum-sucked off the landscape. She would not come up the sidewalk to Sara's house any more, in her long narrow coat, her skirt fishtailing around her ankles. She would not puff behind her on the jogging route. And afterward, at dinner, she would no longer lay her charges against humanity. Charges that were impossible to counter, such as that one's mother had wasted her life and one's man friends were insensitive. Nevertheless, Sara always had argued against them, defending mankind, defending herself really, until finally Jackie would giggle, lay her precise small hand beside the teacup, and say, 'Sara, don't worry. You're exempt. You're in my club.'

What hadn't Jackie said to prepare for this night? Like a child walking into the forest, Jackie had dropped crusts behind her. In that soft mocking voice she'd told Sara everything.

'When I'm depressed,' she had said, washing dishes at the kitchen sink, 'I can only sleep with the lights on.'

'The lights have been on all night,' the landlady had said over the din of party voices.

'I don't do so well, do I?' That one was across the table in a Chinese restaurant. 'You'll have to pick up the pieces, Sara.' 'If I told you all the things I've done you wouldn't like me.'

All the things she'd done. All the things she blamed other people for doing, in fact. Drunk and crying, there would be Jackie saying, 'How many times can you do that to yourself before you're ruined for life?' She might have meant have an abortion or a destructive love affair; she might have meant fail to finish a poem or let down an editor who was counting on seeing her work. She might have meant just about anything. Only Jackie's delivery—the steady violet eyes, the tiny straight mouth, the righteousness that was part child, part methodist—made the melodrama convincing.

Jackie had always regarded herself with a certain fascination, as the only fruit in the garden without a worm. She detailed the spoilage around her, detailed its inroads on her own perfection. 'I don't see how I can live my life,' she would say, 'when there's something wrong with everyone.'

'What's wrong with me?'

'Nothing, Sara. You're my hero. I told you, I worship you.'

'You've said that about people before, but you always find a flaw in the end.'

'People let me down. I get disappointed in them.'

'What disappoints you in me?'

'You're obsessed with having nothing get in your way.'

Sara thought about that as she turned over in bed again. Did she mean she had failed Jackie by not letting anything—her, for instance—get in her way? In the way of what? They were not in a race. She swore it to the ceiling: they were not competing, they were not rivals. If Sara was ahead in her career, if she had sold a few stories to magazines, and there was a publisher waiting for her book, it meant nothing. Except perhaps that Jackie kept getting into scrapes and didn't get her work done. Sara had always thought Jackie was the more talented. Jackie was her friend. She loved Jackie; she needed Jackie. She did not need to win.

Finally, she fell asleep. It was more like waking, however. She went back twelve hours to her jogging, feeling the work of it, the sweat, the air on her skin.

She began by tying her shoe laces and shaking her wrists, and then she set off. The taller of the two friends, she was always in front when they ran, but it was more by privilege than by necessity. Hitting her stride, she missed the soft scrape of Jackie's feet behind her own spongy footfalls.

The road was wide and smooth. On either side, the sculpted lawns and huge trees waited, at this time of day dipped in the gilt of the late sun. Sara's milestones along the route would be the grave markers. Coming up, for instance, was Rebecca Coffin. She and Jackie had laughed at her, wife of Isaac Coffin, died in 1919. And there she was, her details written in shallow letters on soft marble and already eroding.

Past that and on Sara ran as she dreamed; she felt the fatigue in her chest. She had gone this route so often, she could run it on a screen like one of those car-driving games where the road sped past. After the long curve and at the beginning of the straight diagonal across the centre of the cemetery, Sara looked over her shoulder, half expecting to see Jackie a hundred paces back, her hair bouncing on her shoulders the way it always did. Jackie ran like a sissy, her hands tiny ineffectual fists circling in front of her breasts, her knees turning inward. She could almost keep up, though: it was surprising. But she wasn't there. Even her ghost wasn't there. Well, thought Sara, commenting on her dream even as she dreamed it, if there's no ghost she can't have died yet.

And then Sara was into the hard part of the run, and the sun was slipping out of sight. Random rays shot out to make a last show, but already the cool damp rising from the ground insinuated itself around her ankles. Always at this point, she felt she couldn't make it. Her legs, her chest, even her arms were aching. Usually about now Jackie groaned and quit. Usually about now Sara would put on a burst and finish the course. In the dream she did just that, but it was harder without Jackie as audience.

And then she was lying in her bed and it was seven-thirty in the morning. By eight o'clock Sara was back at the hospital, where she sat for an hour in the waiting room outside Intensive Care. When the doctor finished his rounds, he came out to speak to her.

'I don't mind telling you now,' he said, 'that last night, it looked as if we were going to lose her.'

Sara blinked.

'However, there's good news this morning. She's responding to pain.'

Around noon, the parents arrived. Jackie's father squeezed one hand in a fist behind his back; her mother spoke in a whisper. He spoke to the doctors as if the issues were entirely in the terminology, as if there were no secrets that the machines could not break down, no burial so deep that medicine could not pull Jackie out of it. Sara watched them for the secret to what was wrong with their child: wasn't it their fault?

'I'm so ashamed,' said Jackie's mother. 'There's really nothing the matter with her, and she's taking up the doctor's time. The other people here are sick.'

They sat in the waiting room and talked to a woman whose husband was eighty and had a stroke. The woman thought he had good colour that day. Neither Sara nor Jackie's mother mentioned the reason they had come. In the late afternoon, Sara left and went home to sleep. She called her office and Jackie's and made excuses. Then she fell into bed. The loneliness came back: Jackie would never return. She got up and took two aspirin, and then she began to dream. People died in the dreams, died in the middle of sentences they were uttering at dinner tables, died like dogs at Sara's feet. She did not believe the dreams while she had them. A part of her stood at the foot of the bed saying, Oh dear, another death dream, this is not very healthy. And then she went very deeply to sleep.

She was entering a room in her house, one that existed behind the closet door, one which she had not noticed before. There was a coffin there, that sinister shape that coffins were, narrow at the top and bottom, wider where the shoulders would be if there were a body inside. The box was covered with dirt. Sara understood that Jackie had buried herself alive and that it was her responsibilty to dig with her fingers and get her out. With earth under her nails she lifted the lid, took Jackie out, and made her stand.

The girl was limp and boneless, but Sara was determined she should walk. She took her by the elbow. Jackie was like rags and rotting wood: she lurched, her mouth gaped, and she fell, finally pulling Sara down too. Then they were joyously under the surface of a clear stream, swimming. Jackie's hair streamed behind her, and Sara gulped hair, choked on it, so that when she woke it was because she thought her heart had stopped.

It was dusk again. She thought about jogging and decided against it. She called the hospital: no change. She didn't want to face Jackie's parents again, so she went out to dinner alone before going down to the hospital. But when she came out of the elevator in front of the Intensive Care unit, they were ready to step into it, on their way to a hotel. Jackie's mother now regarded Sara with hostility. By this time they too must have got around to thinking about reasons, about blame. They looked as if they had decided that the secret lay in Sara, but they were too proud to ask.

Sara had been in the waiting room only a few minutes when the doctor came out.

'She's coming around. You can go in and see her.'

Jackie was not quite conscious, but she had been moving. She'd pushed down the sheet to expose her bare chest. There was a tube in her nose and one in her stomach; blood was caked around her nostrils and lips. She had a big turquoise plastic umbilical cord in her mouth with steam bubbling in it. There was also a wire taped to her breast, a catheter in her arm, and something down her throat. The nurses told Sara they'd tied Jackie's arms to the sides of the bed so that she wouldn't knock the apparatus away. Sara saw Jackie's eyelids flicker, and a flood of gratitude went through her.

'Sit with her, if you like. Talk. Help her come out of it.'

For hours, Sara sat by the bed, holding Jackie's cold hand and burbling as she would to a fussy baby.

'Jackie, you're waking up! It's so good to see you! Can you hear me? Can you? Can you see over there where the nurses are all sitting at their station? They look like a bunch of sparrows on a wire.'

Jackie smiled at that: they often played simile games. Sara tried to keep going, but her friend groaned sometimes and twisted on the bed, thrusting herself backwards like a fish trying to escape the line that pulled it out of the dark. Jackie's eyes were closed, and her lips hardly moved, but she spoke.

'The world's gone mad,' she said. And then, 'Are you going to do a show about it?'

Sara pulled her hand back sharply. Shortly afterward, Jackie began to sob. The nurses asked Sara to leave so they could clean up the patient.

Sara went back to the cemetery. The iron gates were locked after dark, but there was a place where she could get one foot on a cement post and the other in a thick curl of iron. She swung over the top and dropped down into the dark on the other side. The city vanished as her feet hit the grass: the trees absorbed the sky-line, and the lights of the houses close up against the stone walls only winked through the foliage. The deserted roads with their tick, tick, tick of a dotted yellow line gleamed faintly between charcoal shrub and inky ground. It was as if all life had been turned to ash there. The place was utterly dark, utterly sympathetic.

When she saw the light, Sara wanted to hide, but she was afraid to move. It was low to the ground and yellowish: it flickered. She'd read about corpses giving off phosphorescence, or was that the sea? The night was windless, the light the only moving thing. Sara took a few steps toward it. The light did not change.

Now she could see that it was coming from the foot of a grave-stone. She could see the marble it reflected off and a dark wreath. Perhaps a hobo was warming himself at a campfire? But what sort of hobo would hang around a graveyard in the middle of the night? A hobo like herself. She did not wish to encounter such a one: it would be more frightening than meeting the dead.

Ten steps ahead and she could see that no one was there. The flame was a candle enclosed in a glass box, laid by some mourner on a fresh grave. She let her breath out and walked past the spot, over a mound and into a lower pasture of modest stones. Suddenly she was in a meadow of little flames. There must have been two dozen of them, each circled by a small sun which skimmed the dark earth. She stopped to read the names on the stones they lit. Foreign birthplaces, foreign expressions of loss spoke an awful loneliness. But the flames, as she looked over them, were a merry crowd; death was a joining, then, to the lost familiar.

But Jackie wasn't dead. The flames stirred, becoming frantic, as a wind passed over their boxes. Sara walked on into the older part of the cemetery, where the graves were not tended, where they were vast monuments grown over with ivy, idols to the idea of man or woman. Jackie wasn't dead, although she had tried to be. She had flubbed it. She had made an incomplete statement. She had made death a messy, halfway thing. If it was a kind of virginity to be alive, then Jackie, like her innocence, was tainted. Life would appear to come back to her, its vessel would not be intact. Something of it would have leaked away. Maybe part of Jackie's leg or her palm or her tongue would not come back. Maybe part of her brain would not come back. Maybe she would always be a little bit dead.

'So,' said Sara out loud, 'that's what you wanted. To muck up the absolutes some more. To turn one more thing into a fraud.'

When Sara went to the hospital the next morning, Jackie had the tubes out and was sitting up in bed. The nurses had been combing her hair; it was spread out on her shoulders.

'Hi, Sara, what are you doing here?'

'We had a dinner engagement.'

'Oh, no, did I ruin your evening?'

'Jackie, you must have known I'd come looking for you.'

Jackie closed her lips in a pout. 'I knew you would,' she said, beginning to wail. 'I thought you'd come around 8:30. But I thought that by then I'd be . . . well, it would all be finished.'

You miscalculated, Sara thought. 'I didn't get there till eleven,' she said.

Something hard flashed in Jackie's eyes: *are you calling me a liar?* But she put out her arms to be hugged. 'You saved my life!' The sweetness in her voice was gone; perhaps her throat was raw from the tube. 'I must have scared you a lot,' she said in the voice of one making amends.

'You mean you must have hated me.'

'Oh no, not you, Sara. I'd never hate you. I *love* you.'

Sara went out and cried in the toilet. All the things she wanted to say to Jackie and couldn't: *Next time, don't arrange to be rescued. Why choose me to do your dirty work? I'm not your servant. I'm not responsible for the remains*. Now that Jackie was alive, Sara felt like killing her.

There were two more days with Jackie in the hospital. Sara seethed at the arrogance of her friend, lying there disdainfully absorbing hundreds of dollars of medical assistance every hour, too polite to inform the doctors that they were making a mistake to bring her around, that she did not want to live. Because it was clear that Jackie still believed that the world had gone mad and people were faintly despicable for their participation in it. The psychiatrists gathered around and asked Jackie questions about how she felt: they took notes while she expounded. And what about me, Sara thought from the sidelines, what about me?

ELISABETH HARVOR

Our Lady of All the Distances

She sometimes thought of Sam up there. She had one image of
the northern summer—an image of tawny moth-eaten tundra, like
a faded golden carcass partly eaten away by mud, and above it,
rising forever, a shimmering pale sky. All the movies, all the slides,
all the black-and-white stills—all the shots of sea-planes tethered
to fallen wharves, caught against blinding northern lakes, blinding northern suns—that Sam had brought back with him over the
years had done nothing to alter it. And in any case her image was
her own cliché, and therefore a better cliché than ice and snow.

She had an image for Sam, too (in case he didn't have one of
his own), of them, his family, far to the south of him, part of a
congested untidy human tide-mark on the lower part of the sandy
stretch of Mooney's Bay. And although fewer and fewer Americans came to Canada for their summer vacations with skis on the
tops of their cars, few of them could have imagined the oppressive Texan-like heat through which she now led her two young
sons as they worked their way to the water's edge.

She wished she had worn a big loose dress for her ordeal of
walking through the sun-bathers to the beach. Her big white
vulnerable thighs quivered, testy in anticipation of second looks.
But there would be no second looks. There would be no first looks.
It had been years since there had been second looks and almost
as many since there had been first looks. Her children followed
her, each according to his own style. Billie, four, walked eagerly
toward the water, his friend. Shaun, seven, a first child (and
because of that? because of her? because of what?), walked near
her—as if leashed to her own ennui—sour, complaining about all
the things it was not in her power to change—that it was too hot,
that the walk to the beach was too long, that he was tired, that he
wished he hadn't come.

On the terrace of the cabana they paused a moment, paused like far-eyed conquerors, and looked out over the prone bazaar of the beach with all its people felled by sun. People who had transistor radios were there. In force. They lay in little groups on their tight bellies with their Tahitian-flower-blooming bums beamed at the sun. Even to her their eyes seemed too hard, too level, aimed as impersonally as artillery above their jarring fortresses of sound. Shaun, in skirting distrustfully around one of these groups, inevitably came into the radius of another almost exactly like it, and the beach seemed to her then a parody of life itself, an endless plain of overlapping circles, and backing out of one, you backed into another, which, if not the same, was probably worse. Oh, she was in a bad mood today, she really and truly was.

They passed by a whole colony of single girls, falsely bright single girls, wearing wrap-around sunglasses and lying like burnt offerings on their giant Aztec beach-towels, and farther down they passed a woman whose radio sang-growled: 'Tank 'eaven for leetle girls, zey grow up in zee most delightful way.' The woman had caressed herself with oil till her skin shone wetly. She was past the age where she had grown up in the most delightful way, but she seemed to have taken good care of herself all the same; her hair was protected by a smart little head scarf, and her beach-coat—thrown down to one side of her—was made of an impressive fabric, like one of Rousseau's paintings of dreams.

Nearer the water's edge were the young gods and goddesses, and they were so perfect that she could hardly bear to look. They had perfect overall tans. Only when they laughed, only when they bent over in their young convulsive way could you glimpse small winter white slits of skin. She herself had a housewife's tan that came from wearing high-necked sleeveless dresses, so that her legs were tanned below the knee and her arms up to the shoulder, but there was a vast expanse around her bathing-suit that was a slack and sick-room white. And there were a few workmen's tans—tanned torsos, white legs—and there was one alarming man who had one white leg, one brown one. When she noticed that he walked with a limp, she realized that his harlequin look came from his having recently worn a cast.

She settled herself down and got out the children's things. On her beach-bag a stylized blue flounder swam through perfect waves of turquoise rick-rack. Christmas-present beach-bag. And very useful it was turning out to be, too, here on the burning glitter of the sands of summer. She sighed, dispensing pails and warships.

For a while she watched the lifeguards, solid and visored on their wooden towers, their whistles twinkling like lockets in the sun. And there were the people nearby who had brought their terrible efficiency to the beach with them, and who now produced an incredible assortment of containers in plaid vinyl and primary-coloured plastics. She thought she remembered them from last year. She thought she remembered their equipment.

Farther down, Billie squatted at the water's start, gouging the wet sand with his pail. Shaun stood close by, disinterested, tense. Such desperate apathy reminded her of her own childhood, but did not make her sympathetic. She narrowed her eyes against the pewter glare of the water, took out her book, *Encounters with British Intellectuals*, a book she would not be ashamed to leave face-down on the towel when she later went in for a swim. As if anyone cared, she thought, smiling her private smile. She dug a little hole in the wet sand, leaned over, smelled it, decided to use it as an ashtray. Perhaps she had better oil herself before her encounter with the British intellectuals. She ferreted around blindly in her beach-bag for the spill-free container, found it, absently and patchily rubbed oil on herself while she watched her children. At last she began to read.

The afternoon wore on. Serious children's construction work was going on along the sandcastle-line, but nine times out of ten the castles were smashed by huge boys chasing thuddingly after girls who had thrown sand in their faces in the first place. The builders of the castles squatted bewildered, their droopy wet bathing-suits sugared with sand, but soon began again to firm up their crumbled dreams. The sad but patient children made her think of people in bombed cities. She was having a bad day. She was only seeing the sad things. But then the happy things didn't seem to make her feel any better either. Lovers lying nearby didn't cheer her up, only brought to the surface the thought that she had expected more from this trip to the beach than merely giving her children a swim. Reading her book, *trying* to read her book, she was sometimes disturbed by a wincing deep inside her. She lit her cigarette and with her match-stick scratched I WANT deep in the dark sand. But she couldn't finish it, what it was she wanted, even though she had always known what a good censor sand is, had known since she was very young how with one swoop you could smear out the legend of a wish in the sand and no-one would ever know what the wish had been. Sand was even better than snow, that way. She erased I WANT thoroughly, what she wanted being for some lean intelligent man to lower himself down on the blanket beside her. To begin with the book, but to end with her.

On the shoreline there was a casual parade of girls. They came in twos, usually in bikinis, sometimes smoking, plowing the shallow water with their feet. They had made their unawareness of admiring glances almost an art. Watching them, watching the men they promenaded for but pretended not to notice, she wondered if liaisons were formed here. She could not see that they were. And yet at that moment, one of the walking girls, hands on first-rate hips, stopped below the lifeguard's tower and called up to him. He leaned out like a sky king, gesticulating, pointing, describing. The girl winced uncomprehendingly for the noise of the swimmers was truly (and conveniently) deafening. The lifeguard climbed down from his wooden tower, put a protective arm around her, pointed, explained. Yes, liaisons were made, then, and all that walking was not in vain. She sighed, envious, contemptuous, and then suddenly, panic-stricken, tried with her eyes to search out her own children. She found them at last. Shaun seemed after all to be having a happy day, was talking to two similar-sized children, and Billie was on some touching secret mission, still gouging out wet sand with his pail, still tottering to a chosen spot on the lower beach to dump it, still rushing back in a desperate serious way for more, from down where the water made its mindless bright beginning. A tremendous tenderness for him made her throat tense up, bound all the stalks of vocal cords and tendons tightly together.

After a while she called the children in to get something to eat. They sat caped in towels, eating quietly, watching everything. She herself had forgotten, over the winter, so many of the sounds of the river, the interweaving of screams and giggling, the shouts of the young men, the quick way the water throttled their laughter. Not far from them, three boys were wrestling a girl in a yellow blouse and blue jeans toward the water. This had happened every single time she had come to this beach. The same moves. The same counter-moves. Only the players changed.

'Don't!' the girl in blue jeans screamed, loving every minute of it. Her elbows were held high and jutted out, her body was arched back and she dug her heels protestingly into the sand as they dragged her waterwards. Phony, phony, phony. They got her into it thigh high. 'Stop it!' she shrieked happily, in her element. 'Don't you dare throw me in!' They threw her in. She bobbed up, a happy, vicious, flustered Venus, and started flailing them all with great silver sails of water. Shaun and Billie watched, missing no detail. And through the tea-coloured glass of her sunglasses she also watched—but with a jaundiced eye.

After food they went back to play and she went back to her book. Some time later, the sky darkened, and she turned her attention away from the river and toward the grass where some people were playing volleyball. There was a Negro girl in a dark green tartan bathing-suit and a girl with long brown hair who had on a bikini that had designs on it like black and brown Japanese brush strokes. Oh, to be young again, she thought, watching them. And yet when she had been young, she had not been like them—she had never been any good at games, she had been an awkward sideliner always, thinking that life would come with being grown-up, just as she now seemed to think it went with being young. Nothing went with anything! When would she ever learn that? It was all part of the mustard with hotdog myth! It was all part of the love with marriage myth! Her mother had been a great believer in that one. And yet it must be wrong to teach your children that life was a series of inevitable and beautiful combinations. Whatever else it *was*, life was not *that*. And it was busy proving it to you twenty times a day. She called her children in to get dressed.

The afternoon was slanting across itself by the time they went to catch their bus. And when they got home their house smelled closed-in, sour. They would have to get some breezes through it. After she had opened the kitchen window, a marvellous ribbon of late summer wind blew through the house; she could feel it on one of her bare shoulders as she stood watching over the bean-sprouts and hamburger heaving and bubbling in the frying pan. She was remembering when she had been a nurse. She had not been a good nurse, and she had been grateful when Sam had come out of the North and rescued her. In some ways she had been too smart to be a nurse, in other ways not smart enough. She seemed never to have got the knack of distances, an important thing for a nurse to get the knack of. There were two kinds of distances, she now realized—the distance that had to be gauged when you raised frail shoulders with one arm while with the other arm you eased in under them with a great cool wedge of hospital pillow, or when you pivoted a 200-pound patient on its quivering axis while with your other hand you did some kind of sleight-of-hand with the bed linen, making it taut as a trampoline. That was one kind of distance, and a kind she had been clumsy with. Then there was the other kind, the emotional kind, and there too her gauging had been out of kilter. Caring too much (or so she had then thought), lifting the frail shoulders with one arm, she had sometimes banged the fat hospital pillow into the wobbling damp head, in her terrible clumsy anxiety to relate, to care. It was the cool-eyed ones (who thought of it as a job) who did it all best. And for the first time it occurred to her that the two distances were interdependent, more interdependent than mustard and hotdogs, more interdependent than love and marriage. She was remembering when she had worked in the delivery room. A happy place where birth was the rule. But there had been a death while she worked there, a death she still remembered. Except to think of it as a death was perhaps inaccurate—and certainly melodramatic—since it was a death-before-birth, the spontaneous abortion of a three- or four-month-old fetus. It was strange she could remember it so clearly. There must have been many similar cases. It was around five o'clock in the morning, she had been cleaning up the utility room to make it ready for the day-shift, and it lay there among all the debris of birth—among all the other things to be flushed away, among the uprooted placentas, the umbilical cords that looked like telephone cords, among the clots like shiny wine-dark jelly, there it was, this pre-human that looked more like a plant than a human being, that looked, in fact, like a bloated white sprouting bean. She stirred the bean-sprouts in the frying pan, acknowledging them as a source of her rememberings. And in the wards beyond the delivery room there was a curious paradox, one that she now remembered. To the left corridor had been the public mothers—the poor ones—to the right had been the middle- and upper-class mothers. And it was in the public ward that you heard loud scientific discussions on the merits of various kinds of anesthetics and formulas—twilight sleep versus spinals, Carnation milk versus soy—whereas in the private wards almost all the mothers had gone primitive, were having natural childbirth, were breastfeeding and spoke no jargon at all. And she remembered some of the shy rich mothers, backed by their ribboned florists' jungles, the way they jerked like startled gazelles at the first hard pull of the baby's mouth on the nipple. Then a conversation she had had with Sam just before he went away. He had been listing the attractions of Eskimo women. And he had been telling her that the highest honour an Eskimo host could pay a visitor (and there would be a lot of settlements where Sam would be a visitor) was to lend his wife to his guest for the night. She had heard those wife-lending stories before. Hot tales from the cold North.

'But do they still do that, now that they're living in all those pre-fab houses?'

'Men lend their wives in pre-fab houses *here* don't they?' he had said, 'right in our very own suburbs.'

She had sat silent, thinking of Sam and the Eskimo women. 'But what about *me*?' she had cried at last, sitting cross-legged on the immense white plain of their bed, 'What am I supposed to do while you're away?'

'Fuck yourself,' Sam had said, testing the straps of his knapsack.

Now the children were in bed. Not that they had settled to sleep. Well, Shaun had, obliterating the whining day with some tender and original remark that she could not now recall. But with Billie the day could not be so easily given up.

'Come into my room!' he now called, imperious, seductive.

'I've already been to you room twice,' she pointed out firmly, from her white haven in the bathroom.

'I've something to tell you.'

'Tell it from there.'

'Can you hear me?'

One two three testing. 'I can hear you,' she said.

'I have a riddle for you.'

'Alright, ready,' she said.

'What colour is a tired elephant?'

She knew this was her cue to play stupid, to incite his joyful, incredulous four-year-old laughter, to guess 'chocolate purple' or 'Macintosh plaid,' but she was too tired. A tired elephant. 'Grey,' she said.

'Do you give up?'

'I give up.'

'Grey,' he said.

'Good,' she said, briskly, 'Now good-night, Billie. No more talking.'

'No more talking?' He was cunning as an 83-year-old.

'Big day tomorrow!' she called, trying to make her voice robust with encouragement.

'Mummie?'

'Yes, Billie?' Even her blood seemed to sag in her veins.

'Just come into my room for only one more time?' Sweet and plaintive.

'*Billie*, I *can't* come, I'm doing pooh.' This was an activity he had some respect for. Sometimes it took him almost an hour to do it himself. And in what she hoped was a kind but firm voice she said: 'Good-night now, darling.'

'Good-night, darling,' he said.

After five minutes of silence, she went quietly down the hallway to her own room. Outside, darkness was slowly taking charge of the streets, the city's sky. Night fed the shadows. She could imagine lovers, on the slopes of parks, on the slopes of car-seats, being felled by darkness. She turned on the bedside lamp and jolted the outside world (what was left of it) into night. She worked her feet out from her warped sandals and sat on the edge of the bed, looking sideways at a fashion magazine. The pages flapped heavily by. Fashion models wearing white satin dresses were posed against black skies, Brontë landscapes. On one page a girl peered into a seething pool of her own hair—or what appeared to be her own hair—and there were many pages of thick stockings that looked as if tractors had been driven over them, stockings being worn by girls who strode clear-eyed through streets and fields. But out of the corner of her eye, it was the poetry that caught her. All the poems were made up of simple words, words she knew, yet words made to pyramid strangely—into joy, into pain. And although she couldn't always understand the poetry, she felt certain that the poetry *understood her*. That gave her a strange feeling. She closed the magazine and looked up to one wall that had on it a handsome photograph of an arctic church. Taken by Sam. It looked like a Byzantine igloo, something clever had been done with translucent bricks, for the impression you got was of the muted struggle of light shining dimly through thick blocks of snow. She had named this photograph 'the Basilica of the Frozen Blood.' She got up and went over and looked at herself in the curly gilt-framed mirror. All around the mirror—for contrast—Sam had pasted a photo-collage of Eskimo faces—fine, tough Eskimo faces squinting against an unseen sun. So surrounded, she stood watching herself comb her fair dull hair. For a while she thought of Sam's North and imagined the jarring squeak of boats grating against wood wharves, and waiting on the wharves, men with hair like fur, men wearing the blurred blue plaids of much-washed flannel shirts. Then for no reason that she could think of, she suddenly remembered the one attractive man she had seen at the beach that day, a man who had squatted gently by a small girl at the water's edge. They had stayed there together for some time, the man squatting, the little girl (how old? two?) with that pronounced pregnant-looking stomach that very small girls usually have, and her hands clasped high on it, looking peacefully out at the swimmers. A pot-bellied Renaissance child in a bright red bathing-suit. She had found the father and child curiously touching. And even from that distance, beached on her towel, she had almost felt she was there with them, feeling with them the warm gift and retreat of water lapping at her feet. After a while, and again for no reason that she could fathom, she began to cry. The day had pyramided like the poetry. She was on the painful point. She would have to let herself cry. So she did not sniff it back or wipe at it. It was the beginning of something that she could feel how she was caught in the skein of all the distances. It was the beginning of something that she could cry. There were beginnings here that must be honoured.

And with her bare feet planted on the flowered carpet in the high bright bedroom in the summer night she stood there crying on and on while the Eskimo faces squinted politely all around her.

JANETTE TURNER HOSPITAL

You Gave Me Hyacinths

Summer comes hot and steamy with the heavy smell of raw sugar to the north-east coast of Australia. The cane pushes through the rotting window blinds and grows into the cracks and corners of the mind. It ripens in the heart at night, and its crushed sweetness drips into dreams. I have woken brushing from my eyelids the silky plumes that burst up into harvest time. And I have stood smoke-blackened as the cane fires licked the night sky, and kicked my way through the charred stubble after the men have slashed at the naked stalks and sent them churning through the mill. I have walked forever through the honeyed morning air to the crumbling high school—brave outpost of another civilization.

The class always seemed to be on the point of bulging out the windows. If I shut my eyes and thought hard I could probably remember all the faces and put a name to each. One never forgets that first year out of teachers' college, the first school, the first students. Dellis comes before anyone else, of course, feline and demanding, blotting out the others; Dellis, who sat stonily bored through classes and never turned in homework and wrote nothing at all on test papers. 'Can't understand poetry,' she said by way of explanation. There were detentions and earnest talks. At least, I was earnest; Dellis was bored. She put her case simply: 'I'll fail everything anyway.'

'But you don't *need* to, Dellis. It's a matter of your attitude, not your ability. What sort of job will you get if you don't finish high school?'

'Valesi's store. Or the kitchen at the mill canteen.'

'Yes, well. But they will be very monotonous jobs, don't you think? Very boring.'

'Yes.' Flicking back the long blonde hair.

'Now just supposing you finished high school. Then what would you do?'

'Same thing. Work at Valesi's or in the mill canteen. Till I'm married. Everybody does.'

'You could go to Brisbane, or even Sydney or Melbourne. There are any number of jobs you could get there if you were to finish high school. There would be theatres to go to, plays to see. And libraries. Dellis, this town doesn't even have a library.'

Silence.

'Have you ever been out of this town, Dellis?'

'Been to Cairns once.'

Cairns. Twenty thousand people, and less than a hundred miles away: the local idea of the Big City.

'Dellis, what are you going to do with your life?'

No answer.

I felt angry, as though I were the one trapped in the slow rhythm of a small tropical town. 'Can you possibly be content,' I asked viciously, 'to work at the mill, get married, have babies, and grow old in this shrivelled-up sun-blasted village?'

She was mildly puzzled at my outburst, but shrugged it off as being beyond her. 'Reckon I'll have to marry the first boy who knocks me up,' she said.

'You don't *have* to marry anybody, Dellis. No doubt you could fall in love with some boy in this town and be quite happy with him. But is that all you want?'

'Dunno. It's better'n *not* getting married.'

I knew her parents were not around; perhaps they were dead; though more likely they were merely deserters who had found the lure of fruit picking in the south too rewarding to resist. I knew she lived with a married sister—the usual shabby wooden cottage with toddlers messily underfoot, everyone cowering away from the belligerent drunk who came home from the cane fields each night. The family, the town—it was an intolerable cocoon. She simply had to fight her way out of it, go south. I told her so. But her face was blank. The world beyond the town held neither fascination nor terror. I think she doubted the existence of anything beyond Cairns.

In the classroom the air was still and fetid. There was the stale sweat of forty students; there was also the sickly odour of molasses rolling in from the mill. An insistent wave of nausea lapped at me. Dellis's face seemed huge and close and glistened wetly the way all flesh did in the summer. She looked bored as always, though probably not so much at her detention as at the whole wearying business of an afternoon and evening still to be lived through—after which coolness would come for an hour or two, and even fitful sleep. Then another dank day would begin.

'Dellis, let's get out of here. Will you go for a walk with me?'

'Okay,' she shrugged.

Outside the room things were immediately better. By itself, the molasses in the air was heavy and drowsy, but pleasant. We crunched down the drive and out the gate under the shade of the flame-trees.

'I love those,' Dellis said, pointing upwards where the startling crimson flaunted itself against the sky.

'Why?'

She was suddenly angry. 'Why? You always want to know why. You spoil things. I hate your classes. I hate poetry. It's stupid. Just sometimes there is a bit I like, but all you ever do is ask why. Why do I like it? And then I feel stupid because I never know why. I just like it, that's all. And you always spoil it.'

We walked in silence the length of the street, which was the length of the town, past the post office, Cavallero's general store, Valesi's Snack Bar, and two pubs. The wind must have been blowing our way from the mill, because the soot settled on us gently as we walked. The men swilling their beer on the benches outside the pubs fell silent as we passed and their eyes felt uncomfortable on my damp skin. At the corner pub, someone called out 'Hey, Dellis!' from the dark inside, and laughter fell into the dust as we rounded the corner and turned toward the mill.

Halfway between the corner and the mill, Dellis said suddenly, 'I like the red. I had a red dress for the school dance, and naturally you know what they all said. . . . But the trees don't care. That's what I'd like to be. A flame-tree.' We went on in silence again, having fallen into the mesmeric pattern of stepping from sleeper to sleeper of the narrow rail siding, until we came to the line of cane cars waiting outside the mill. Dellis reached into one and pulled out two short pieces. She handed one to me and started chewing the other.

'We really shouldn't, Dellis. It's stealing.'

She eyed me sideways and shrugged. 'You spoil things.'

I tore off strips of bamboo-like skin with my teeth and sucked at the soft sweet fibres.

We had passed the mill, and were on the beach road. Two miles under that spiteful sun. Close to the cane there was some coolness, and we walked in the dusty three-foot strip between the road and the sugar plumes, sucking and chewing and spitting out the fibres. The dust came up in little puffs around our sandals. We said nothing, just chewed and spat. Only two cars passed us. The Howes all hung out of one and waved. The other was a pick-up truck headed for the mill.

About one and a half miles along, the narrow road suddenly emerged from its canyon of tall cane. A lot of cutting had been done, and a farmhouse stood alone in the shorn fields, white and blinding in the afternoon sun. The haze of colour around the front door was a profusion of Cooktown orchids, fragile waxen flowers, soft purple with a darker slash of purple at the heart. 'Gian's house,' said Dellis as we walked on, and into the cool cover of uncut cane again.

Gian! So that was why he always had an orchid to tuck brazenly behind one ear. He was seventeen years old, a Torres Strait Islander: black, six feet tall, a purple flower nestled against his curly hair any time one saw him except in class. Gian, rakishly Polynesian, bending over that day after school till the impudent orchid and his incredible eyes were level with mine.

'Did you know that I killed my father, Miss?'

'Yes, Gian. I was told that when I first arrived.'

'Well?' The eyes were incongruously blue, and watchful under the long silky lashes.

I knew the court verdict was self-defence, I knew his father had been blind drunk, a wife-beater on the rampage.

'Well?' Gian persisted.

I said lamely: 'It must have been horrible.'

'I hated him,' Gian said without passion. 'He was a bastard.'

'I gather many people thought so.'

'Well?'

'What are you asking me, Gian? How can I know what was the right thing to do? Only you can know that.'

'I am the only person in this town who has killed a man. Do you realize that?'

We stared at each other, and then outrageously he let his eyes wander slowly down my body with blatant intent, and walked away. I was trembling. After that I was always afraid to look Gian in the eye, and he always dared me to. When I turned to write on the board, I could feel two burning spots on the back of my neck. And when I faced the class again, his eyes were waiting, and a slow grin would spread across his face. Yet it was not an insolent grin. That was what was most disturbing. It seemed to say that we two shared a daring and intimate secret. But he knew it and I didn't.

Dellis and I had reached the beach. It was deserted. We kicked off our sandals, lay down, and curled our toes into the warm sand. The palms cast a spindly shade that wasn't much help, but a tired wisp of sea breeze scuffled up the sand refreshingly from the calm water. So amazingly calm inside the reef. I never could get used to it. I had grown up with frenetic surf beaches, but from here you had to go a thousand miles down the coast before you got south of the Great Reef.

'Dellis, you must visit Brisbane this summer, and give yourself a swim in the surf for a Christmas present. You just can't imagine how exciting it is.'

'Let's go swimming now. It's so bloody hot.'

'But we don't have swimsuits.'

'Just take our clothes off.'

'But somebody might come.'

Dellis stood up and unbuttoned her blouse. 'You spoil things,' she said. It hurt when she stood naked in front of me. She was only fifteen, and it wasn't fair. I almost told her how beautiful she was, but envy and embarrassment stopped me. This is her world, I thought; she is part of it, she belongs. She was tanned all over; there were no white parts. She ran down into the water without looking back.

I stood up and slipped off my dress, but then my heart failed me, and I went into the water with my underwear on. We must have swum for half an hour, and it was cool and pleasant. Then we ran along the water's edge for ten minutes or so to dry out. We dressed and lay on the sand again. 'It's good to do that,' Dellis murmured. 'It's the best thing when you're unhappy.'

'Are you often unhappy?'

The look she gave me suggested that if I had to ask such stupid questions, why did I call myself a teacher?

'What I meant, Dellis, is that I'd like to . . . if you're unhappy, I would like to . . . I mean, if there's any way I can help. . . .'

'You don't even know how to chew cane properly.' She was looking at me with a kind of affectionate contempt, as though I were an idiot child. 'You don't know anything. You really don't know *anything*.' She shook her head and grinned at me.

I smiled back. I wanted to tell her how much I was learning. I would have liked to speak of poetic symbols, and of the significance which flame-trees or Cooktown orchids would henceforth have for me. Instead I said: 'Dellis, today. . . . Who would have thought? How could I have guessed, this morning, that today would be so . . . would be such a . . . ? Well, a *remarkable* day.'

'Really? Why?'

'You spoil things. Don't ask me why.'

She giggled. 'But really, why?'

'It's very complicated. It has a lot to do with a religious and sheltered background that you couldn't even begin to imagine, and it would take a lot of explaining. But to put it briefly, it is a truly extraordinary thing for me to have gone swimming naked with one of my students.'

'You didn't even take all your clothes off,' she laughed.

Now the silence was close and comfortable, and longer and drowsier. We must have dozed, because when I sat up again the humidity was even more oppressive and monstrous dark clouds had billowed up out of the sea.

'There's going to be a thunderstorm, Dellis. We'd better get home quickly.'

'Too early in the year,' she said sleepily. And when she saw the clouds, 'It'll ruin a lot of cane.'

We were walking quickly, and nearly at Gian's house again, when Dellis pointed into the shadowy green maze of the cane field and said, 'That's where Gian and I did it.'

'Did what?'

'*Did* it. He laid me.'

'Oh! . . . I . . . I see. Your first. . . ?'

She looked at me, startled, and laughed. 'He's the only one I loved. And the only one I wouldn't take money from.'

Virgin and child in a field of green. No madonna could have beheld the amazing fruit of her womb with more awed astonishment than I felt. Something hurt at the back of my head, and I reached up vaguely with my hand. There was a whole ordered moral world there somewhere. But I couldn't find it. It wouldn't come.

I said, inanely: 'So you and Gian are in love?'

'He was going to give me money and I wouldn't take it. But he was gentle. And afterwards he took the orchid from behind his ear and put it between my legs. I hoped I'd have a baby, but I didn't.'

The storm was coming and we fled before the wind and the rain. At the mill we separated, but Dellis ran back and grabbed my arm. She had to shout, and even then I thought I hadn't heard her properly. Our skirts bucked about our legs like wet sails, runnels of water sluiced over our ears. She shouted again: 'Have you ever been laid?'

'Dellis!'

'Have you?'

'This is not . . . this is not a proper. . . .'

'Have you?'

'No.'

'Gian says you're beautiful. Gian says that you. . . . He says he would like to. . . . That's why I hated you. But now I don't.'

Then we ran for our lives.

All through my dinner and all through the evening, the rain drummed on the iron roof, and the wind dashed the banana palms against the window in a violent tattoo. For some reason I wanted to dance to the night's jazz rhythm. But then surely there was something more insistent than the thunder, a battering on my door. She was standing dripping wet on my doorstep.

'Dellis, for God's sake, what are you doing here? It's almost midnight.'

'They were fighting at home again, and I couldn't stand it. I brought something for you.'

She held out a very perfect Cooktown orchid. Somebody's prize bloom, stolen.

'Come inside, out of the rain,' I said vaguely, listening to the lines from Eliot that fluted in my head—fragments and images half-remembered. I had to take down the book, so I showed her the passage:

> 'You gave me hyacinths first a year ago;
> 'They called me the hyacinth girl.'
> —Yet when we came back, late, from the Hyacinth garden,
> Your arms full, and your hair wet, I could not
> Speak, and my eyes failed, I was neither
> Living nor dead, and I knew nothing,
> Looking into the heart of light, the silence.

'Dellis,' I said, as (teacherly, motherly) I combed out her wet tangled hair, 'for me, you will always be the hyacinth girl.'

'*Poetry*!' she sniffed. And then: 'What do hyacinths look like?'

'I don't know. I imagine they look like Cooktown orchids.'

ISABEL HUGGAN

Into the Green Stillness

The summer I was nine my mother and I spent nearly four weeks in Streetsville looking after my three cousins. Their mother had died the year before, along with another of my mother's sisters, in a dreadful car accident near Clappison's Corners. My Uncle Rennie was having a hard time getting over his grief. Memories of Aunt Mabel lurked in closets and kitchen cupboards, hovered over her jars of jams and jellies in the basement so that he could not bear to open and eat them. He couldn't stand the charitable offers of help from the neighbours, the sympathetic eyes of the minister each Sunday, the well-meant invitations out to bridge parties to meet new widows and divorcées. He'd rave and rage, sitting at our kitchen table with my mother, and finally they decided that what he should do was drive out west and look for work in Alberta or B.C. My father agreed. 'A complete change of scene, that's what I'd do,' Frank said.

Uncle Rennie got a week off without pay to add to his vacation, packed up his Studebaker and left my mother, Mavis, in charge of his children. She wanted them all to come to Garten—she may not have wanted to dwell with her sister's ghostly presence any more than Rennie did—but in Streetsville my cousins had their own rooms and our house couldn't provide that. So it was decided that she and I would go there the middle of July.

I had mixed feelings, for although I liked my cousins well enough I hated giving up my swimming-lessons at the Rotary pool. On the other hand, the idea of getting out of Garten was attractive even at that age. I'd only been to my cousins' house a handful of times but I loved it—a grey brick bungalow on the farthest edge of a new development, with only a school playground between it and a maple bush. There were no trees at all on the streets, as if having the bush so near provided sufficient greenery, and something about the stripped-away bareness was appealing.

I liked too the smell of fresh plaster that seemed to linger in their house over the years, and the ivory-coloured venetian blinds on the windows, and the pastel carpets covering all the floors.

Unlike my mother or uncle, I did not mind Aunt Mabel's house for fear of being reminded of her at every turn. I was not sad that she was dead and gone—I rather welcomed the chance to enjoy the house without her there always pricking sharply at us children: 'Shoes off at the door! How many times have I told you? . . . No cookies in the bedrooms! Crumbs everywhere! . . . Really, Elizabeth, would you do that at *home*?' The very worst aspects of my mother, it seemed to me, were magnified and intensified in her older sister. I inevitably felt grateful for Mavis after an encounter with Mabel, just as I had always been made discontent after a visit from Rita, the younger sister who was 32 and still unmarried at the time of the accident. She had been a teacher at the school for the deaf in Milton, and would teach me and my cousins how to sign rude words, which we would then do in front of our untutored parents while she smiled and winked at us. Rita was the one I missed, I mourned—not Mabel.

My cousins, however they felt, knew a good thing when they saw it, and played up their position as motherless children during that whole year after the accident. The eldest, Ted, who'd been eleven at the time Mabel died, always took full charge of the recital of events surrounding the accident, and Charlene, two years younger, filled in details, emotional fragments that worked to flesh out the story and give it immediacy.

'Mom and Aunt Rita had gone over shopping to Hamilton,' Ted would begin, and Charlene would add dramatic punch: 'And Dad had told them to be real careful because of all the construction on Highway 5.' Between the two of them they sorted out melody and harmony, motif and refinements, so that as their tale progressed my teeth would be on edge with anxiety even though I knew the ending.

'Dad was pacing up and down the kitchen saying, ''Those dang fool women shoulda been home an hour ago,'' ' Ted would say. 'By then rain was coming down something awful and the lightning was making us jump like crazy,' Charlene would provide, giving Ted a moment to pause.

'I was looking out the window so I was the first to see it, the police cruiser,' Ted would resume. 'I saw the red light flashing out there in the storm and it didn't hit me till I turned around to tell Dad there were two cops getting out of their car and coming up the driveway. He was just at the doorway to the living-room when the doorbell rang then and . . .'

'His face went white as white.' Charlene, all breathless. 'And he said "Oh Christ, no." Just like that.'

Then would follow all the gruesome details of the accident itself, the overturned transport truck, the slippery highway, the badly marked detour, the rain, the blood, the women flung into their windshield. In all this, my cousin Grace, who was six months younger than me, never said a word. Not because she couldn't speak, but because she had the mind of a three-year-old and didn't have very much to say. 'Brain-damaged' we were taught to explain if anyone ever asked about her. And so her part in the family recital was simply to weep softly, spontaneously, from the heart, for Gracie knew only that her Mom had gone forever. Her Mom, who had been told by the nurses to hang on, keep that baby in, don't push yet, the doctor will be here any minute . . . and hadn't pushed, had kept that baby in its birth canal too long, had deprived it of oxygen, had stunted its poor brain forever. I wasn't told all that until I was an adult—at the time, the distinction merely was made that Gracie was not a moron, it was not a flaw that ran in families, it was only an accident at birth. She was the same as the rest of us except she was a little slow.

In fact, she was the prettiest of us all, and but for a vacancy in the eyes, and a kind of slackness that came to her mouth and cheek muscles in later years, hers was the sort of appearance that would have been the conventional ticket to success, had life turned out a little differently. Her fair wavy hair, her even features and wide-set grey eyes would have made her a teacher's pet, a prom queen, a heart-breaker. I loved the way she looked, the pretty ruffled dresses she was allowed to wear even though she was chubbier than I was—Mavis always said chubby girls shouldn't wear ruffles. I think once it became clear to Aunt Mabel what the score was she allowed Gracie to wear anything she liked and to eat all she wanted, either to allow her some small pleasures in life or, as likely, to minimize the chances of her growing up to be so attractive that she 'got in trouble'.

My mother really wasn't comfortable with Gracie. Slowness of any kind made her impatient, and I think she sometimes thought the child was 'just putting it on to get attention'. Ted, the first-born, was very much her favourite, and could do no wrong in her eyes; but Charlene she found sneaky. 'She's a little too nicey-nice to be trusted,' I heard her say in conversation with my father the night before we left for Streetsville. I was lying in my usual spot at the top of the stairs listening to them talk in the living-room.

It would be the longest separation my parents would have had since the week my mother had spent in the hospital when I was born. In spite of that, Frank didn't seem as upset about our going as I think Mavis might have liked. He'd have his lunches down-town as he preferred to do anyway, and he knew, as did Mavis, that the neighbourhood wives would outdo themselves having him over for evening meals. He promised to come see us one Sunday, and to phone once during each week. He was so cheerful about what he called 'batching it' that I felt less guilty about being glad to leave him too.

When he leaned down to kiss me on the forehead at the bus station the day we were leaving, he didn't say he'd miss me, or that he hoped I'd have a good time with my cousins. 'You behave yourself, Elizabeth,' is what he said. 'Do as your mother tells you and no talking back, you understand?'

I squinted up at him balefully in the way I knew infuriated him. 'Yes, Daddy.' Wondering if Mavis had put him up to it, if she had said, 'You had better have a word with her, Frank, before we go. She'll listen to you better than me. What *will* I do with four to look after?' Or whether that was really all he had to say to me ever, any time. 'Behave yourself.' As if he were suddenly aware of the harshness of his tone, he reached out and straightened the shoulder strap of my sundress. 'There now, away you both go.'

We got our seat near the front, and my mother waved her handkerchief so that he could see where we were through the dusty glass, and then we were off, enclosed in the smoky, musty smell of plush seats and other people's perfume, settling into our-selves for the trip ahead. Mavis was wearing one of her smart little hats and a striped cotton dress that made her look taller, more chic than usual. I wanted to tell her how wonderful I thought she looked, but it sounded false when I rehearsed it in my head so instead I sat silently, flipping over pages of my comic book while she opened out a new issue of the *Ladies' Home Journal*.

Reading on the bus made me feel like throwing up; my usual remedy, sucking peppermints, so annoyed Mavis with its accom-panying smacking noises that in the end I put down the comic and looked out the window. After Guelph the country got flatter, less lush, more open, as if paving the way for the towns and cities to come. I was happy to be leaving home; life in Streetsville was bound to offer me adventures not possible in Garten. I thought about Ted and Charlene, and wondered if they would play with me or not. We had always seemed as much friends as cousins, yet the last time I'd seen them, during the Easter holidays, they had pretty well ignored me, had played games that were too difficult for their sister to understand and had left me to play with her. Somehow, since Aunt Mabel's death, we were no longer in the same league; cousins still, but they had something from which I was excluded and it seemed to make them much older. 'They've been through a lot,' my mother soothed when I complained about feeling left out. 'Don't forget that. Death leaves its mark.' If *she* were to die, I wondered, would we then be equal again?

Uncle Rennie and my mother stayed up very late that night going over the past, organizing the present. He left the next morning after breakfast, and we all gathered out at the end of the driveway to wave goodbye. It was a very hot, clear July morning, and the edges of everything seemed brighter and sharper than normal. As his car pulled away, my cousins followed it down to the curb where they stood, barefoot on the grass, holding hands. Mavis wiped her eyes and put her arm across my shoulders and I knew I was supposed to be feeling something, love or sadness. But I longed only for time to move more swiftly.

'Come now, children, we'll go inside and talk about all our arrangements,' my mother said, and I saw Ted and Charlene raise their eyebrows at each other after she'd turned and opened the screen door. Having an aunt around every minute was going to be a big change in their lives and I recognized that. I wanted to raise my eyebrows back at them in some kind of comradely gesture, to show that I was on their side. But I didn't. I knew, intuitively, the protocol to be observed here was the same as in Garten: one waits to be asked to enter the charmed circle, the secret society; one does not attempt to wink and weasel one's way in.

We sat down around the kitchen table and looked at each other. Ted played with his spoon in the remaining cereal and milk in his bowl, stirring it around and mashing it, a habit I knew drove my mother wild. But she didn't say a word to him, she was busy with a pad of paper and a pencil, checking the notes she and Uncle Rennie had made. Ted was very much like his father in appearance, angular and square-headed, with fair hair that wanted to grow at right angles along the back ridge of his scalp. His hair was greasy, and although he wouldn't turn thirteen until the end of the summer his face was already blotchy and bumpy. I didn't know anything about puberty at that point, I only recall thinking that he had become, as if under some awful enchantment, horribly ugly.

Unlike Charlene, who at ten was long-limbed and slim, whose hair was combed back smoothly into a pony-tail that flicked back and forth as she tossed her head and chewed her gum. She had a way of sauntering that made you think she wasn't scared of anything, and I envied her wholeheartedly; even her clothes lay loosely on her body, did what they were supposed to, didn't stick and bind and wrinkle the way mine did in this hot weather. She began stacking the breakfast dishes by the sink, and looked back over her shoulder.

'I don't mind doing the dishes every morning before I go to day camp, Auntie,' she said, 'if that would be a help. I'm used to doing chores.'

'Oh no, dear, there's no need for that. You could clear the table for me, of course,but that'll be fine. You and Ted just take care of getting yourselves ready. We'll make up your lunches the night before and put them in the fridge, wouldn't that be smart?' Mavis smiled, at her kindly, efficient best.

The two older ones would be gone every day from nine until four, leaving me to play with Gracie. Or, as Mavis put it, 'being responsible for your cousin'. I didn't mind at all; Gracie was far and away the easiest one to get along with, and I rather liked the status of being her caretaker. Besides, Ted and Charlene had made it clear since my arrival, by ignoring me and lumping me in with their sister, that they wanted nothing to do with me. Trailing around after them would only end in heartbreak, I felt sure of that.

It was decided that I would share Gracie's room instead of staying in my mother's bed—a move I heartily approved. Aunt Mabel had made the room a mauve-and-white bower with floral wallpaper, white furniture decorated with gold scrolls and curli- cues, fluffy curtains and ruffled cushions, and shelf after shelf of stuffed dolls and toys. Gracie had such a placid generous nature I knew she would let me play with all her things—she never argued or wanted to do things 'her way' the way other children did—and she might even give me a doll to take home. No wonder everyone loved her, I thought wistfully. What must that be like? Maybe if there was something wrong with me Mavis and Frank would give me whatever I wanted, would give me ruffles and stuffed toys. It must not be so bad having the mind of a three-year-old. I tried to remember what it had been like to be three, but all that came was a fluttering of shreds and scraps, like torn-out pictures from a book or bits of cloth being tossed from a ragbag. Maybe that's what it was like, just not remembering much. Well, I wouldn't mind that, I thought.

'Can Gracie and I play in the woods?' I asked, seeing in that the opportunity for adventure. My mother looked hesitant, and glanced at Ted and Charlene as if for their sanction.

'Oh sure, Auntie, the little kids play at the edge of the bush there by the school all the time. You just have to be sure that Grace doesn't wander off, Elizabeth,' Ted said. 'You have to keep an eye on her because sometimes she'll go off and then not know the way back.'

'Do not,' said Gracie, offended. 'Do not. Gracie's a good girl.'

'Of course you are, dear,' my mother said, reaching over and patting her arm. 'And you must be good when you are with Elizabeth and stay with her every minute so that *she* doesn't get lost in the woods. Do you see?' Mavis thought she was being so clever, I thought, and it was such a transparent ploy I was sure even Gracie could see through it as well. But we all smiled then and nodded at each other and finished our orange juice and went out. Ted and Charlene went off on their bicycles to their day camp at the Y, riding side by side down the street at exactly the same speed. They swerved their front wheels slowly in sweeping rhythmic movements leaving a trail of invisible *esses* in the air behind them. There was a smooth, effortless quality to their riding, as if they had practised this routine so often they could do it with their eyes closed.

Mavis stood at the door behind Gracie and me, and when I turned to say goodbye I thought how worn down and lonely she looked, how out of place. I wondered what she would do without her Garten friends to talk to on the phone. Would she sit at the kitchen table now and sip coffee by herself and miss her dead sisters? Well, there was nothing I could do. I couldn't make her feel better. I would just get out and away.

I held my cousin's hand crossing the street to the school-yard and then we ran across the open grass to the fence at the far end where the bush began. There was a section of fence pulled up so that it was easy to crawl under into the long uncut grass on the other side. Queen Anne's lace and milk vetch and sweet clover, I could name all the flowers for Gracie. And then out of the tickle of grass against bare legs, into the enveloping shadow of the trees. At the edge of the woods there was very little undergrowth, but as we went farther it became thicker and heavier, the saplings crowding for every last bit of soil and light. The farmer who owned the bush must have stopped clearing it out once he saw the direction the development was taking; he must have known that he'd soon be a richer man than he'd ever have been from lumber or maple syrup.

I wanted to keep going, right into the dense heart of the woods, where I imagined there'd be a clearing, a small tranquil pool. But in some places the thin wiry branches were so interwoven that we could barely get through, and Gracie whimpered as they whipped against our arms and faces. 'Don't cry, Gracie,' I said. 'We'll turn round in a minute.' I felt dizzy with new sensations, the heavy scent of growth, the closeness and overwhelming sameness of all the green around us. What if we *did* get lost? They would find us here, huddled beneath a tree, starved to death, our souls gone to heaven. Like the babes in the wood. The illustration from my nursery storybook flashed into my head then, and I saw two sleepy, chubby children cuddling by the roots of a tree on the edge of a path. A path. That's what we would do. We would make a path and then Gracie wouldn't cry any more and she wouldn't get lost. It would look just like the picture in the book.

'Do you want to make a path, Gracie?' I asked. 'Do you want to help make a beautiful path?' She nodded, enthusiastic about anything to put a stop to this trudging forward through the underbrush. We turned back, and sat on the edge of the woods while I thought about what we'd need. Just clearing the leaves away from the forest floor wouldn't be enough, we'd need clippers too and maybe a trowel. I was sure Uncle Rennie would have everything we needed in the garage, and I warned Gracie not to tell anybody what we were going to do. 'My Mom would think you might hurt yourself with the clippers or something,' I said, 'so we'll just borrow things without telling for now. You understand? It's our secret. Our secret path.' The idea became more and more appealing, and I began to see a small hut at the end of the path, with walls and a roof made of twigs. The summer started to take on the shape and colour I'd been hoping for.

It was easier than I'd imagined to get the tools out to the wood without anyone noticing. Mavis was often on the backyard patio of a neighbour, drinking iced tea or lemonade and talking about dear Mabel. Ted and Charlene didn't come out to the bush—they treated me as if I were as babyish as their sister—in case they'd get stuck with us, and although occasionally at supper one of them would ask 'What do you *do* out there?' an answer such as 'Just playing' was always sufficient, barely acknowledged. Even when Mavis missed the little whisk broom we borrowed for sweeping the leaves away, it never occurred to her that we might have it. And to Gracie's credit, she never once volunteered to help find it.

The only trouble with Gracie was her slowness. Unless you kept reminding her, she'd forget what she was doing and sit and daydream in that blank-faced way of hers. Sometimes I wanted to shake or pinch her, but it was impossible to get really angry with her. It would have been like punching mist; there was no resistance in her at all.

She did try to work very hard, and would help me yank at the larger saplings when the clippers failed to break a woody stem. We tried to clip everything right down close to the roots so that the path, which was nearly two feet across, would be as smooth as possible. After the small seedlings were pulled out we turned to the anonymous greenery left after spring flowers had stopped blooming, the green leaves of wild leeks, dog-toothed violets, bloodroots, and hepaticas. The path made two or three abrupt twists around patches of trillium leaves, which we knew we mustn't pull on pain of death, ours or the flowers' we weren't quite sure. And we left a little group of jack-in-the-pulpits and decorated around them with some stones we took from the school-yard. But all else vanished under our busy hands, until we were down to the bare soil.

The removal of the leaves was the task we both loved. The scooping up of the first light dry layers of soft brown and yellow like bits of fragrant paper, and then under that the leaves nearly turned into humus, dark and moist and smelling rich and heavy. Secret. A smell that made me want to bury myself in the leaves and just lie there and be. Only that, just be. I think Gracie felt the same things, for we would lift handfuls of leaves to our faces at the same time, kneeling on the ground together, and breathe in the smell and then smile at each other. Two small animals, noses buried in the wet, dark pre-earth. I didn't know anyone else in the world with whom I might share such moments.

After that layer had been off for a day and the ground below allowed to dry, we would sweep it all with the whisk broom and straighten the edges with small twigs. Except for the occasional knobby stub where a sapling's life had ended, the path was smooth, looking exactly as I had imagined it would. It was hard work, but so perfectly satisfying we kept at it day after day, doing little else. Obeying, perhaps, some primitive, atavistic urge to clear the land that our ancestors must have had pushing them on to make fields out of forests when they came from Germany and England in the last century. The repetition of an ancient dream, being played out by children in a bush on the edge of a city. But all I knew then, at that age, was that we had to keep going, we had to push farther into the centre of the woods.

On Sunday morning at the end of that first week, Mavis got us all ready for Sunday school and church at some cost to her composure. She wasn't used to four children getting washed and dressed at once, and she became edgy and flustered. As we were standing by the door for a final review, she opened her purse to put in the necessary handkerchief and peppermints, and to check, she said, that she had enough change for the collection plate. At home, she and Frank gave each week in little paper envelopes on which the offering was marked for use at home or abroad. But here she would need a dollar for herself and quarters for us. As she opened her change purse, her face wrinkled in puzzlement and then flared in anger.

'I had several dollar bills in here only yesterday,' she said. 'Somebody has been in my purse and taken them.' She looked right at me and I hated her with all my heart. How dare she accuse me in front of these cousins? I hadn't ever taken money from her in my life.

'It wasn't me, Mommy, honest,' I said, my face flaming and the backs of my eyes feeling on fire.

'No-one said it was, Elizabeth,' she said, in that calm voice I knew was meant to sound clever, as if she had caught me out. 'But *someone* took this money and I want to know who. Now.'

Silence. Ted and Grace and Charlene standing at the door looking back and forth at each other and at me. 'Oh Auntie, we'd never do anything like that,' said Charlene, her eyes wide open with hurt at the idea of being a suspect. 'And you mustn't think, just because, you know, Gracie doesn't understand everything . . . she still knows the difference between right and wrong, she would never steal, would you Gracie?' She knelt before her sister, who was nearly as tall as she was, so that Gracie had to look down at her. 'You wouldn't take anything from Auntie's purse, would you?'

Gracie began to cry and Ted said, 'Look what you've made her do, Charlene, you've started her bawling.' Mavis dabbed at Gracie's eyes with her handkerchief and patted her cheek. 'There, there,' she said. 'I know Gracie's a good girl. She wouldn't take money to play with, would she?'

'Gracie's a good girl,' Gracie sobbed, as the cousins turned and glared at me as if it were all my fault. I stared back, squinting and blushing, wondering how I would ever get even with them for this. It had to be one of them and I was sure it was Charlene; sneaking money was the kind of thing I could imagine her doing. I wondered if Ted knew, if he was in on it too. I'll bet he is, I thought. They're always in things together now. They're going to make sure I get blamed.

My mother gave up and said we'd discuss it after church, and that what each one of us better do was pray to God for forgiveness and for the strength to confess our sins, whichever of us it had been. We marched down the sidewalk in silence, a sad little band, Gracie no longer crying but sniffling and wiping her nose with her hand. 'I love you Gracie,' I whispered, and took her hand when we got to the curb and then didn't let go. 'You are my favourite.' That made her smile and we squeezed our fingers together and lagged behind the others—Ted all awkward and skinny, his white cotton shirt sticking to his shoulderblades in the heat, and Charlene mincing along in her crisp turquoise sundress beside Mavis, whose back was stiff as she walked, as if all her distress had concentrated itself in her spine.

At lunch, oddly, Mavis didn't mention the money and we all waited for the topic to come up—you could tell by the way that none of us looked at each other and kept talking about other things. And again at supper, nothing. I could barely swallow from anxiety and I noticed that no-one else seemed very hungry either. Mavis spent a long time talking to my father on the extension phone in the bedroom and when she came out she said, 'Oh,

Elizabeth. I meant to let you say hello to Daddy.'

'That's okay, Mommy,' I said, and tried to look wounded but brave. In truth, I was immensely relieved; the idea of listening to Frank lecture me on the telephone was too awful to contemplate.

The next day came cool and cloudy, a kind of temporary relief. I was eager to get back to the woods after the weekend, to see how the path looked, whether it would be as perfect as it had been when we left it. I lived in constant fear that other neighbourhood children would come into the woods there and find it and mess it up or claim it for their own. But none of them ever came; they were all off at camp or swimming-lessons, or else they felt that since Gracie had someone to play with they didn't have to, and so they left us alone.

One or two days that week it rained, and there was always a lot of work to do after that, for the path would be strewn with new leaves and twigs and in need of careful cleaning. We'd brush and pluck and pull together, munching on snacks of carrot sticks and occasional arrowroot biscuits. Our hands and knees were always dirty when we arrived home and my mother would say, 'How *can* you get so dirty?' but in that exasperated way that didn't expect an answer.

At the end of the second week the worst heat wave of the summer settled down to stay in the flat treeless streets of the subdivision; the little bungalows shimmered in the sun and became airless traps. Mabel's house, which had seemed so wonderfully modern and bright, now showed itself for the nasty little box it was. 'What I wouldn't give to be back in my own house this minute,' my mother said, as she set the electric fan in the hallway to 'stir up some circulation'. I thought about our old-fashioned house with its wide front verandah and all its wooden trim painted green, the snowball bushes and spirea that I hated for their drabness. The lawn and the house seemed to sit in a pool of shade cast by the big maples that grew along Brubacher Street, leaning over to form an arch above us, hemming us in. But it *was* cool under that canopy. I smiled at Mavis. 'Me too, Mom,' I said. 'I miss it too.' We looked at each other with affection and marvelled.

On the Friday afternoon she took to her room for a nap after lunch, with a cool cloth to put on her forehead, and urged both of us to do the same. 'I'll leave a note on the kitchen counter for Ted and Charlene to tell them we're resting,' she said, 'and maybe they'll put their feet up before supper too.' Gracie obediently went off with her damp washcloth to lie down and within minutes fell asleep. I roamed about the house, restless and uneasy, until I could bear it no longer. I went out to the bush with a plastic glass full of lemonade and ice but by the time I drank it, it was warm. The heat had seeped in through the trees and lay close to the ground; there was no coolness in the shade, only heaviness. Mosquitoes nipped at the back of my knees and neck, insects hummed everywhere in the air, everything seemed too alive and sticky. I looked at the path, the intricate design it made through the brush, and felt very tired. Without Gracie along it didn't seem fun and I didn't know why. I decided I would go back and sit in the basement the way Nana, my grandmother, did at her house when it was hot. She kept a rocking-chair down there and in summer often took her knee chores, as she called those jobs she did in her lap, down to her cool cellar to get them done. I had sometimes helped her shell peas and snap beans in the grey halflight.

The house was still except for the whirr of the fan in the hallway. I went down the steps carefully, my eyes unaccustomed to the darkness. It *was* cooler; it had been a good idea. I crawled behind the furnace in the farthest corner, behind a pile of suitcases and boxes, and imagined myself hiding on board a ship—a runaway orphan, a stowaway bound for who knew where.

There was a slightly sharp odour to the basement, a clean cement smell that was at odds with the dark dampness I knew in the woods. It was so impersonal and anonymous I felt safe and hunched down happily, grateful to have found a place where I could avoid everyone upstairs. Ted and Charlene kept acting as if they were waiting for me to confess that I had taken the money, and they had all kinds of ways of making me feel guilty. Sometimes Charlene would sidle around the doorway to Gracie's room and would lean there, looking at me without speaking. I put my thumb in my mouth for comfort in the dark then, and thought about how to get her to admit that she had done it. I must have fallen asleep like that and dozed for some time, for I woke to voices nearly next to me on the other side of the furnace. Ted and Charlene.

'Don't twist my arm, you're hurting!' She was hissing with anger.

'Give me a dollar then,' he whispered.

'I don't have any left, I really don't,' she said. She seemed now to be nearly crying. I was going to come out at that point and accuse her and say that I was going to 'tell', but I was frightened, the way you are when you wake out of a bad dream and then can't make it go away. I was frightened of what they might do to me if they thought I had meant to spy on them. So I huddled down and tried to stop breathing.

'Don't tell, Teddy, please,' she was saying. 'I'll give you something else, I will, I will. Just don't tell.' Then I heard her gasp as if he had twisted her elbow behind her back even harder. It was the kind of torture I most feared, that wrenching, burning pain as your arm nearly gets pulled from its socket. Why did boys always do that?

'Okay, but you have to do everything I say or I tell,' he said. 'Promise. Swear to God.'

'I promise, swear to God, Amen.'

Then the rustle and slide of cotton against skin, the zzzzt of a zipper, the sound of their intake and outtake of air. Ted's breathing fast and shallow, Charlene's a kind of gulping sob.

'You have to, you said you would do anything I said,' he was saying, and she was whimpering. I heard a kind of thud of flesh and bone on concrete, as if one of them had knelt down, but I couldn't tell which one.

'I'll just rub it for you, okay, Teddy?'

'No. Suck it. Put it in your mouth.' His voice was rushed and urgent, like the beginning of a windstorm.

'I can't, I can't, I'll be sick!' Charlene's voice a whine, like the mew of a cat. Then a kind of swallowing sound and Ted moaning. The most grotesque images flooded my mind. I was picturing something that had never entered my head before. She had *it* in her mouth. What if he peed? I felt my stomach heave and my throat fill with acrid, burning vomit. 'Aaagh. . . .' In my little corner behind the trunk and boxes I threw up between my feet, shuddering with disgust. Behind me I heard noises as they moved boxes to get to me, the gasping of Ted and Charlene's sobbing.

'You little puke!' he said, yanking at my hair. 'You little spying puke! We'll get you for this Elizabeth, we'll get you, just you wait. We'll kill you if you ever tell your mother. If you ever tell anything to anybody I'll make you do it too. I will!'

I retched again, this time at his feet, more terrified than I knew how to be. My eyes had become used to the dim basement light and I could see Charlene's pale face behind his, pleading with me not to tell. But . . . if I didn't tell, then Ted would keep on making her do this. She *had* taken the money; maybe this was meant to be her punishment. God always evened things out, I knew that. But what had *I* done wrong? What was going to happen to me?

I made my solemn vow never to tell and promised to clean up the vomit and sat there shivering and crying long after they left. I heard Mavis walking around the kitchen upstairs and finally found some rags and newspapers to clean up the mess and threw the whole works in a cardboard box and put it in the garage. I went outside and lay on the lawn until I was called in to set the table for supper.

That night Mavis served us cold canned salmon and lettuce with yellow Jell-o for dessert, and we sat in the late afternoon heat and tried to eat. None of us could, and finally she said it was okay, and gave us ice cubes to suck instead. We sat out on the porch and watched the sun sink behind the maple bush, a violently red ball promising more heat for the next day and the next after that. There was no wind at all; we were too far from Lake Ontario to get even the faintest breeze. Only the falling of the dark and the oppressive heat bearing down.

Lying in bed in Gracie's room that night I asked her who she loved the best. 'My dead Mommy,' she said.

'Who next?' I pressed. 'Who else?'

'You,' she said, and started to cry.

'Don't, Gracie, it's too hot,' I said. 'I love you too. I love you the best of anybody.' And we fell asleep.

The next morning I could barely wait through breakfast to get out to the woods. I made Gracie bring her last piece of toast with her, and in a bag full of dolls and toy dishes, in case Mavis looked to see what I was carrying, I hid a jar of nails and a hammer from Uncle Rennie's workshop. It was time, I suddenly knew, to build a little shelter at the end of the path. A place where Gracie and I could hide and be safe if we had to. I saw myself fashioning something out of branches nailed together and perhaps bound with rope, if I could just get some rope somewhere. I had found four small trees growing in such a way that they made the corners of a rectangle, and I imagined a roof attached, somehow, to each trunk. There would be ferns and moss on the floor for mats, and we would live on beechnuts and berries, and water from a nearby stream. Or we might have to bring food from home . . . but we would think about all that later.

I explained to Gracie that her job today was to clear the path from beginning to end while I organized our new hut. She took the whisk and began, on her knees, to clear away the debris, patting the dry soil with her hands to make it smooth. We were both content, in control.

Late in the day, into the green stillness came the sound of voices, Ted and Charlene. Why were they coming? Would they wreck the path? Were they going to do something to me? They stood, Ted with his arms folded across his chest, several yards away from where Gracie knelt, scraping away at the ground. She looked up, happy to see them, to have the secret over, able now to show them how much she and I had accomplished. 'Look, Teddy,' she said. 'See what I can do.' And she dug with furious energy, pulling up plants and scattering dry leaves in the air.

'Does Elizabeth make you do that?' Ted asked.

'Yes, she makes me. I'm a good girl,' Gracie said, not understanding the intent of his question as I did. There was a cutting tone to his voice that made me feel very alert, as if something had altered the slant of light through the trees, as if the whole scene was changing before my eyes. I smelled danger.

'I don't *make* her do anything,' I said. 'She likes doing this. We both do. She's good at it. Leave us alone, we're having a good time and we're not hurting you.'

They stood for a moment, as if unsure whether to join us or run, and then they moved off, wordlessly, leaving Gracie sitting on the dirt floor, digging with a spoon, looking sad.

'They didn't like our path?' she asked me. 'Not pretty?'

'No, no, they liked it all right. Never mind, Gracie. It's me they don't like any more.' I turned back to the hut, and the unsolvable problem of how to make the branches and twigs stick together onto the tree trunks. It was going to be much more difficult than I had thought, and I wished Ted were still my friend so that I could get him to help. We gave up finally and gathered up our bag of dolls and toy dishes and went home.

After supper that night Ted and Charlene offered to help Mavis do the dishes while Gracie and I were sent to a neighbour's garden to pick green beans. When we came back with our full baskets, my mother's manner had changed—she had become tight-lipped, aloof, and her eyes were red. She told Gracie to go upstairs and get into the tub she had readied for her, and she told me to come to her room.

'Your cousins have told me what you've been up to,' she said, as soon as she closed the door behind her. Her face was taut, and she had the kind of expression on her face that I knew from experience would soon give in to full-blowing rage. Sure enough, as I sat on the edge of the bed looking confused, her voice became louder, harsher, the words came faster and faster. 'The *idea* of you taking advantage of that poor child when she can't think for herself makes me sick, Elizabeth. Sick. To think that a child of mine could be so heartless, so unfeeling. . . .'

'But what did they say that I *do*?' I broke in. 'I don't even know why you're mad at me. I haven't done anything bad, I really haven't!'

'Calling your cousin Grace your slave and making her grovel in the mud, Elizabeth? You don't call that *bad*?' She stopped and shuddered. 'If I had had any idea of what was going on out there. . . . Oh, it's all my fault, I should have kept an eye on you. I've been too preoccupied with the older two, keeping the house straight and yes, chatting next door. It really is my fault. I've just let you go your own way, I should have known you'd disgrace us. But I never thought . . . really, Elizabeth, your own cousin!'

They had convinced her. I could see I didn't stand a chance of explaining anything. They had told her that Gracie was too frightened of me to tell her what was going on, that I had threatened her, that I had twisted her arm behind her back to make her do what I wanted. 'They feel very responsible for their little sister, you know, Elizabeth, because she can't always tell when she's being taken advantage of. Oh, where have I gone wrong with you?' The sorrowful gaze, her hands to her face, her head shaking back and forth—I knew all these movements intimately, could predict her next words. 'I've failed, I've failed.'

When I tried to speak, she asked me to keep still. 'Your father is coming tomorrow. I'll take him out to the woods and we'll see these roads you've made your poor cousin work at. We'll see what he thinks, but I'm afraid we'll have to send you home, Elizabeth, we'll have to work out some kind of arrangement, I don't know. . . .' Her voice trailed off; the whole awful thing was becoming far too complicated for both of us.

Gracie emerged from her bath, being towelled dry lovingly by Charlene, as my mother opened the bedroom door. 'G'night, Auntie Mavis,' she said, and came toward us to give my mother a kiss, her rosy naked body still damp and shining.

'Put your nightgown on, dear,' Mavis said, 'and then we'll say goodnight. Elizabeth, you go and get washed up.'

After it was dark, and I heard Gracie's breathing change to the deep rhythms of sleep, I lay very still and waited for the rest of the household to settle. I heard their voices, Ted's and Charlene's, and I tried to remember what it had felt like, back before Aunt Mabel died, when I had liked them, had wanted them to like me. And now it had all changed. I knew these terrible things, and we would never like each other again. We couldn't even look at each other. They were going to get me sent home so I wouldn't know any more about what they did, so I couldn't tell. Did they really think I would tell Mavis about *that*?

It was nearly midnight when the light under my mother's door went out, and then another hour after that passed before it seemed safe to move. It had been so hard keeping my eyes open—but the anger and hate I felt seemed like a kind of energy, strengthening my resolve. I was not a creature of stealth by nature, so that getting down the stairs was difficult and I was thankful for the thick carpet. I chose the back door out of the laundry-room for my exit, moving the lock with careful, careful fingers. Then out through the garage and down the side of the driveway, looking up only once to see whether anyone was watching from a window. No-one. I was safe. Barefoot, worrying about the sharp gravel sticking up through the asphalt on the road and the thistles in the schoolyard, I kept going. It didn't matter if my feet hurt. Nothing mattered but what I had to do.

A three-quarter moon hung in the sky, a white and fleshy thing giving off bright light and pale shadows so that I was able to see where I was going. I was surprised not to be frightened. It occurred to me that I was more frightened of the people in the house behind me than of anything in the woods.

The little path shone out in the moonlight, a silvery ribbon through the leaves and underbrush. I walked on the velvety soil, occasionally feeling the stub of roots under my feet, having to bend sometimes over the overhanging branches. It was beautiful, just right. The very kind of path Hansel would have scattered his crumbs along. I got to the place where the hut was to be, and gathered up the rest of the tools we had hidden there, the spoons and clippers; then with the whisk broom and my hands began sweeping leaves and twigs back over the bare ground, covering it over, making the path disappear. It took a long time and my arms got tired, but finally I reached the edge of the bush where our work had begun and I looked back where I had just been.

There was no path. You could tell there was a clearing of under-brush here and there, but it might have been natural; the path had been so twisting and winding it had never made a straight clear course. It would have looked like this again in the fall—but now, right *now* there was nothing, nothing to show for our days spent here. Only now to go back and put the tools in the garage and get into bed without getting caught. I would have to clean my feet, I thought, and my hands, but I would manage somehow. Suddenly, I was very tired, and my limbs ached from the exertion I had made. I turned slowly and bent down to crawl under the hole in the fence. And saw another pale nightdress in the moon-light, another pair of bare feet, another tear-stained face. I scram-bled through and got up as fast as I could.

She stood there, looking at me, weeping quietly, her chin qui-vering as she tried to speak.

'Oh Gracie, I had to, I had to,' I said. 'I can't explain why. They were going to spoil it all anyway, they had already spoiled it. Everything is ruined. Can you understand?'

'My path,' she said. 'You broke my path. I'm a good girl and you broke my path!' And she began to sob in earnest.

'Please Gracie, don't cry. I love you. I had to. It was my path too and I had to. . . . Please. Honest, please.' I reached out and turned her shoulder so that she was looking right at me again, and we were face to face, out there in the open on the edge of the bush. The same height, head to head, and I couldn't make her see. Ever. I couldn't do anything about it.

JANICE KULYK KEEFER

Mrs Putnam at the Planetarium

Tuesdays Mrs Putnam locked her flat, walked three city blocks to the subway; passed, with the sombre airiness of a ghost, through grilles and spokes and greedy-mouthed machines, and rode from Jane and Bloor to Museum. Rode in summer, when the cars were full of tourists with cameras clotting their necks and the pale yellow tiles made the station seem a morgue, ice under the hammer heat of asphalt overhead. Rode in winter when the closeness of the cars made Mrs Putnam, in her Merino wool coat, her black mink toque, clammy, dizzy, ravaged like a book with pages razored out. Did not ride in spring and autumn since those flighty seasons no longer existed for her now. Once there had been day trips to Niagara-on-the-Lake in Tulip Time, or Autumn Splendour in Muskoka with the boarders from St Radigonde's or, more rarely, much more rarely, outings with Adam to the Island in late May, early September. Long before there'd even been a Planetarium, back when the Museum walls had been the colour of greased soot, and stone lions snarled in the Tomb Garden.

On this Tuesday—mid-November, snowless, skyless—Mrs Putnam claimed the seat reserved for veterans, pregnant women, and old-age pensioners and started for the Planetarium. Across the aisle from her were advertisements for office temps, notices for putting your newborn through university, and pamphlets about Careers without College. Mrs Putnam glued milky brown eyes to them. For the past ten years she had been retired on a pension sufficient for her to maintain her flat, though not to repair the cracks in the plaster or buy poison enough to terminate the roaches. She had neither nieces nor nephews with babies requiring to be sent to Victoria or Trinity College, and since she'd come by her post as English Mistress and later Language Specialist with only a Grade 13 Diploma from Harbord Collegiate Mrs Putnam had no need to consult pamphlets at all. Yet it was imperative to do so—otherwise she would have had to look upon her fellow travellers, and Mrs Putnam had no interest in anybody else's story but her own.

Twelve year olds with pink or green or orange hair, Jamaicans looking resolutely uncolourful in raincoats, Lebanese waiters mournful as blank television screens, Pakistanis with babies on their laps, babies with perfectly round faces and eyes like black moons in the dank heat or chill of the subway car. Arms sweating, legs jolting, Mrs Putnam holding tight and tighter to the silver pole in front of doors out which her stop would show as welcome as the ram to Abraham, and in another sort of thicket altogether.

Changing trains she noted men at the newspaper kiosks who reminded her of Adam—no similarity whatsoever in colour of hair or lack of it, no slightest resemblance in build or height, but perhaps the cut of the overcoat, the precise indentation of the fedora. She was not the sort who would have held a lover's hand or gazed into his eyes, but often after he had left her side and was safely showering she would take up his hat from her dresser and press her fingertips along the crease his own had made in the felt. His wife had the vexing habit of presenting him with a new fedora every Christmas. She ordered them by telephone from Creeds; it was one of the few things she could do for him. The little else she could do Althea had told while waiting in Mrs Putnam's office one rainy Sunday afternoon for Uncle Adam to take her to tea with Aunt Rosamund.

'She's awfully pale, of course, being an invalid, but it's amazing how strong her hands are—she does yards of crochet and knits scarves and vests and things, none of which Uncle Adam can wear, since he's allergic to wool (*though he wore cashmere mufflers and Harris tweeds, as Mrs Putnam could have told her*) but he does have his office filled with crocheted doilies and coasters everywhere, even under the secretary's typewriter, which shows how devoted they are to one another. Aunt Rosamund's made me all kinds of tablecloths and comforters for my own hope chest—she says I'm like a daughter to her, since she hasn't any children of her own, which is sad, don't you think Mrs Putnam? Maybe you feel the same—I mean, having no children, not even a husband even. I mean, of course you did have a husband once, at least you *say* you did, I mean—no offence Mrs Putnam—'

Mrs Putnam took none. Pimply, placid Althea, who hadn't the

imagination of a pincushion and thus, any notion of the fact that while Aunt Rosamund was crocheting quiet mounds of doilies, Uncle Adam was taking more than tea with Hilary Putnam. Althea, thick as three planks, who couldn't recite a line of poetry to save her soul (*a soul the colour and consistency of clotted cream, thought Mrs Putnam*) but who nevertheless passed all of Mrs Putnam's classes for the six years she was at St Radigonde's and her uncle at Mrs Putnam's. Tuesday and Thursday evenings, from six to ten, and, perhaps half a dozen times a year, an entire Saturday or Sunday when Rosamund could be persuaded there was pressing work to be done at the Trust Company of which her husband was vice-president. Kind Althea, who hadn't meant anything by her remarks, since she hadn't the intelligence to think ill of anyone's peculiarities, but who merely parroted schoolgirl gossip about the English Mistress' marriage, which, as Mrs Putnam knew extremely well, all the girls and over half the staff believed to be a harmless fiction, if not an outright lie.

Southbound to Museum Mrs Putnam stared at her reflection in the window as the train racketed through a tunnel. The mink toque had been a present from Adam, the last she'd ever had from him. The first had been a ring—one topaz in a (twelve carat) band. To match her eyes, he'd said—and her hair, which was a watered blond, definitely not 22 carat, but then, all her own at least, and hadn't it made the first grey hair scarcely noticeable? Though he'd not been there to notice anything the night that Mrs Putnam's mirror finally ambushed her. A massive coronary at his desk, or so Althea had announced the day after the funeral to which, of course, his niece's English teacher had not been summoned. Rosamund—Rosamund was still sipping the small beer of invalid life in Rosedale, having, to counterbalance her fringed nerves, an amazingly strong heart. Althea had vouched for it—of all her former pupils, Althea was the only one who still sent Christmas cards to Mrs Putnam, rang her up on shopping trips to town, and never sounded disconcerted by the minute and peculiar questions put to her—not on the subjects of how many children she had, and of which sex, but of whether there had been any change in her Aunt's condition. There never was.

Mrs Putnam's was a different case. She had been a carelessly handsome, strong-blooded young woman and it had been to her the strictest form of punishment to watch as, year by year, the slow blue veins that Adam had once traced along her arms and breasts struggled up to the very surface of her skin like drowning swimmers. Liver spots over her hands, the peevish slouch of skin, cracks in her lips which, in the caustic light over the bathroom mirror, seemed to be fissures or crevasses down which her very soul might slip—these were to Mrs Putnam stages of a cross made of real and not symbolic wood; they left scars and splinters in her shoulders. Her colleagues at St Radigonde's would not have noticed—she had no friends among them and no confidantes; they, for their part, regarded her merely as an English Mistress renowned for the strict discipline she kept within her class, and for the tedium of the material she set her students. Not even Adam had known that, while she buried his niece under slabs of Pope and all of Milton's *Aereopagitica*, at home, alone, she'd finger a vellum Swinburne, recite from memory the lusher lyrics of Tennyson or read aloud from Keats in a special edition, gilt-edged with plump, fawn-coloured, soft suede covers.

Pigeons were wheeling over the Museum steps, or skittering after bits of popcorn that schoolchildren, on their way home from a session with dinosaurs or dusty Indians in the anthropologist's bargain basement, had bought from the Italian vendors. At their yellow-painted cars, crenellated with candy apples, fragrant with the steam from roasting chestnuts, Mrs Putnam did not so much as glance—nor at the faces of the children, flushed against the chill of this grey air outside, sharp as icicles against her cheeks. Mrs Putnam liked neither popcorn nor children overmuch—on the one she had lost a quarter of a tooth some twenty years ago; on the other she had wasted 40 years. In none of her students had she bred a love of Shelley, Scott, or Swift, though she had done a creditable job in teaching them what sentence fragments, comma splices, and malapropisms were. For, some fifteen years ago, the Headmistress of St Radigonde's had decided that English Literature would have to be hatcheted and Contemporary Culture (plus remedial grammar) put in its place if the school were to hold its own against the more prestigious, if less venerable, private girls' schools in Toronto. Mrs Putnam had lately read that no-one taught *Edwin Drood* or *Silas Marner* to schoolchildren these days—it was all Contemporary Song Lyrics and Shakespeare Comic Books. A colleague of hers, retired now from Weatherstone School, had got up a petition against it and asked Mrs Putnam to sign, but she hadn't. *I do not care, I do not care*, was all that Mrs Putnam had written in reply.

No-one asked Mrs Putnam for the extravagant sum it cost to get a ticket to the Planetarium: on Tuesdays old-age pensioners were admitted free—into the Museum as well, though Mrs Putnam refused to set so much as the toe of her ankle boots inside the place, now that they'd changed everything round and destroyed the garden. On Sunday afternoons after Adam's death Mrs Putnam had walked under the arches and the stone lions, listening to snow or leaves fall as if they'd been the bells that had hung from the roofs of the tombs. Once a man not much older than herself had watched her from the window of the garden door and asked her, after she'd returned, to have tea with him downtown. From his accent she had diagnosed him as Eastern European, and refused, not out of loyalty to Adam's memory, but because she'd been raised in the belief that people whose names ended in *off* or *ski* or *vich* might be highschool janitors but hardly the social equals of a Stuart or Jones or Putnam—she'd had visions of the man stirring his tea with his index finger. Foreigners had been barred from St Radigonde's since its founding by an interim Anglican bishop in 1833, though somewhere in the middle of Mrs Putnam's term at the school *that* had changed as it had everywhere—Mrs Putnam understood that the country's Prime Minister was married to an emigrant from that country whose flag looked like a checkerboard.

Once inside the Planetarium she walked up and down corridors painted the colour of milk frozen in the bottle, ignoring the displays of information on the walls and joining the small queue in front of the Projection Room. Waiting for the doors to open she looked down at her hands, then lifted them a little cautiously to her face, stroking her cheek with the leather, inhaling its rich, almost meaty scent. Real kid, none of that pigskin business—though she had to eat macaroni and skimp on the cheese four days a week, Mrs Putnam would have her necessary luxuries, mere tokens of the things she could have had if Adam hadn't betrayed her at his desk that Tuesday morning, or, at the very least, if Rosamund's nerves had done her in before he had to die.

Particles of rouge like motes of rosy dust clung to Mrs Putnam's gloves; all the heating and air-cleaning machines whirring through the foyer made her eyes feel papery, her skin crisp under the powder she had pressed on that morning. Why wouldn't they open the doors, why must they make her wait—70 years old and with the dignity, the presence of a dowager queen, yet they kept her in line as if she were queuing up for cigarettes at the five and ten. Where on earth was the Manager, he would have to be talked to, he would have to—. Someone in front of her began to whistle— further down the line she heard, distinctly, a belch. Mrs Putnam drew tighter the collar of her good, her excellent cloth coat, pulled the mink toque down so it covered her ear lobes—shrivelled, hard now like dried apricots—and waited. If Adam had been with her, if ever he could have been with her. . . . But then, if there was anything she detested it was whining women, watering their tea with tears over the mistakes they'd made. *She* had made up her mind when she was thirteen—just after her mother had died—that she would marry well or never marry at all, having learned from her parents' case that life as or with a bank clerk was no great addendum to the sum of human happiness.

Adam had been charming to her—it hadn't been his fault that Rosamund had had the tenacity of a wire-haired terrier in her grip on life, on Adam, and on the president of Adam's company: Rosamund's father. And yet if desire, need and hope had anything to do with our lot on earth; if there were justice under the stars. . . . The subjunctive mood, Miss Putnam had drilled into her students' heads, is always used for things that one merely wishes or hypothesizes to be true.

But now it was as if the gates of a post-modernist heaven had been opened for the pensioners and straggling students. The inner doors of the Planetarium swung slowly apart and gathered them in like the great skirts of a Mater Misericordia. As quickly as her dignity and arthritic hip would let her, Mrs Putnam found her customary seat, three rows back from the front, and at right angles from a certain twist in the crumpled metal that projected stars on the egg-shaped dome over her head. She drooped into the chair like a bird to its nest on a darkening winter afternoon; back she tilted, closing her eyes until her head had found its cradling place and the low music rising from the projector crept across her like a hand stroking her brow. And then she looked up at the great black bowl, not hard and blank as the subway window but soft, dewy, gelid—like a membrane to which Mrs Putnam could raise up her hands, poking fingers through to touch the stars.

Lights dimmed, the music faded and a voice fountained from the projector, talking about Pole stars and Betelgeuse and Charles' Wain. The names didn't matter to Mrs Putnam; she was lying in the grass on the Island with Adam—they had rented one of the small canoes and paddled out to the hand's breadth of land that was now a bird sanctuary; they had beached the canoe and were lying on their backs in wild, tall grass, watching the stars. For once he was not wearing his fedora; she had on her finger a ring with one diamond and a band of 24-carat gold. Rosamund was in Mt Pleasant and even Althea had been sent back home to Thunder Bay, to parents who had at last decided that the advantages of a private education did not outweigh the loving kindness to be found only in the bosom of one's family. Softly Hilary opened lips that time had not so much as crumpled:

Now sleeps the crimson petal, now the white. . . . Now lies the earth all Danae to the stars. . . .

and the stars sang back to her. They were not crystal splinters as children imagined them, but round, fragrant as waterlilies you might pick off the mirror of a lake and hold up to your face, breathing in their succulence and fragrance. . . .

Across the table from her someone began to snore, with all the violence of a chain-saw massacre. It was hot in the darkened room, the leatherette under Mrs Putnam's hands began to feel like fur and she was floating somewhere between floor and stars. The voice was talking now about satellites and lasers. Mrs Putnam remembered hearing on the radio that before long man would be able to orbit messages in space—celestial billboards advertising Pepsi or the other Cola, *billets-doux* or messages of condolence that could circle earth forever, forcing their stories down peoples' very eyes. If it were possible, floating through a darkness cut to ribboned light—what would they say were she to chisel it into the night sky: *Rosamund, detested of Adam who loved Hilary alone*, Hilary who loved Keats and Tennyson and silk against her skin, and all the powders and perfumes of Araby she could not wear to St Radigonde's, but which she would apply each evening upon coming home, whether Adam were coming or not, whether she believed in him or not, coming or going, leaving or loving, Betelgeuse and Charles' Wain, Miss or Mrs Putnam, Althea and detested Rosamund and petalled stars in the night sky, looking down where she lay, in her story, nobody else's story—head lolling against the squashed leatherette as a voice explained the simulated stars shifting, blooming, exploding on the painted ceiling over the sleeping dark in which Mrs Putnam lies curled tight, a newborn's fist around some fiction of a finger to grab onto, climbing steep, black spaces in between the stars.

BHARATI MUKHERJEE

The Lady from Lucknow

When I was four, one of the girls next door fell in love with a Hindu. Her father intercepted a love note from the boy, and beat her with his leather sandals. She died soon after. I was in the room when my mother said to our neighbour, 'The Nawab-*sahib* had no choice, but Husseina's heart just broke, poor dear.' I was an army doctor's daughter, and I pictured the dead girl's heart—a rubbery squeezable organ with auricles and ventricles—first swelling, then bursting and coating the floor with thick, slippery blood.

We lived in Lucknow at the time, where the Muslim community was large. This was just before the British took the fat, diamond-shaped subcontinent and created two nations, a big one for the Hindus and a littler one for us. My father moved us to Rawalpindi in Pakistan two months after Husseina died. We were a family of soft, voluptuous children, and my father wanted to protect us from the Hindus' shameful lust.

I have fancied myself in love many times since, but never enough for the emotions to break through tissue and muscle. Husseina's torn heart remains the standard of perfect love.

At seventeen I married a good man, the fourth son of a famous poet-cum-lawyer in Islamabad. We have a daughter, seven, and a son, four. In the Muslim communities we have lived in, we are admired. Iqbal works for IBM, and because of his work we have made homes in Lebanon, Brazil, Zambia, and France. Now we live in Altanta, Georgia, in a wide, new house with a deck and a backyard that runs into a golf course. IBM has been generous to us. We expect to pass on this good, decent life to our children. Our children are ashamed of the dingy cities where we got our start.

Some Sunday afternoons when Iqbal isn't at a conference half-way across the world, we sit together on the deck and drink gin and tonics as we have done on Sunday afternoons in a dozen exotic cities. But here, the light is different somehow. A gold haze comes off the golf course and settles on our bodies, our new house. When the light shines right in my eyes, I pull myself out of the canvas deck chair and lean against the railing that still smells of forests. Everything in Atlanta is so new!

'Sit,' Iqbal tells me. 'You'll distract the golfers. Americans are crazy for sex, you know that.'

He half rises out of his deck chair. He lunges for my breasts in mock passion. I slip out of his reach.

At the bottom of the backyard, the golfers, caddies, and carts are too minute to be bloated with lust.

But, who knows? One false thwock! of their golfing irons, and my little heart, like a golf ball, could slice through the warm air and vanish into the jonquil-yellow beyond.

It isn't trouble that I want, though I do have a lover. He's an older man, an immunologist with the Center for Disease Control right here in town. He comes to see me when Iqbal is away at high-tech conferences in sunny, remote resorts. Just think, Beirut was once such a resort! Lately my lover comes to me on Wednesdays even if Iqbal's in town.

'I don't expect to live till ninety-five,' James teases on the phone. His father died at ninety-three in Savannah. 'But I don't want a bullet in the brain from a jealous husband right now.'

Iqbal owns no firearms. Jealousy would inflame him.

Besides, Iqbal would never come home in the middle of the day. Not even for his blood-pressure pills. The two times he forgot them last month, I had to take the bottle downtown. One does not rise through the multinational hierarchy coming home in midday, arriving late, or leaving early. Especially, he says, if you're a 'not-quite' as we are. It is up to us to set the standards.

Wives who want to be found out will be found out. Indiscretions are deliberate. The woman caught in mid-shame is a woman who wants to get out. The rest of us carry on.

James flatters me indefatigably; he makes me feel beautiful, exotic, responsive. I am a creature he has immunized of contamination. When he is with me, the world seems a happy enough place.

Then he leaves. He slips back into his tweed suit and backs out of my driveway.

I met James Beamish at a reception for foreign students on the Emory University campus. Iqbal avoids these international receptions because he thinks of them as excuses for looking back when we should be looking forward. These evenings are almost always tedious, but I like to go; just in case there's someone new and fascinating. The last two years, I've volunteered as host in the 'hospitality program'. At Thanksgiving and Christmas, two lonely foreign students are sent to our table.

That first evening at Emory we stood with name tags on lapels, white ones for students and blue ones for hosts. James was by a long table, pouring Chablis into a plastic glass. I noticed him right off. He was dressed much like the other resolute, decent men in the room. But whereas the other men wore white or blue shirts under their dark wool suits, James's shirt was bright red.

His wife was with him that evening, a stoutish woman with slender ankles and expensive shoes.

'Darling,' she said to James. 'See if you can locate our Palestinian.' Then she turned to me, and smiling, peered into my name tag.

'I'm Nafeesa Hafeez,' I helped out.

'Na-fee-sa,' she read out. 'Did I get that right?'

'Yes, perfect,' I said.

'What a musical name,' she said. 'I hope you'll be very happy here. Is this your first time abroad?'

James came over with a glass of Chablis in each hand. 'Did we draw this lovely lady? Oops, I'm sorry, you're a *host*, of course.' A mocking blue light was in his eyes. 'Just when I thought we were getting lucky, dear.'

'Darling, ours is a Palestinian. I told you that in the car. This one is obviously not Palestinian, are you, dear?' She took a bright orange notebook out of her purse and showed me a name.

I had to read it upside-down. Something Waheed. School of Dentistry.

'What are you drinking?' James asked. He kept a glass for himself and gave me the other one.

Maybe James Beamish said nothing fascinating that night, but he was attentive, even after the Beamishes' Palestinian joined us. Mrs Beamish was brave, she asked the dentist about his family and hometown. The dentist described West Beirut in detail. The shortage of bread and vegetables, the mortar poundings, the babies bleeding. I wonder when aphasia sets in. When does a dentist, even a Palestinian dentist, decide it's time to cut losses.

Then my own foreign student arrived. She was an Indian Muslim from Lucknow, a large, bold woman who this far from our common hometown claimed me as a countrywoman. India, Pakistan, she said, not letting go of my hand, what does it matter?

I'd rather have listened to James Beamish but I couldn't shut out the woman's voice. She gave us her opinions on Thanksgiving rituals. She said, 'It is very odd that the pumpkin vegetable should be used for dessert, no? We are using it as vegetable only. Chhi! Pumpkin as a sweet. The very idea is horrid.'

I promised that when she came to our house for Thanksgiving, I'd make sweetmeats out of ricotta cheese and syrup. When you live in as many countries as Iqbal has made me, you can't tell if you pity, or if you envy, the women who stayed back.

I didn't hear from James Beamish for two weeks. I thought about him. In fact I couldn't get him out of my mind. I went over the phrases and gestures, the mocking light in the eyes, but they didn't add up to much. After the first week, I called Amina and asked her to lunch. I didn't know her well but her husband worked at the Center for Disease Control. Just talking to someone connected with the Center made me feel good. I slipped his name into the small talk with Amina and her eyes popped open, 'Oh, he's famous!' she exclaimed, and I shrugged modestly. I stayed home in case he should call. I sat on the deck and in spite of the cold, pretended to read Barbara Pym novels. Lines from Donne and Urdu verses about love floated in my skull.

I wasn't sure Dr Beamish would call me. Not directly, that is. Perhaps he would play a subtler game, get his wife to invite Iqbal and me for drinks. Maybe she'd even include their Palestinian and my Indian and make an international evening out of it. It sounded plausible.

Finally James Beamish called me on a Tuesday afternoon, around four. The children were in the kitchen, and a batch of my special chocolate sludge cookies was in the oven.

'Hi,' he said, then nothing for a bit. Then he said, 'This is James Beamish from the CDC. I've been thinking of you.'

He was between meetings, he explained. Wednesday was the only flexible day in his week, his day for paperwork. Could we have lunch on Wednesday?

The cookies smelled gooey hot, not burned. My daughter had taken the cookie sheet out and put in a new one. She'd turned the cold water faucet on so she could let the water drip on a tiny rosebud burn on her arm.

I felt all the warm, familiar signs of lust and remorse. I dabbed the burn with an ice cube wrapped in paper towel and wondered if I'd have time to buy a new front-closing bra after Iqbal got home.

James and I had lunch in a Dekalb County motel lounge.

He would be sixty-five in July, but not retire till sixty-eight. Then he would live in Tonga, in Fiji, see the world, travel across Europe and North America in a Winnebago. He wouldn't be tied down. He had five daughters and two grandsons, the younger one aged four, a month older than my son. He had been in the navy during the war (*his* war), and he had liked that.

I said, ' ''Goodbye, Mama, I'm off to Yokohama.'' ' It was silly, but it was the only war footage I could come up with, and it made him laugh.

'You're special,' he said. He touched my knee under the table. 'You've already been everywhere.'

'Not because I've wanted to.'

He squeezed my knee again, then paid with his MasterCard card.

As we were walking through the parking lot to his car (it was a Cougar or a Buick, and not German or British as I'd expected), James put his arm around my shoulders. I may have seen the world but I haven't gone through the American teenage rites of making out in parked cars and picnic grounds, so I walked briskly out of his embrace. He let his hand slide off my shoulder. The hand slid down my back. I counted three deft little pats to my bottom before he let his hand fall away.

Iqbal and I are sensual people, but secretive. The openness of James Beamish's advance surprised me.

I got in his car, wary, expectant.

'Do up the seatbelt,' he said.

He leaned into his seatbelt and kissed me lightly on the lips. I kissed him back, hard. 'You don't panic easily, do you?' he said. The mocking blue light was in his eyes again. His tongue made darting little thrusts and probes past my lips.

Yes, I do, I would have said if he'd let me.

We held hands on the drive to my house. In the driveway he parked behind my Honda. 'Shall I come in?'

I said nothing. Love and freedom drop into our lives. When we have to beg or even agree, it's already too late.

'Let's go in.' He said it very softly.

I didn't worry about the neighbours. In his grey wool slacks and tweed jacket, he looked too old, too respectable, for any sordid dalliance with a not-quite's wife.

Our house is not that different in size and shape from the ones on either side. Only the inside smells of heavy incense, and the walls are hung with rows of miniature paintings from the reign of Emperor Akbar. I took James's big wrinkled hand in mine. Adultery in my house is probably no different, no quieter, than in other houses in this neighbourhood.

Afterwards it wasn't guilt I felt (guilt comes with desire not acted), but wonder that while I'd dashed out Tuesday night and bought myself silky new underwear, James Beamish had worn an old T-shirt and lemon-pale boxer shorts. Perhaps he hadn't planned on seducing a Lucknow lady that afternoon. Adventure and freedom had come to him out of the blue, too. Or perhaps only younger men like Iqbal make a fetish of doing sit-ups and dieting and renewing their membership at the racquet club when they're on the prowl.

October through February our passion held. When we were together, I felt cherished. I only played at being helpless, hysterical, cruel. When James left, I'd spend the rest of the afternoon with a Barbara Pym novel. I kept the novels open at pages in which excellent British women recite lines from Marvell to themselves. I didn't read. I watched the golfers trudging over brown fairways instead. I let the tiny golfers—clumsy mummers—tell me stories of ambitions unfulfilled. Golf carts lurched into the golden vista. I felt safe.

In the first week of March we met in James's house for a change. His wife was in Madison to babysit a grandson while his parents flew to China for a three-week tour. It was a thrill to be in his house. I fingered the book spines, checked the colour of sheets and towels, the brand names of cereals and detergents. Jane Fonda's Workout record was on the VCR. He was a man who took exceptional care of himself, this immunologist. Real intimacy, at last. The lust of the winter months had been merely foreplay. I felt at home in his house, in spite of the albums of family photographs on the coffee table and the brutish metal vulvas sculpted by a daughter in art school and stashed in the den. James was more talkative in his own house. He showed me the photos he wanted me to see, named real lakes and mountains. His family was real, and not quite real. The daughters were hardy, outdoor types. I saw them hiking in Zermatt and bicycling through Europe. They had red cheeks and backpacks. Their faces were honest and marvellously ordinary. What would they say if they knew their father, at sixty-five, was in bed with a married woman from Lucknow? I feared and envied their jealousy more than any violence in my husband's heart.

Love on the decline is hard to tell from love on the rise. I have lived a life perched on the edge of ripeness and decay. The traveller feels at home everywhere, because she is never at home anywhere. I felt the hot red glow of blood rushing through capillaries.

His wife came back early, didn't call, caught a ride from Hartsfield International with a friend. She had been raised in Saskatchewan, and she'd remained thrifty.

We heard the car pull into the driveway, the loud 'thank yous' and 'no, I couldn'ts' and then her surprised shout, 'James? Are you ill? What're you doing home?' as she shut the front door.

We were in bed, sluggish cozy and still moist under the goose-down quilt that the daughter in Madison had sent them as a fortieth anniversary gift some years before. His clothes were on top of a long dresser; mine were on the floor, the stockings wrinkled and looking legless.

James didn't go to pieces. I had to admire that. He said, 'Get in the bathroom. Get dressed. I'll take care of this.'

I am submissive by training. To survive, the Asian wife will usually do as she is told. But this time I stayed in bed.

'How are you going to explain me away, James? Tell her I'm the new cleaning woman?' I laughed, and my laugh tinkled flirtatiously, at least to me.

'Get in the bathroom.' This was the fiercest I'd ever heard him.

'I don't think so,' I said. I jerked the quilt off my body but didn't move my legs.

So I was in bed with the quilt at my feet, and James was by the dresser buttoning his shirt when Kate Beamish stood at the door.

She didn't scream. She didn't leap for James's throat—or mine. I'd wanted passion, but Kate didn't come through. I pulled the quilt over me.

I tried insolence. 'Is your wife not the jealous kind?' I asked.

'Let's just get over this as quietly and quickly as we can, shall we?' she said. She walked to the window in her brown Wallabies. 'I don't see any unfamiliar cars, so I suppose you'll expect James to drive you home.'

'She's the jealous type,' James said. He moved towards his wife and tried to guide her out of the bedroom.

'I'm definitely the jealous kind,' Kate Beamish said. 'I might have stabbed you if I could take you seriously. But you are quite ludicrous lounging like a Goya nude on my bed.' She gave a funny little snort. I noticed straggly hairs in her nostrils and looked away.

James was running water in the bathroom sink. Only the panicky ones fall apart and call their lawyers from the bedroom.

She sat on my side of the bed. She stared at me. If that stare had made me feel secretive and loathsome, I might not have wept, later. She plucked the quilt from my breasts as an internist might, and snorted again. 'Yes,' she said, 'I don't deny a certain interest he might have had,' but she looked through my face to the pillow behind, and dropped the quilt as she stood. I was shadow without depth or colour, a shadow-temptress who would float back to a city of teeming millions when the affair with James had ended.

I had thought myself provocative and fascinating. What had begun as an adventure had become shabby and complex. I was just another involvement of a white man in a pokey little outpost, something that 'men do' and then come to their senses while the *memsahibs* drink gin and tonic and fan their faces. I didn't merit a stab wound through the heart.

It wasn't the end of the world. It was humorous, really. Still, I let James call me a cab. That half-hour wait for the cab, as Kate related tales of the grandson to her distracted husband was the most painful. It came closest to what Husseina must have felt. At least her father, the Nawab-*sahib*, had beaten her.

I have known all along that perfect love has to be fatal. I have survived on four of the five continents. I get by because I am at least moderately charming and open-minded. From time to time, James Beamish calls me. 'She's promised to file for divorce.' Or 'Let's go away for a weekend. Let's go to Bermuda. Have lunch with me this Wednesday.' Why do I hear a second voice? She has laughed at me. She has mocked my passion.

I want to say yes. I want to beg him to take me away to Hilton Head in his new, retirement Winnebago. The golden light from the vista is too yellow. Yes, *please*, let's run away, keep this new and simple.

I can hear the golf balls being thwocked home by clumsy mummers far away where my land dips. My arms are numb, my breathing loud and ugly from pressing hard against the cedar railing. The pain in my chest will not go away. I should be tasting blood in my throat by now.

MADELEINE
OUELLETTE-MICHALSKA

The Cat

On Sunday afternoons the dining room of the Belvedere looked sad. The tables, lined up in monastic rigidity, seemed to await the arrival of a horde of tourists. They were expecting hundreds, but not one had shown up. The bay reflected a white light that flattened objects, congealing them in dull unreality. The crackling of the sun, still lively on the roof, made the air heavy. Barbara and Genevieve stopped and surveyed the room, suddenly struck by a shared experience.

'You'd never think we'd danced here last night.'

'No, you'd never think that.'

To one side lay the sea. To the other, the patio edged with bougainvillea which led to the rooms. The play of shadow and phosphorescence forced them to make a choice between two contradictory worlds: the day and its mundane, horribly persistent reality and the night with its possible openings toward dreams and the needs of the heart. Unable to reconcile this emptiness with the animation of Saturday evening, Barbara discontinued this train of thought. She began to talk, hoping to ward off the oppressive silence. Genevieve answered in an acrid tone of voice that revealed fatigue and exasperation. At the far end of the room two men were leaning on the bar, drowsy. They, too, seemed to be in slow motion, suspended between the dead time they had no influence over, and a present they were indifferent to. Barbara approached them, looked at the foam that topped their glasses and made a gesture of disgust.

'You're drinking that!'

'Yes, ma'am. Cheers!'

The taller of the two raised his glass and made a deep bow. The other one imitated the gesture hardly bending his shoulders. Genevieve commented on his lack of enthusiasm. He replied that not once in his life had he kneeled to anyone, but she seemed not to grasp his meaning. He was insistent, repeating: 'Me, that's who I am.' She realized that this was not his first drink. She knew the refrain well.

'We should go.'
  'Go now, before we've emptied our glasses? You're crazy.'
  'You won't be able to drive anymore.'
  'All I need is one more drink to have perfect vision.'
  'Hurry up and finish.'
  'There's no rush. Waiter, would you get them a drink.'
The waiter got two bottles of Fanta out of the refrigerator and brought them to the two women. He knew that alcohol would be out of place. For economic reasons as much as for reasons of principle, they refused it every time the men abused it. They accepted the lemonade graciously. Experience had taught them that an annoyed husband drinks twice as much. They turned toward the sea. The sun, still high, was quickly going down. Shadow was already covering a part of the beach. The bathers moved away from the rocks and got nearer the waters where no tree tempered the warmth of the day's end.
  'It's depressing,' Barbara remarked.
Shouts rose from the base of the cliff, muffled by the distance, and a hum spread along the shore. A group of children ran to throw themselves into the water one last time. Goats left the grass around the lemon trees and came down to stretch out under the eucalyptus. Something irremediable was happening. The weekend holiday was being engulfed by the sea. Tomorrow's worry and work were approaching.
  'I could go and sleep for an hour.'
  'Impossible. We have to be getting back.'
  'You only have one life, and you can't even sleep it in peace.'
  'Oh, don't make phrases. Coming from you, they sound hollow.'
  'Come now, children, be good and finish your drinks without arguing. We've got two hours of driving ahead of us.'
Genevieve disliked sharp exchanges that she hadn't initiated between what she called 'a couple'. The men ignored her advice. They commented that they always started home too early, that the visibility was nil when the sun hit the windshield horizontally

and that that was dangerous. In this argument the women recognized the prelude to another beer. They looked at each other hopelessly.

'Did you pay for the rooms?'

'Good thing you're here. We were going to forget.'

The waiter brought the bill respectfully pointing at the bottom line.

'I left it blank for the beers.'

'Left it blank for the beers! How thoughtful. And only one bill, as usual.'

'You are brothers, no?'

Since the hotel personnel had decided they were brothers, it was no use arguing the point. The colour of the skin, the eyes and the beard carried more weight than any discussion. As for the hair, it was well known that roomies had the habit of splitting hairs. They always got tangled in obtuse convolutions explaining that they weren't of the same stock and didn't even come from the same place. They apparently did not belong to any clan or town. They were born alone and they died alone, as they had done for centuries.

'Cheers, brother!'

Barbara sighed. She knew already how this would end. An hour would pass, and the men would still be at the bar mulling over their gripes about the local administration. They'd spout their usual reflections on the native population, juggle their grievances, run out of talk and return to town, dazed and depressed. Powerless against the real culprits, she made the room responsible.

'Sundays, there's not even a cat in this tomb!'

Hardly had she finished the sentence when a small plump man appeared in the doorway. He had a round head, feline eyes and a moustache pulled toward his cheeks. He said 'Hello' and headed straight toward them. Then he looked at them and held out the claws of his short chubby hand to both of them.

'Good thing you're here! The last time I came it was completely dead.'

His sudden, rather bizarre presence created an unexpected diversion. He licked his lips, looking for pleasant things to add. He spoke French with a strong foreign accent.

'You're an American?'

'No, but I have lived in America. I've got around just about everywhere, you know.'

'You have an English accent.'

'Accents, I must have five or six of. I can say I love you in any language. Even in Japanese.'

'Go ahead. Don't wait to be asked.'

'I'm afraid I'll make the ladies blush. Actually, should I say the ladies, or the girls?'

'That's for you to decide.'

'I'm not deciding. I'm stating. You have the freshness of young girls, but you're wearing wedding bands. Take them off and I'll call you "Miss." '

'Me, that's who I am,' one of the men began to shout, anxious to defend his rights.

'I didn't want to annoy you. Let's just say I was congratulating you on your good taste.'

'Me, that's who I am. And take care what you say!'

'Of course. But what are you drinking? Beer? Cognac is what you need at this time of day. Waiter, five double cognacs.'

He led them to a table set in the bay window overlooking the terrace, sat down first, and invited the men to take a seat. He kept the women on either side of him, content to pat their shoulders.

'I like to be surrounded by pretty women. Life is short, you have to make the most of it.'

'Are you working here?'

'Working. Not really. Actually, I make others work.'

'In what field?'

'I'm an engineer. A project involving 300 men. And as for working, I can guarantee you they work. As soon as they start to slacken up, I shout "*Emshi!*" and send them packing to their father.'

'Do you find other workers easily?'

'It's not work, it's training. When they arrive, they hardly know the difference between a straight line and a curve. Last week I had the same string laid three times, and it was still off. Okay, I said, that's it for you, wog.'

'You're a hard man.'

'That's how I am with men. With women I am sweetness personified.'

He laid one paw around Barbara. She laughed, stiffening a little. The waiter put the cognacs on the table. Four yellow stains appeared on the table cloth. The afternoon wore on comfortably thanks to this man who spoke six languages and let them forget the time.

'Cheers! It's been a long time since I had a drink in such agreeable company. And God knows I've made toasts in my life. I've clinked glasses in the best cabarets of the world. Paris, London, Istanbul, Tokyo, Baghdad. Do you know the belly dance?'

'It's not great here, and you know, we've never made a trip around the world.'

'You should. Take me, I'm just like God, I want to see everything.'

'Another one who thinks he's the prophet. How many women have you had?'

'I haven't got enough fingers to count them on. I've had them in all colours, but I have a weakness for Japanese women. Nothing can beat them. At Osaka, I kept one with me for a week. When I left, she cried like crazy.'

'You must be quite irresistible.'

'It's a question of style. You have it or you don't. And you two, I bet you don't have it.'

Both men leapt up and hit the table with their softened fists. The shorter one sat down again quickly. The other one stood there, ready to strangle this intruder who allowed himself to address him in that tone.

'That's an insult. You don't know who you are talking to. You forget we've got Viking blood in our veins?'

'Viking blood? I have some too. My maternal grandfather was a Breton. That's been of help to me in my life. Thank God, I had Breton blood in my veins at Shiprock.'

'What were you doing down there?'

'Smuggling gold. In two weeks, I made half a million.'

'Don't you have a little left? We could split it.'

'No. I lost everything in Reno in three days. Kaput! I didn't have a penny left. I told myself it's not the end of the world, I'll have to start again at zero. I found a guy to pay my ticket and left for Rhodesia.'

'Where you put a quite insignificant little diamond into your pocket.'

'Yes, a diamond, and it was worse than if I'd found gold. A prospector accused me of having stolen it and told me to clear out. Two hours later I offered him a special drink. He left first.'

'You're a real fiend.'

'A fiend? No. I'm a pussycat. I can squeeze through spots where others can't even get a little finger.'

Barbara looked at the man. He did look like a cat and he had a cat's reactions, its face, its suppleness. His chubby hands softly stroked the glass and rose to cross under his chin that purred out a rough whistle between sentences. In darkness his eyes had to be green. The sun was no more than a thin fiery band above the sea. She shivered in spite of the heat, thinking he might well become dangerous once night fell.

'We should get going if we don't want to be on the road in the dark.'

'Go? How dare you say such a thing? We're just starting to get to know each other.'

'Don't provoke her. She starts roaring like a panther.'

'A blond panther. I've never seen one of them. And never with such lovely eyes either. But I know enough about hunting to tell you she reminds me more of the young guanacos on Tierra del Fuego. A gentle disposition, charm, kindness, but if you approach them too roughly, they'll bite your hand or spit in your face.'

'Me, that's who I am. And if you're rude to my wife, I'll make you pay for it.'

'How much are you asking?'

'Take that back, right now!'

The man pounded furiously on the table, but his alcohol-soaked fist didn't frighten anyone. The stranger pretended not to hear or see anything. He got out his wallet, pulling out a wad of hundred dinar bills. He riffled the money skillfully yet indifferently as though it were a pack of cards, but the greed in his eyes belied the indifference. Below the arch of his eyebrows, his little eyes sparked wih lust. He brandished his wallet.

'This is the source of power! There are two categories of men in the world: men and wogs. And to be a man you can't do without this.'

'Nor this,' said Barbara, indicating her head.

'Intelligence makes your capital yield a profit. Am I shocking you? You're young and you haven't travelled. This is where the future of the underdeveloped countries is, and nowhere else. If you don't learn the art of ownership and how to count your possessions, you are condemned to stay sub-human.'

'Quite a simple ethic.'

'Ethics, that's for the priests. For other people there are only situations you have to know how to take advantage of.'

Genevieve, who had been content to listen up till then, began to wake up. Her laughter cut through the air. The stranger saw this as an encouragement to seduce her and stroked her thighs. At the same time, his other hand held Barbara's wrists.

'I am a romantic, you know. See that sunset? That's nothing beside all the ones I've seen in my life. From country to country, they were never the same colour. In China, they were purple. In Mexico, they tended more to apricot and orange. In the Congo, violet was the main colour. Turkey, that was the ultimate! At Edirne, the sun drops into the Maritsa like a fiery ball swallowed by a green eye.'

'Green?'

'Green, lots of green. The most beautiful sunsets are green. It was a rare green. Something like the colour of your eyes.'

'They've never been green.'

'When you look at the Mediterranean, they turn green. It's too bad you have to get back. I would have taken you out for a little cruise, all four of you. I like to please people.'

'An iron hand and a soft heart. The perfect combination, wouldn't you say?'

'What can I do, it's stronger than I am. You wouldn't believe it, but every time I leave, I send my wife a postcard. She's got about 2000 of them. Here, this is a photo of her.'

He took a wallet he'd left on the table and removed a tiny photograph taken by an ID-card machine. A young dark-haired, dark-skinned woman looked at them sadly. She had a low forehead and a drooping mouth. Her look of a frightened doe put her undeniably into the wog category. A moment of embarrassment hung over the group followed by a long silence. The cat put the photograph back into his wallet.

'Are you surprised that I've got such a young wife? It's natural. Women always wish they could marry their fathers.'

'Age is not an important difference.'

'The difference! That's what is important. Take these two beauties. If they underwent a sex change, we'd never get over it.'

The taller one of the men raised his voice and made large gestures.

'They couldn't allow themselves to be lacking in intelligence either. Let's keep our women the way they are, they're irreplaceable.'

'Well said. Really. I love you. Those words say everything. You had good taste. I like them.'

The man got up, unsteady.

'I repeat, they are not for sale and I am who I am.'

'That's just what breaks my heart. I would still like to see the four of you again. Do you come here to dance now and again?'

'To dance? That's all they do. Our wives discovered their vocation in North Africa. They were born to dance.'

'Is that so? So we'll see each other again? When will you be back?'

'Thursday.'

The two men gave a start.

'Because now, besides going dancing on Saturdays, we're going on Thursdays too?'

'From now on, we're not coming on Saturdays anymore, just on Thursdays. That way we'll get home earlier.'

Under this threat the men had got up .They said their goodbyes to the cat with somewhat sagging knees. The women shook his hand and fled, repeating 'See you Thursday!' He replied 'I'll be there' quivering with pleasure. They turned their backs on him and took a last look at the sea. The water had turned gray. An opaque silence reached the coastline and enveloped the Belvedere. Within the hour the road would be in darkness. Barbara whispered into Genevieve's ear.

'Are we really coming here to dance on Thursday?'

'No, that was a trap.'

'What a revolting man! I feel like puking and we haven't even got to the bends yet.'

Barbara put her hand to her mouth and suppressed a hiccup. Genevieve burst out laughing and admitted that the cognac had gone to her head. Once through the door, they turned to look back. He was standing beside the table making them a sign with his hand. Against the matte background of the window, he had the shape of an alley cat.

Translated by Luise von Flotow-Evans

MONIQUE PROULX

Feint of Heart

Might as well come right out with it: love stories don't do much
for me. They rarely loosen my tear ducts. Other people's love
stories, that is, the ones Guy des Cars will be cranking out until
Cupid himself, with heaving stomach, sticks him full of arrows to
shut him up. Or the ones that limp across our movie and TV screens
and fill our nights with sweet, gritty fantasies. Love stories are
personal, if you want my opinion: either you have one or you
don't, and if you don't have one life's disgusting enough without
some honey-tongued sadist purring his into your ear. But a love
story of your own: well, that's another matter altogether. Once
you've known love in all its force and fragility, words just can't
describe the dizzying eddies that sweep us to the heights—and
who cares about other people's love stories when you're drifting
in the regions of interstellar bliss, which is perhaps the only reality
that matters after all. But enough of that. Whether you like it or
not I'm going to tell you the story of Françoise and Benoît in love:
because you're a bunch of hopeless romantics—yes, I can see it in
your eyes that drip with emotion whenever you see a beautiful,
banal young couple exchange a peck on the cheek, not to mention a cavernous kiss—because fresh-sliced heart served up with
no matter what revolting sauce is your favourite gourmet treat,
you sentimental anthropophagist creeps, and for a lot of other
reasons that are none of your business.

But let's get one thing straight right away: this is a perfectly
ordinary story, not at all rife with dramatic incident. The 'heroes'
are heroic in name only: there isn't a single case of creeping,
insidious leukemia, and neither protagonist suffers from even the
tiniest fatal cerebral lesion. They're normal, ordinary folks, as
healthy as can be expected, given their propensity for alcohol,
nicotine, animal fats and the various controlled substances they

turn to for life's little pleasures. So you've been warned, and don't come whining to me if the conclusion isn't bloody enough for your liking.

Among today's young intelligentsia there's an impressive clique of misguided perfectionists who, in the name of Independence, complicate their lives beyond belief. I'll get back to that. For the moment, let's just say that Françoise and Benoît were members in good standing when they first met in a little bar on rue Saint-Jean, which will remain anonymous unless the owner offers me drinks on the house for at least ten days running.

It was a Monday night in winter—quiet, nothing out of the ordinary. As soon as Françoise walked into the bar with a suicidal-looking friend at her side, her sleepwalker's shuffle—was it chance or fate—took her to the very back, right next to the seat where Benoît was peacefully reading. On the chair beside him sat an ill-defined individual, considerably the worse for drink, the sort of quiet old bum you often see in bars, who occasionally turns out to be a PhD in mathematics or a former Nobel Peace Prize laureate. Françoise took a seat without looking at anyone, the friend flopped down beside her with a melodramatic whoosh, Benoît's eyes stayed glued to his book and the bum muttered something unintelligible. Time passed.

The friend—let's call her Marie, she's just a bit player here—had been delivering an endless, monotonous litany of complaints about life, love, death, and other profound matters for some time, to judge by Françoise's weary silence, when suddenly the bum made a sound like a death rattle—guttural and rather frightening. All heads turned his way, including those of a small group of individuals—the only other customers in the bar—sitting a few tables away. The septuagenarian dipsomaniac hadn't succumbed to a run-of-the-mill heart attack. On the contrary, his cheeks had suddenly gone purple and he was pointing, stupefied, at the walls of the bar, emitting lugubrious noises all the while. Finally he yelped something intelligible: 'Horrible! Hideous! Horrible!'

Curious heads turned away from the bum and converged upon the apparent cause of this vast spill of emotion: the walls of the bar. There was nothing special about the aforesaid walls, aside from the fact that they were covered with paintings by a local artist. It's true that the artist in question was inordinately prone to formless, provocative dribbles and smears, but who, in these troubled, permissive, and culturally undistinguished times, can boast of his or her ability to distinguish the beautiful from the ugly? So. The bum did *not* approve of the work of the artist in question; in fact, he clearly disapproved. The small group a few tables away from Françoise, Benoît, and company resumed their discussion somewhat resentfully. Benoît gave the bum an approving snicker, Françoise gave the sorry-looking pictures an amused glance, friend Marie tried to resume her dreary soliloquy—in short, everything was just about back to normal. The old man wasn't impressed: he stood up and started shrieking insults at the pictures, threatening to slice them to shreds if they weren't removed from his sight.

'Garbage!' he yelled. 'Trash! Makes me puke!'

And so forth. Now, among the small group of individuals seated, as I mentioned, a few tables away, were some friends of the maligned artist, and they were beginning to think the joke had gone a bit far. A tall, bearded man got up, almost knocking over his chair in the process, and waved his fist at the bum.

'If that old wreck doesn't shut up, I'll bust his jaw!'

The old wreck, delighted and encouraged by the attention, only stepped up the abuse, producing new, even more eloquent epithets. The tall, bearded man stomped over to him.

Then Benoît stood and calmly laid his book on the table.

'I think they're ugly too,' he said blandly. 'In fact, I think they're hideous, repugnant and stercoraceous.'

Which cleared the decks for action. The artist's fan club sent their table flying, Benoît and the bearded man prepared for battle, the panic-stricken waiter burst into the fray—and the little old man, with a snort, began to take the pictures off the wall.

Suddenly a firm, strident voice rose from the budding scuffle and, surprisingly, paralyzed the crowd.

'Monsieur Riopelle! That's enough! Sit down, Monsieur Riopelle.'

Françoise was tugging gently at the old bum's arm, forcing him to leave the pictures be. She pushed him onto a chair, holding him in a firm yet respectful grip.

'Calm down, Monsieur Riopelle. Young artists deserve a break too—don't they, Monsieur Riopelle?'

After a long, stunned silence, the artist's fan club slowly took their seats again, and it's here that my story, or rather the story of Françoise and Benoît, really gets underway.

Now you weren't born yesterday and you're well aware that

the bum was no more Jean-Paul Riopelle than I'm Simone de Beauvoir. Françoise and Benoît found themselves at the same table, doubled over—discreetly—in the same uncontrollable laughter. Friend Marie had finally gone, the group at the other table was gradually breaking up, the old bum—who was nothing more or less than a full-time rubby—sank into a comatose slumber. For our hero and heroine, though, their chattering, their mutual glee, and their delight in each other's wit were endless, and now Françoise's hand finds its way, as if by chance, onto Benoît's thigh, and in their eyes there dances an odd sort of shared glimmer that now and then reduces them to silence, and here they are, a little later, fused and confused in Françoise's big double bed, laughing harder and harder through all the blazing pores of their skin.

Now let's be frank. This nocturnal liaison was not, in itself, exceptional—not for Françoise, and not for Benoît. Both were happily bound for thirty and they were accustomed to light-hearted, effervescent flings, tossed off as voraciously as champagne, just for a few spins of the clock. They were familiar with sudden yearnings for passion that would draw them inexorably into the bed of a stranger with an ever-so-sensual voice encountered in some smoky bar.

At times the fling would have happy consequences: a one-night stand would turn into a regular lover, for a while at least, and the relationship would develop into one of affectionate complicity, free of hassles.

Other times, the fling would turn out to be a full-fledged disaster: after awakening to a vague anxiety bordering on disgust, one would be astonished to find oneself beside some pale, nondescript stranger with whom no communication was possible, but who, behind the veil of the previous night's alcoholic vapours, had seemed brilliant.

To get back to the case in question, everything had been proceeding as smooth as silk from the moment Françoise and Benoît first made contact until the next day when they parted. In fact, they hadn't slept very well. It was as if, in the course of their mutual explorations, their bodies had set off a series of flash fires they couldn't extinguish, and their consuming hilarity kept them awake all night. Hunger finally tugged them from bed the next morning, their eyes rimmed in black, aching all over, but in a splendid mood regardless, and they carried right on with their giggles and winks and confessions. The omelette was good. Benoît—

surprise!—knew how to make filtered coffee, and Françoise—oh, joy!—wasn't a grow-your-own-granola type. In a word, they were enraptured as they parted at Françoise's door, repeating how enjoyable it had been and so on and so forth. Then came the last peck on the cheek, the final wink and giggle, and a nonchalant, 'Be seeing you. Take care.' And so it began.

Françoise devoted the rest of the week to her usual activities with a surplus of energy and zeal that she didn't, at the time, find suspect. Her 'usual activities', it should be said, would normally have been enough to consume the vitality of half a dozen less dynamic souls. Françoise was a born activist, and the financial problems of one Philémon Tremblay, Third Avenue, unemployed—one-armed, asbestositic, tubercular—and the tribulations of one Roberte Roberge, rue Couillard, tenant—grappling with rent increases directly proportional to the size of her giant cockroaches—gave her serious difficulty in sleeping. Françoise could be found in any association that proposed direct action to improve the fate of the world in general, and the quality of her neighbours' lives in particular.

Benoît didn't sit still either, in the days that followed, but was active in his own inward and reflective way, which often resembled mere daydreaming. He was a teaching assistant at Laval University, in the literature department actually, but what he did there was closer to revolutionary sociology than literary studies. There was a kind of serene, spontaneous authority in his most innocuous presentations ('Why are the poor not interested in reading?' 'Is feminist literature authentically progressive?' 'Who really stands to profit from the book-publishing industry?') that had the knack of stimulating passionate discussions among his students and even, at times—to his great astonishment—provoking outside the university stormy demonstrations and the distribution of frankly subversive tracts that claimed to be inspired by him.

Whatever, the week passed normally, or almost: it wasn't till Friday night that Philémon Tremblay's money problems and Roberte Roberge's bugs aroused in Françoise only a sort of irritable indifference, and she suddenly started thinking about Benoît and the night they'd spent together. In fact, she realized she'd been thinking about it nonstop, insidiously, despite the variety of tasks she had compelled herself to carry on with, and that wasn't normal for a why-not-round-off-the-evening sort of fling. She even caught herself glaring at her phone, which was silent—or might as well have been, if you know what I mean—and getting vaguely depressed and wondering if he'd call and telling herself he wouldn't and remembering his hands so soft and velvet and that adorable dimple in his chin and thinking maybe she ought to go back to the little bar 'cause you never know and then saying no, he probably has a wife and five kids—the interesting ones always do.

As there'd been a tacit agreement not to broach the subject of another meeting or any formal commitment, and as he himself hadn't dared to contravene it—out of pride or God knows what ridiculous principle—Benoît, for his part, was concocting, along with his lecture notes, some complex manoeuvres that would allow him to see Françoise again, without making it too obvious. There was the telephone, of course—because he'd made a note of her number without being too obvious—but wouldn't such a primitive mode of communication risk the displeasure of a woman who transcended, without effort, it seemed, such petty, practical details of everyday life? (I know . . .) There remained—of the measures that wouldn't seem too obvious—the chance encounter. Benoît had peeked several times inside the little bar on rue Saint-Jean—which will remain anonymous unless the owner, etc.—and he hadn't seen Françoise (she wasn't there, she was waiting, at home, by the telephone), and that was all it took to convince him that she didn't care if she ever saw him again, she was so beautiful, so free, so far above the petty, practical details of everyday life, and undoubtedly had her hands full coping with the earnest attentions of a dozen men more interesting than he was.

Right. A pair of idiots, I grant you. But be patient, there's worse to come.

As there's a limit to everything, even to the blackest streak of lousy luck and the crassest stupidity, they finally ran into one another at the newsstand near Françoise's apartment, where Benoît—oddly enough—had been buying his papers for two weeks. They recognized each other at once, obviously, but didn't even exchange a peck on the cheek, overwhelmed as they were by an all-consuming stupefaction that had them stammering nonsense about the snow that would or wouldn't fall and the weather past and future. But they did manage, with an unconvincing air of nonchalance, to make a date for that evening. 'If you aren't tied up, that is. . . .' That night found them at his place or hers, it really doesn't matter, and this time Cupid's aim was right on target. He took their breath away, turned their legs to jelly, flung them together like molten lava. They saw each other the next day and the day after that and every night afterwards for weeks and weeks and always there was the same electrifying ardour, the same unalloyed delirium.

This might be the place to bring up independence again, with a capital 'I'—no, my lambs, you haven't been forgotten—in the name of which we make so many sacrifices, especially once it's hardened into a virtue.

It pleased both Françoise and Benoît to consider themselves— eyes modestly lowered, though, as befitted their leftish convictions—part of a mature and highly developed élite, utterly dedicated to the examination and liberation of the self, which had learned how to function on its own (that's what Independence means after all, or something pretty close, with all due respect to my two-volume dictionary). On the subject of love, it follows that they both had airy theories (rather unlike those of John Paul II), which condemned both systematic lumping into couples and unhealthy possessiveness. I'm not telling you anything new when I point out that, when you profess to hold to certain theories with even a modicum of sincerity, the trouble starts when you have to make them conform with reality.

In the beginning, euphoria came easily. It was its own begetter. They were swept along by an incredibly powerful current they hardly dared believe in, that left them exhausted and fulfilled.

Every day as dusk began to fall, Françoise would pick Benoît up at the university or wait for him with a pretended nonchalance at the back of a café or throw herself into the preparation of a gargantuan dinner for two that she knew she'd only pick at, for the emotions of love paralyzed her stomach and her appetite as surely as a bout of nausea. Every day, Benoît would twitch with impatience until late afternoon when he'd see Françoise's indefinable smile, and he never wearied of swooping her up in a violent embrace, of feeling her reel with desire against him, of cooing spectacular trivia into her ear that would melt both their hearts and cause them, with sudden gravity, to exchange a look that left them all a-flutter.

Until . . . Right. Until they take fright as they realize to what extent the well-oiled gears of their lives have unquestionably been disturbed. They start to daydream, to find more and more suspect the peace of mind and security in which they've lately been submerged up to the neck. Françoise, who's always been a lyrical advocate of the need for creative independence and sanctifying solitude, glumly discovers that she NEEDS Benoît: she turns to him at night with undeniable eagerness and rapture that leave her awash with guilt; he turns up at any hour of the day, nesting at the very core of her thoughts, even though she was sure she was safe among her tenants and her jobless. . . . She seems to be in the process of succumbing to feminine atavism, getting caught in the time-worn role of the near-wife devoured by the Other.

As for Benoît, he finds himself overreacting to a friendly jibe by one of his students who saw him with Françoise. He suddenly has the disagreeable impression that his image has betrayed him, that he's gradually lost control of his own emotions, that he's playing the bashful lover in a caricature of a melodrama that has nothing to do with him, that's totally at odds with his libertarian principles. . . . He begins to doubt the authenticity of his inexplicable, all-consuming feeling for Françoise. He thinks it's unhealthy, mawkish, restricting—in a word, conformist. The evidence is clear: he's well on the way to giving in to petit bourgeois happiness.

In short, it's Benoît who strikes the first blow. Boldly and manfully. He unplugs his phone and plays dead for several days. Françoise, concerned and saddened by his abrupt silence, finally runs into him one night as she's strolling, woebegone, through the Latin Quarter. Having spotted him through a café window, she unthinkingly heads inside and makes her way toward him. He greets her with torrents of affection, as if nothing has changed, enquires about her health and the well-being of the unemployed Philémon Tremblay. He gets lost in a woolly discourse on the latest Altman film which he's just seen at the Cartier with Manon or Sandra or Marie who, as it happens, is even now at his side and whose thigh he is almost absent-mindedly patting. Françoise plays along as if nothing was wrong, smiles pleasantly at Manon or Sandra or Marie, dazzlingly outdoes him on the subject of Altman's style—so peculiarly engaging and so unexpectedly American—then finally gets up, gives Benoît an excessively polite kiss, flashes a charming smile at Manon or Sandra or Marie, and leaves the café—distraught, knees quaking, and with an uncontrollable desire to throw up and scream. She drags herself home, upbraiding herself aloud and giving herself inward kicks to ward off the real pain. Oh, it was nothing to get worked up about, just a passing fancy she'd inflated like some prepubescent crush, that's all. . . . Françoise is almost relieved, despite the frightful ache that's spreading through her belly: now, at least, she can go on believing there's no such thing as love. She stretches out on her bed, flicks on the TV, forbids herself to cry and eventually falls into a dreamless sleep, as though nothing had happened: stoicism is a precondition for Independence.

First thing the next morning, though, who should phone but Benoît—all sweetness and light, and secretly ravaged by a nagging anxiety that kept him awake all night. What if Françoise was so hurt by his inexplicable behaviour that she refused to see him again. . . . But no—Françoise speaks in her usual voice, pleasant and warm, tells him she's fine, and they make a date for that night. Miraculously, they get together as if nothing had happened: with their usual passion and fire, laughing and embracing like old accomplices. Françoise asks no questions, Benoît offers no confession. They maintain a tacit silence about what *may* have happened the night before—and the days before that.

And so the tone is set. Benoît is convinced he was right to introduce those breathing spaces into their relationship—not only does Françoise not hold it against him, she seems to be welcoming the change with her unshakeable good humour; perhaps deep down she was even hoping for it. And so Benoît multiplies his meetings with Manon or Sandra or Marie, sets up others with Sylvie, Laura and Julie, and banishes guilt from both his vocabulary and his daily life. By behaving as if nothing has happened, Françoise finally convinces herself she's living through a healthy, normal situation, one that's even somehow privileged (traditional couples are so quick to give in to possessiveness and neurotic jealousy . . .) and that her relationship with Benoît is turning out to be, basically, completely satisfying, giving her exactly what she needs. After all, don't they see each other at least twice a week, and isn't it absolutely sensational, fantastically passionate, every time? What more could she ask? It's only the remnants of romantic culture, decadent vestiges she hasn't had time to shed, that still make her start painfully and feel an acute, inexplicable anguish whenever she sees Benoît exchange familiar, tender gestures with someone else. . . . And then she decides that a meaningful quickie or two would do her a world of good, so she goes back to cruising, a tried-and-true activity at which, I might add, she excelled before Benoît came into her life. So now it's Benoît's turn to feel something like an icy swell rising in him as he sees Françoise's indefinable smile reflected in someone else's eyes, as he sneaks a peek at her sensual hand brushing against a leg other than his. But there are new ground rules now, and there's nothing to do but carry on in the same offhand, swaggering manner, to nervously gulp down the rest of his beer and look around for a woman to go home with tonight, so he won't be outdone.

And then one night Françoise is sitting with a friend—sure, let's call her Marie. Why not?—in the little bar from the beginning of the story, and as a matter of fact she's just launched into a loud, clear discourse on the merits and advantages of her relationship with Benoît when who should walk in but . . . He spots Françoise and gives her a knowing wink. He sits at a table with a gorgeous blonde—yet another one—whom he clearly already knows, as he starts up a passionate conversation punctuated with furtive fondling and inconsequential little kisses—inconsequential, Françoise tells herself, recognizing at once the vague cramp that even now is clenching her guts, though it doesn't stop her from pursuing with increased fervour her discourse on the fidelity, yes, the sort of inner, visceral fidelity, that marks her relationship with Benoît, even though, from all appearances, even though . . . And then, suddenly, she stops talking. Breaks off in mid-sentence with no warning, just like that. She doesn't even pretend to be following the conversation, but slumps into an odd sort of torpor from which her friend Marie can't shake her. When the gorgeous blonde gets up to go to the can or straight to hell—who cares—Françoise glides over to Benoît and tells him in a hoarse little voice, without giving him time for a smile or a kiss, that she has just discovered that she doesn't have the knack for being super cool, so she's pulling out, giving up, she's tired of stomach aches, she's exhausted from making up stories for herself. Benoît is silent, she utters a definitive goodnight that sounds like a farewell, and now she's outside, encased in an Olympian calm, friend Marie hard on her heels.

We find them both much later, in another bar, needless to say, unwinding into strong drink the never-ending skein of female rancour—he was never capable of love, I should have known, when I think of what I invested in that relationship, God, women are crazy to love the way we do, so much for nothing, waiter, five more beers, five beers to help me forget that times are tough and men are wimps. . . . Françoise is awash in a sort of lyric intoxication. She's found herself even though she's lost Benoît; at least this pain is unequivocal, with no little tricks, it'll be easier to assuage, to cauterize it, starting tonight with that dish with the bedroom eyes who's been hovering around, whom she brutally decides to pick up—for her libido, only her libido, and also to warm up the left side of her big double bed—the nights are so chilly now.

When she eventually goes home on the arm of the stranger who may with a little luck turn out to be a good lover, Françoise finds Benoît—who else!—haggard and shivering on her landing, his eyes distorted by something wet that looks like tears. He tells her he loves her—what else!—that he doesn't want to lose her, all in a tone that cannot be mistaken, on the landing of an aging apartment, in the slanting pre-dawn light, with a stranger planted there like a coatrack, who finally takes off because nobody's paying any attention to him.

So there it is. I've reached the epilogue, dear hearts. But where's the ending, the real ending, how does it *really* end (a bang? a whimper? fireworks or cold shower?), you ask with the look of a lustful pterodactyl. All right. I can see right through your new-wave hairdo. I know what's on your mind. Maybe Françoise and Benoît get married—sure, why not—it's still done. It's been all the rage for the past few years, in fact, amazingly popular with the under-twenty-fives. Don't get your hopes up, my little badgers. After all, I did make it clear that Françoise and Benoît were intelligent youngsters, well aware of life or, at least, a few of the primary truths, starting with this one: the marital arts are inevitably, every single time, transformed into martial arts. Okay, fine, so you resign yourselves, sighing like a duck-billed platypus being stroked the wrong way. Whether they marry or not, whether they have children or not, Françoise and Benoît might well enjoy a long and flawless happiness, for all eternity. Sure. Don't get me wrong—I'd like that, too. But things don't turn out that way in real life, where love isn't organized by those chaps from Hollywood or Harlequin. So let me tell you what happens to Françoise and Benoît: after all the twists and turns and tortuous manoeuvres through which we've followed them, they finally reach a workable compromise between independence and commitment—which is rare, ultra-rare. In fact, their relationship is very special, a passionate, gripping love affair that lasts three years. Or five. Or eight. And then one day they decide to split up because it's time, because they'd only hurt each other if they tried to revive what's already dead between them, because nothing lasts forever, alas, and they have high standards and abhor pretense. I'm not saying they burned all their bridges. No. When you've achieved an intense, almost total communion with someone—which is rare, ultra-rare—when you've lived a real-life love story, in a word, you never really leave each other altogether: there's a neatly laid-out compartment in your heart that no one else can fill.

Listen: only last year, on the anniversary of the day they met, Françoise received from Benoît—special delivery—a big rectangular package. She was home with some friends and a passing lover—Max, let's call him, or Pierre or Victor-Hippolyte—when she opened the parcel. It was a print, a reproduction of a weird-looking hairy owl, pasted like a party favour onto a hazy landscape. When she recognized the picture that had got Monsieur Riopelle so worked up, Françoise laughed. Then, if you must know, she started to blubber, blubbered like a calf, like a Magdalene, blubbered hard enough to bust a gut, tirelessly, inconsolably, till we had to call Benoît to help us calm her down.

And that's why alcohol and Colombian gold and lovely lavender stories exist. That's why I've told you about Françoise and Benoît, and that's why I'm on my way to down a few little carafes of plonk. There are truths that are difficult to digest, there are truths to be swallowed a spoonful at a time, slowly, slowly, so as not to upset the stomach. This one, for example.

If you're strong, you know that life's a road on which you're always alone, even with love, even if people have halted along the way to engage our emotions. We must carry on, carry on to the end, till we can touch the little light that's shining just for us, till we can embrace its light, a special little light for each of us, at the end, at the very end of the road.

Translated by Sheila Fischman

ROBYN SARAH

The Pond, Phase One

What do husbands, sitting on the porch in the dark, talk about while their wives take a late night walk down a country road? One at a time, they rise abruptly and go into the house to freshen their drinks; they return, ice cubes clinking in their glasses, and settle down to take their ease; the dark beyond the edge of the deck is alive with lightning-bugs. A match flares, then another, and blue smoke of Sobranie wafts from one's pipe; the other's cigarette is a point of orange tracing the movement of his hand as he gestures across the valley, at house lights perhaps, to say who lives there, or maybe he's really indicating something nearer, the place they've bulldozed recently for a pond, not visible in the dark; he describes it to his guest.

I believe that for long periods they are silent, either because they do not feel the need to talk or because they think there is nothing very much to say; they're past that, they think, they're not young men any more. Probably when a child begins to wail in the bedroom upstairs where all three have been put to sleep, it doesn't register right away, it goes on for a little while before they remember that the women are not in the house. They think of it at the same moment and incline their heads—'Is that one of mine?' 'No, I think it's mine,' and the host gets up and goes inside to check.

Their wives have been friends for upwards of twelve years; they met working in the same department for one of the larger weeklies in the city. Helen writes for a different paper now; Rosalie has been living in the country for two years, free-lancing in her spare time, rueful to report she doesn't have the kind of spare time she expected to have. They miss their frequent long lunches together in the city, the telephone conversations that left receivers warm in their cradles in both houses—conversations comparing notes on everything from writing assignments to pediatricians and daycares to past loves, with long vivid digressions about their childhoods. They've seen each other through divorce, remarriage, pregnancy, childbirth, miscarriage, and family illness; there is nothing they're afraid to say to each other. And now they find themselves the mothers of three children born within two years of each other, children who play together like cousins.

It has taken Rosalie two years in the country to be able to walk out at night without being driven back by a primitive dread of the dark—even on a night like this, starry, with a clear half-moon, and all the lightning-bugs twinkling on either side of the road. But Helen feels she could walk forever, she's utterly at home, she feels embraced by this country dark. Why? In the city, night gives her the creeps, even in her own neighbourhood. Here it's as if she could come to no harm; she imagines walking alone, breathing the fragrant air, following a road without knowing or caring where it may take her, just walking on and on into daybreak. She longs to do it. She feels immune, protected. Her husband, on the other hand, she tells Rosalie, gets spooked in the country at night. Once they took a walk down a road in Vermont, it was so beautiful, their first time in the country in years, and then he wanted to go back. Because there was that kind of a moon, a smokey moon, smothered in cloud. Rosalie says she knows exactly what kind of a moon. She gets spooked too.

They're quiet for a little while, then they begin making plans for the next day, for the three days Helen and Tom and the children can stay this time, before they have to go back to the city. It'll be wonderful next summer, when the pond has filled up. Is that all it takes? Helen wants to know; will one year's melting snow really make a pond? No, says Rosalie, but the hole is full of springs. You'll see tomorrow; we dug there because it was always marshy, and it turned out there are four or five underground springs. Right now it's just a big hole in the ground, with a hard mud buttom. But it's funny—Benjamin has been spending whole days down there playing, it's such a boon I almost wish we could leave it a mud-hole!

Little by little their talk moves to other things, the things they've been waiting to talk about, now they're over the first rise and far enough down the road that they can be sure their voices won't carry back towards the house. They speak fondly and ruefully of the state of their marriages, tentatively of the men they are currently in love with: in Rosalie's case her first cousin, a painter, recently divorced and living in the next township, in Helen's a colleague, also married, with whom she used to car-pool—a man lately fired for political reasons, and in the process of filing a grievance.

They tell of recent exchanges, they are amazed at the parallels; they laugh at themselves. It's a relief to be able to talk about it. What's the matter with us? It's so stupid. Do you think it's the same for everyone? Helen has a friend who's in love with a priest; Rosalie says so-and-so told her she and her husband haven't slept together for four months and she's in love with a doctor at the hospital where she works. God, says Helen, four months, that's even worse than us. And a doctor. Couldn't she do better than that? They laugh because it's a long-standing joke between them, their indifference to the professional set, their preference for the crazy ones, artists, politicos, dreamers—the ones they left the first time around.

The damp gravel crunches under their sandals. Rosalie yawns. Do you think we should turn back now? Maybe we'd better. They might worry. Do you suppose the kids ever settled down? They were so excited to see each other. Funny how light it seems now, I can see everything. I'm getting eaten alive by mosquitoes, what about you?

2.

The hole has been dug right to hardpan, with banks that slope, though it's to be expected that the sides will give somewhat when the pond fills up. At bottom the mud is mostly firm, traced by rivulets from the springs. The water is icy cold and good to drink; one of the springs bubbles up from under a rock, you can catch the water in your hands. Any quick spots? Tom wants to know. A few, Daniel says, but nothing dangerous to the childen—the hole's too deep for that. They could sink in maybe half a foot, probably not even that.

Nevertheless Amy, the youngest, loses no time in finding one; before breakfast eggs have even hit the pan the boys come running, banging the screen door, Mummy, Daddy, Amy's stuck in the mud and she can't get out!

Ludicrous in her nightgown and Wellingtons, Helen runs out

after them into morning mist, down into the raw gash in the landscape behind the house. She feels her own foot give as she steps out onto the flat where Amy, arms upraised and wailing, stands with mud nearly to the tops of both red gum-boots. Backing up, she tests for solid footing and leans over to get her hands under Amy's arms. The suck of the mud is surprisingly strong; twice she loses her balance, and in the end lifts Amy clear minus one boot, and has to go back for it.

She recognizes that there's no real danger, Tom and Daniel josh her out of that, but after breakfast, when the children indicate they're heading back down there, she wants to go too, to see for herself just how much trouble Amy is apt to get into if left on her own there. Rosalie says she'll come too, she likes the mud-hole. It's not the way you'd think, she says, it's really kind of an interesting thing to have in one's back yard. I feel like it wouldn't be a complete disaster if it *didn't* fill up.

The children troop ahead, jubilant explorers; the women, skirts catching in the tops of their Wellingtons, pick their way down along the tracks the bulldozer left on its way out. They'll come back in the fall, Rosalie explains, to bank up the far side where the springs drain off; the idea is to give the sides some time to harden.

At the bottom of the hole, an expanse of gleaming wet mud, variously textured. The silts are red and brown and grey and black, streamlets of water have deposited traces and superimposed them to create a marbling effect. Where springs bubble up, the silt is held in suspension; small fountains, small eddies of velvety mud. Mostly, it's surprisingly firm to walk on, but there are those spots near the springs where sediment has built up; when you step on them the mud gives, you sink rapidly, a little sickeningly, but not very far: to half the depth of her own boots, Helen discovers; Amy was about as far in as she could have gone. She finds it's hard, but not very, to extricate herself unaided, even without leaving a boot behind.

She tells Amy and Jeremy to stay away from the squishy parts. The only danger, agreed, is that they could lose their balance and tumble: more nuisance than danger. After all, we have a washing machine, says Rosalie.

They follow behind the children, who are exploring the run-off, where rivulets merge into a shallow stream that wanders away crookedly among cattails towards the lower meadow. This is the part that will be blocked off in the fall. There will still be drainage, through a pipe, but not the same amount of water—only the overflow from the pond. You see what I mean, Rosalie says, it's a fabulous place for them to play. There's all that mud for a stomping-ground, and then a whole stream to follow out of it. Frogs. Pretty pebbles. A whole forest of cattails to hide in. And I can let Ben play by himself down here. Once the pond fills up, I'll always worry a little. Yes, it's wonderful, agrees Helen. They stand side by side in the deepest part of the stream, watching the water trickle over the toes of their boots, bending to pick up the occasional rock glinting wet in the sun. At a distance now, the children's heads bob in and out among the cattails. A cicada, the first of the day, hones his drill somewhere above them.

3.

Kyona. I've never heard of it. It's a Japanese green, says Rosalie. Taste it. I ordered the seeds from our catalogue. Helen breaks off a feathery, antler-shaped leaf. Mmmm. It tastes a bit like Chinese lettuce. What a beautiful name, kyona. You could name a child that. You could, says Rosalie, only it probably means lettuce-like, or something, in Japanese.

They're squatting side by side in the garden, pulling leaves into a collander for a dinner salad. What else will you need for the quiche? Rosalie wants to know. Helen, nibbling another leaf of kyona, considers. You can put almost anything in it. Zucchini and carrots will be fine. Maybe some chard. Some fresh parsley, if you have any. Tons, says Rosalie, over there at the end of the herb plot, behind the chives. See the chives? The purple puff-balls. Aren't they huge, says Helen. They must be strong enough to get up and walk.

What else goes with quiche? Oh, says Helen. You don't have to make anything. Please. A big salad will be fine. Let me do it, I want to. All right, says Rosalie, then I'll do a lasagna tomorrow. I have a marvelous recipe. Did I show you the book last time you came out? The one from that restaurant in Ithaca? Everything in it is fabulous. There's a vegetarian chili, it uses bulgur instead of meat. Really? I'd like to try that. Sure, I'll show it to you later, you can write it down.

Absently they are chewing on raw green beans, snow peas, breaking them off the vines as they move along the rows. It feels funny, Helen says. What does? To be talking about recipes. Are we that far gone? They laugh. I know what you mean.

They're thinking about when they first met, about foreign films, political demonstrations. About all-night pizza joints, rooms without furniture, dinners on the floor. They sit back on their heels and gaze up at the house, nestled among the trees, the soaring timbers of the new addition still raw, blond in the sun. When did it become necessary, Rosalie wonders, this elaborate shell, this extension of self?

A perfect zucchini, glossy, deep green, not too far yet, with the furled drying blossom still stuck to its end. Feel it, don't they feel strange when you first pick them? Almost prickly. Oh, I know, says Rosalie, it's a riot, do you know Benjamin won't touch them? He can't stand the feeling, it drives him completely wild. Even green beans. I can't get him to pick green beans for me, he says they're hairy. Green beans! Helen exclaims. But it's hardly noticeable on green beans! It is to him, I can understand it, I'm sort of the same, says Rosalie. When I was a kid I wouldn't go near peaches. I think I was twenty-two before I could touch a peach without climbing walls. I mean, I still don't *buy* them, but if someone gives me one . . . Well, I find that mildly amazing, says Helen. What is it, an allergy? Not of the usual sort, says Rosalie. I wonder if there's a name for it? Yes, says Rosalie, I think they call it texture.

4.

Benjamin, Jeremy, red head, dark head, over the garden fence. Benjamin's a year younger but nearly a head taller. Jeremy's gap-toothed, radiant through sweat and mud. They've taken their shirts off, mud streaks their torsos. Where's Amy? Why did you leave her by herself?

Mummy, the backs of my shorts is soaking. Mummy, there's water in my boot. We're making mud things, Mummy. Come and see. They're drying on a rock. Mummy, we like the squishy parts. We won't get stuck. We can just take our boots off. Can we take off our boots, Mummy? Amy already has hers off. The best mud for making mud things is the squishy parts. Can you come and see? Please?

Go, says Rosalie, I'll put these things in the fridge and come down in a few minutes. Is there anything we need from town?

Swiss cheese. Right. I'll tell Daniel, he has to drive in for some plumbing parts.

There's a downward-sloping shelf of rock, large enough for both of them to sit on, embedded in the east bank of what will be the pond. They tuck their skirts in around them, brace their heels to keep from sliding, and hug their knees. The afternoon heat is intense. Slowly Helen slips her feet, one at a time, out of her boots; she peels her socks off and wads them and stuffs them inside, flexes her toes into the breeze. Good idea, says Rosalie. The children, already freed of boots, are almost knee deep in one of the quick spots, stomping and squelching gleefully. Chanting something. How can they stand to do that *barefoot*?

Like monks stomping on grapes, says Rosalie. No, says Helen, they're softening it up to make a trap for monsters. They told me.

They've made mud meatballs and mud potatoes and mud sausages, misshapen blobs drying in a row in a groove of the rock. Here come more. We'll show you how we make them, Mum. See this mud? See how you squish the water out? That's a very nice mud-ball, dear, but please get it away from my skirt. Squish the water out over there. Not in my hair. Mummy, you're knocking our dry potatoes down the hill. Look, Mum, it rolled right down and it didn't break! Look, Benjamin! Mine didn't break. Let's see if yours does. Let's see whose breaks. Amy, come! We're playing Potato Rolling Down The Hill!

Tom and Daniel have driven to town, Rosalie says, they may drive around a bit before coming back. They promised to be back in time for supper. There's a garage sale on in Dunsmuir they might check out, we're looking for bicycles. Benjamin, I like your mudball very much but I told you to take it over there. No, *further*. Where it won't drip on me.

Here, Mummy, hold this, I have to get some more of the wet stuff. Jeremy, I don't *want* to hold it. Put it down. Anywhere. Ouch, don't *lean* on me, honey, it's hard to keep my balance on this rock—Rosalie, will you listen to us. Helen laughs suddenly, you'd think we'd never read Summerhill. Really—just like a couple of *mothers*, sitting primly on our nice dry rock. Aren't you afraid we're going to stifle their creative spirit?

A whoop from Rosalie. I know, aren't we awful? They don't look very stifled to me. I suppose if we were really enlightened, we'd sit down in the mud and make potatoes with them. She waves a deerfly away from her head. Well, so there you are, says

Rosalie, suddenly serious, the career, the kid, the countryhouse. Everything I always said I wanted. You'd think I could sit back now and enjoy it all.

Can't you? asks Helen. Why can't you? She shifts her position on the rock; another potato rolls down the slope. I don't know, says Rosalie, I'm consumed with restlessness. She picks up one of the smaller dried mudballs and presses it between thumb and forefinger to see how hard it is. It explodes softly, showering damp sand in her lap; she brushes it off her skirt.

I am too, says Helen. Ever since the kids stopped being babies. Give me one of those. They're sort of neat, aren't they? It cracks between fingers like a soft nut, slightly off-center; the two halves, each intact, lie in her palm. One of them has a small pebble imbedded in it; that's what it cracked around.

What do you think, asks Rosalie, would you have an affair with Peter? Helen is leaning over the edge of the rock, scooping some of the wet mud into her palm. She spreads it carefully with a finger, picking out all the tiny pebbles, every little irregularity. I don't know, she says slowly. It hasn't exactly come up. There's a lot at stake for both of us, we don't seek each other out. When I see him it's nice, is all.

She's squeezing the mud in her fist, it molds to her hand, holding the ridges where it pressed between her fingers. She reshapes it into a ball, more perfectly formed than the ones the children have made, and sets it in the groove to dry. There must be a lot of clay in this. It has a wonderful texture. Has it? says Rosalie. They both lean over, digging with their fingers for handfuls.

I think about Martin all the time, says Rosalie. I even think about having another kid just to get him off my mind. And then I think— well, *no.* You're right, there must be a lot of clay in this. It feels almost alive. No wonder the kids are so enthralled.

They discover that tossing the mud from hand to hand is a good way to get the excess water out. At first it has a slick wet slap to it; it's elastic, the momentum pulls it into odd loose shapes in the air. But as it gets drier, it firms up, it packs into a smooth dense ball, a small planet, you can squeeze it and it will keep its form. Suppose we baked these, says Helen, would they harden like clay does? Let's keep a few and try, says Rosalie. Let's make a few specially, with the smoothest mud we can find.

They leave the rock and wade across the web of little streams, holding up their skirts. The mud is sun-warmed now, smooth as skin, and near the source of the main spring there's a part that seems to breathe beneath them; they feel it give a little and surge back with every step, retaining its surface tension. It's like walking on somebody's stomach, says Rosalie. Isn't it? says Helen. You can see why this is the stuff God is supposed to have made Adam out of.

5.

The children's voices are far away down the stream, they've evolved out of the mud, moved on to other things. Here and there you can see the print of a small foot that sank in sideways; the quick spots are all churned up, they're a lighter colour than the rest. Helen and Rosalie are squatting by one, they've tucked the bottoms of their skirts up into their waistbands; their hands, their wrists, their forearms are plunged deep in mud. There's something hypnotic about it, they aren't even making mudballs any more.

They look at each other suddenly and begin to giggle. What is this, play therapy? I don't know, but it sure is fun. How long have we been down here, anyway? You've got some in your hair. Well, you've got some on your forehead. What are we going to tell the guys when they ask what kept us from starting dinner earlier? If we don't get up to the house soon and wash, says Rosalie, we won't have to tell them anything.

Oh, who cares what they think! says Helen. I haven't had so much fun in ages. Can you believe it? A whole afternoon! Hey, says Rosalie, look over there, the kids have come back around by the field. They're over by the rock. Hey, don't touch those, she yells. Those are *our* mudballs. Leave them alone, we want to bake them!

Don't touch our mudballs! they yell, and then they're collapsing, gasping, holding their stomachs, their hands are so mucky they can't even wipe their streaming eyes. Rosalie, says Helen, when she can talk again, as long as we've regressed this far, why not take off our clothes and get right in? I mean, they're going to think we're crazy anyway. Can you imagine? What on earth would they make of it?

You just reminded me, says Rosalie, that when I was in college, in the dorm, I used to fantasize about taking a bath in chocolate pudding. I even got as far as measuring the tub and figuring out how many packages it would take.

You did? Honest? How many packages *was* it? Helen sounds amazed, subdued. Did you ever do it? No, says Rosalie sadly, it was too expensive.

They're clutching themselves again, they're doubled over, when they finally straighten up it's as though something has gone out of them, they're limp, drained; they feel wobbly and innocent as newborn colts.

Well? says Helen.

I will if you will.

I will if you will.

They untie their cotton wrap-around skirts, they slip out of their nylon bikini-briefs, they throw off their halter-tops and fling them up the bank towards the rock. Flimsy summer fabrics, ballooning, bright, arc upward to tumble in a heap. Breasts bouncing, they splash across the stream to the deepest quick-spot; solemnly, dispassionately, they watch their feet disappear; with whoops, they fall to their knees in velvet bubbling mud.

The hum of a car engine, just become audible in the distance, will be Tom and Daniel. They've got two used ten-speeds roped through the windows to the roof of the car, and they're taking it slow and easy over the hill.

CAROL SHIELDS

Mrs Turner Cutting the Grass

Oh, Mrs Turner is a sight cutting the grass on a hot afternoon in June! She climbs into an ancient pair of shorts and ties on her halter top and wedges her feet into crepe-soled sandals and covers her red-gray frizz with Gord's old golf cap—Gord is dead now, ten years ago, a seizure on a Saturday night while winding the mantel clock.

The grass flies up around Mrs Turner's knees. Why doesn't she use a catcher, the Saschers next door wonder. Everyone knows that leaving the clippings like that is bad for the lawn. Each fallen blade of grass throws a minute shadow which impedes growth and repair. The Saschers themselves use their clippings to make compost which they hope one day will be ripe as the good manure that Sally Sascher's father used to spread on his fields down near Emerson Township.

Mrs Turner's carelessness over the clippings plucks away at Sally, but her husband Roy is far more concerned about the Killex that Mrs Turner dumps on her dandelions. It's true that in Winnipeg the dandelion roots go right to the middle of the earth, but Roy is patient and persistent in pulling them out, knowing exactly how to grasp the coarse leaves in his hand and how much pressure to apply. Mostly they come up like corks with their roots intact. And he and Sally are experimenting with new ways to cook dandelion greens, believing as they do that the components of nature are arranged for a specific purpose—if only that purpose can be divined.

In the early summer Mrs Turner is out every morning by ten with her sprinkling can of chemical killer, and Roy, watching from his front porch, imagines how this poison will enter the ecosystem and move by quick capillary surges into his fenced vegetable plot, newly seeded now with green beans and lettuce. His children, his two little girls aged two and four—that they should be touched by such poison makes him morose and angry. But he and Sally so far have said nothing to Mrs Turner about her abuse of the planet because they're hoping she'll go into an old-folks home soon or maybe die, and then all will proceed as it should.

High-school girls on their way home in the afternoon see Mrs Turner cutting her grass and are mildly, momentarily repelled by the lapped, striated flesh on her upper thighs. At her age. Doesn't she realize? Every last one of them is intimate with the vocabulary of skin care and knows that what has claimed Mrs Turner's thighs is the enemy called cellulite, but they can't understand why she doesn't take the trouble to hide it. It makes them queasy; it makes them fear for the future.

The things Mrs Turner doesn't know would fill the Saschers' new compost pit, would sink a ship, would set off a tidal wave, would make her want to kill herself. Back and forth, back and forth she goes with the electric lawn mower, the grass flying out sideways like whiskers. Oh, the things she doesn't know! She has never heard, for example, of the folk-rock recording star Neil Young, though the high school just around the corner from her house happens to be the very school Neil Young attended as a lad. His initials can actually be seen carved on one of the desks, and a few of the teachers say they remember him, a quiet fellow of neat appearance and always very polite in class. The desk with the initials N.Y. is kept in a corner of Mr Pring's homeroom, and it's considered lucky—despite the fact that the renowned singer wasn't a great scholar—to touch the incised letters just before an exam. Since it's exam time now, the second week of June, the girls walking past Mrs Turner's front yard (and shuddering over her display of cellulite) are carrying on their fingertips the spiritual scent, the essence, the fragrance, the aura of Neil Young, but Mrs Turner is as ignorant of that fact as the girls are that she, Mrs Turner, possesses a first name—which is Geraldine.

Not that she's ever been called Geraldine. Where she grew up in Boissevain, Manitoba, she was known always—the Lord knows why—as Girlie Fergus, the youngest of the three Fergus girls and the one who got herself in hot water. Her sister Em went to normal school and her sister Muriel went to Brandon to work at Eaton's, but Girlie got caught one night—she was nineteen—in a Boissevain hotel room with a local farmer, married, named Gus MacGregor. It was her father who got wind of where she might be and came banging on the door, shouting and weeping. 'Girlie, Girlie, what have you done to me?'

Girlie had been working in the Boissevain Dairy since she'd left school at sixteen and had a bit of money saved up, and so, a week after the humiliation in the local hotel, she wrote a farewell note to the family, crept out of the house at midnight and caught the bus to Winnipeg. From there she got another bus down to Minneapolis, then to Chicago, and finally New York City. The journey was endless and wretched, and on the way across Indiana and Ohio and Pennsylvania she saw hundreds and hundreds of towns whose unpaved streets and narrow blinded houses made her fear some conspiratorial, punishing power had carried her back to Boissevain. Her father's soppy-stern voice sang and sang in her ears as the wooden bus rattled its way eastward. It was summer, 1930.

New York was immense and wonderful, dirty, perilous and puzzling. She found herself longing for a sight of real earth which she assumed must lie somewhere beneath the tough pavement. On the other hand, the brown flat-roofed factories with their little windows tilted skyward pumped her full of happiness, as did the dusty trees, when she finally discovered them, lining the long avenues. Every last person in the world seemed to be outside, walking around, filling the streets, and every corner breezed with noise and sunlight. She had to pinch herself to believe this was the same sunlight that filtered its way into the rooms of the house back in Boissevain, fading the curtains but nourishing her mother's ferns. She sent postcards to Em and Muriel that said, 'Don't worry about me. I've got a job in the theatre business.'

It was true. For eight and a half months she was an usherette in the Lamar Movie Palace in Brooklyn. She loved her perky maroon uniform, the way it fit on her shoulders, the way the strips of crinkly gold braid outlined her figure. With a little flashlight in hand she was able to send streams of light across the furry darkness of the theatre and onto the plum-coloured aisle carpet. The voices from the screen talked on and on. She felt after a time that their resonant declarations and tender replies belonged to her.

She met a man named Kiki her first month in New York and moved in with him. His skin was as black as ebony. *As black as ebony*—that was the phrase that hung like a ribbon on the end of his name, and it's also the phrase she uses, infrequently, when she wants to call up his memory, though she's more than a little doubtful about what *ebony* is. It may be a kind of stone, she thinks, something round and polished that comes out of a deep mine.

Kiki was a good-hearted man, though she didn't like the beer he drank, and he stayed with her, willingly, for several months after she had to stop working because of the baby. It was the baby itself that frightened him off, the way it cried probably. Leaving fifty dollars on the table, he slipped out one July afternoon when Girlie was shopping, and went back to Troy, New York, where he'd been raised.

Her first thought was to take the baby and get on a bus and go find him, but there wasn't enough money, and the thought of the baby crying all the way on the hot bus made her feel tired. She was worried about the rent and about the little red sores in the baby's ears—it was a boy, rather sweetly formed, with wonderful smooth feet and hands. On a murderously hot night, a night when the humidity was especially bad, she wrapped him in a clean piece of sheeting and carried him all the way to Brooklyn Heights where the houses were large and solid and surrounded by grass. There was a house on a corner she particularly liked because it had a wide front porch (like those in Boissevain) with a curved railing—and parked on the porch, its brake on, was a beautiful wicker baby carriage. It was here she placed her baby, giving one last look to his sleeping face, as round and calm as the moon. She walked home, taking her time, swinging her legs. If she had known the word *foundling*—which she didn't—she would have bounded along on its rhythmic back, so airy and wide did the world seem that night.

Most of these secrets she keeps locked away inside her mottled thighs or in the curled pinkness of her genital flesh. She has no idea what happened to Kiki, whether he ever went off to Alaska as he wanted to or whether he fell down a flight of stone steps in the silverware factory in Troy, New York, and died of head injuries before his 30th birthday. Or what happened to her son—whether he was bitten that night in the baby carriage by a rabid neighbourhood cat or whether he was discovered the next morning and adopted by the large, loving family who lived in the house. As a rule, Girlie tries not to think about the things she can't even guess at. All she thinks is that she did the best she could under the circumstances.

In a year she saved enough money to take the train home to Bossevain. She took with her all her belongings, and also gifts for

Em and Muriel, boxes of hose, bottles of apple-blossom cologne, phonograph records. For her mother she took an embroidered apron and for her father a pipe made of curious gnarled wood. 'Girlie, my girlie,' her father said, embracing her at the Boissevain station. Then he said, 'Don't ever leave us again,' in a way that frightened her and made her resolve to leave as quickly as possible.

But she didn't go as far the second time around. She and Gordon Turner—he was, for all his life, a tongue-tied man, though he did manage a proper proposal—settled down in Winnipeg, first in St Boniface where the rents were cheap and then Fort Rouge and finally the little house in River Heights just around the corner from the high school. It was her husband, Gord, who planted the grass that Mrs Turner now shaves in the summertime. It was Gord who trimmed and shaped the caragana hedge and Gord who painted the little shutters with the cut-out hearts. He was a man who loved every inch of his house, the wide wooden steps, the oak door with its glass inset, the radiators and the baseboards and the snug sash windows. And he loved every inch of his wife, Girlie, too, saying to her once and only once that he knew about her past (meaning Gus MacGregor and the incident in the Boissevain Hotel), and that as far as he was concerned the slate had been wiped clean. Once he came home with a little package in his pocket; inside was a diamond ring, delicate and glittering. Once he took Girlie on a picnic all the way up to Steep Rock, and in the woods he took off her dress and underthings and kissed every part of her body.

After he died, Girlie began to travel. She was far from rich, as she liked to say, but with care she could manage one trip every spring.

She has never known such ease. She and Em and Muriel have been to Disneyland as well as Disneyworld. They've been to Europe, taking a sixteen-day trip through seven countries. The three of them have visited the south and seen the famous antebellum houses of Georgia, Alabama and Mississippi, after which they spent a week in the city of New Orleans. They went to Mexico one year and took pictures of Mayan ruins and queer shadowy gods cut squarely from stone. And three years ago they did what they swore they'd never have the nerve to do: they got on an airplane and went to Japan.

The package tour started in Tokyo where Mrs Turner ate, on her first night there, a chrysanthemum fried in hot oil. She saw a village where everyone earned a living by making dolls and another village where everyone made pottery. Members of the tour group, each holding up a green flag so their tour leader could keep track of them, climbed on a little train, zoomed off to Osaka where they visited an electronics factory, and then went to a restaurant to eat uncooked fish. They visited more temples and shrines than Mrs Turner could keep track of. Once they stayed the night in a Japanese hotel where she and Em and Muriel bedded down on floor mats and little pillows stuffed with cracked wheat, and woke up, laughing, with backaches and shooting pains in their legs.

That was the same day they visited the Golden Pavilion in Kyoto. The three-storied temple was made of wood and had a roof like a set of wings and was painted a soft old flaky gold. Everybody in the group took pictures—Em took a whole roll—and bought postcards; everybody, that is, except a single tour member, the one they all referred to as the Professor.

The Professor traveled without a camera, but jotted notes almost continuously into a little pocket scribbler. He was bald, had a trim body and wore Bermuda shorts, sandals and black nylon socks. Those who asked him learned that he really was a professor, a teacher of English poetry in a small college in Massachusetts. He was also a poet who, at the time of the Japanese trip, had published two small chapbooks based mainly on the breakdown of his marriage. The poems, sadly, had not caused much stir.

It grieved him to think of that paltry, guarded nut-like thing that was his artistic reputation. His domestic life had been too cluttered; there had been too many professional demands; the political situation in America had drained him of energy—these were the thoughts that buzzed in his skull as he scribbled and scribbled, like a man with a fever, in the back seat of a tour bus traveling through Japan.

Here in this crowded, confused country he discovered simplicity and order and something spiritual, too, which he recognized as being authentic. He felt as though a flower, something like a lily, only smaller and tougher, had unfurled in his hand and was nudging along his fountain pen. He wrote and wrote, shaken by catharsis, but lulled into a new sense of his powers.

Not surprisingly, a solid little book of poems came out of his experience. It was published soon afterwards by a well-thought-of Boston publisher who, as soon as possible, sent him around the United States to give poetry readings.

Mostly the Professor read his poems in universities and colleges where his book was already listed on the Contemporary Poetry course. He read in faculty clubs, student centres, classrooms, gymnasiums and auditoriums, and usually, part way through a reading, someone or other would call from the back of the room, 'Give us your Golden Pavilion poem.'

He would have preferred to read his Fuji meditation or the tone poem on the Inner Sea, but he was happy to oblige his audiences, though he felt 'A Day At The Golden Pavilion' was a somewhat light piece, even what is sometimes known on the circuit as a 'crowd-pleaser'. People (admittedly they were mostly under-graduates) laughed out loud when they heard it; he read it well, too, in a moist, avuncular amateur actor's voice, reminding himself to pause frequently, to look upward and raise an ironic eyebrow.

The poem was not really about the Golden Pavilion at all, but about three midwestern lady tourists who, while viewing the tem-ple and madly snapping photos, had talked incessantly and in loud, flat-bottomed voices about knitting patterns, indigestion, sore feet, breast lumps, the cost of plastic raincoats, and a previous trip they'd made together to Mexico. They had wondered, these three—noisily, repeatedly—who back home in Manitoba should receive a postcard, what they'd give for an honest cup of tea, if there was an easy way to remove stains from an electric coffee maker, and where they would go the following year—Hawaii? They were the three furies, the three witches, who for vulgarity and tastelessness formed a shattering counterpoint to the Pro-fessor's own state of transcendence. He had been affronted, angered, half-crazed.

One of the sisters, a little pug of a woman, particularly stirred his contempt, she of the pink pantsuit, the red toenails, the grapefruity buttocks, the overly bright souvenirs, the garish Mexi-can straw bag containing Dentyne chewing gum, aspirin, breath mints, sun goggles, envelopes of saccharine, and photos of her dead husband standing in front of a squat, ugly house in Winnipeg. This defilement she had spread before the ancient and exquisitely proportioned Golden Pavilion of Kyoto, proving—and here the Professor's tone became grave—proving that sublime beauty can be brought to the very doorway of human eyes, ears and lips and remain unperceived.

When he comes to the end of 'A Day At The Golden Pavilion' there is generally a thoughtful half second of silence, then laughter and applause. Students turn in their seats and exchange looks

with their fellows. They have seen such unspeakable tourists themselves. There was old Auntie Marigold or Auntie Flossie. There
was that tacky Mrs Shannon with her rouge and her jewelry. They
know—despite their youth they know—the irreconcilable distance
between taste and banality. Or perhaps that's too harsh; perhaps
it's only the difference between those who know about the world
and those who don't.

It's true Mrs Turner remembers little about her travels. She's
never had much of a head for history or dates; she never did learn,
for instance, the difference between a Buddhist temple and a
Shinto shrine. She gets on a tour bus and goes and goes, and
that's all there is to it. She doesn't know if she's going north or
south or east or west. What does it matter? She's having a grand
time. And she's reassured, always, by the sameness of the world.
She's never heard the word *commonality*, but is nevertheless fused
with its sense. In Japan she was made as happy to see carrots and
lettuce growing in the fields as she was to see sunlight, years
earlier, pouring into the streets of New York City. Everywhere
she's been she's seen people eating and sleeping and working
and making things with their hands and urging things to grow.
There have been cats and dogs, fences and bicycles and telephone
poles, and objects to buy and take care of; it is amazing, she thinks,
that she can understand so much of the world and that it comes
to her as easily as bars of music floating out of a radio.

Her sisters have long forgotten about her wild days. Now the
three of them love to sit on tour buses and chatter away about
old friends and family members, their stern father and their
mother who never once took their part against him. Muriel carries
on about her children (a son in California and a daughter in
Toronto) and she brings along snaps of her grandchildren to pass
round. Em has retired from school teaching and is a volunteer in
the Boissevain Local History Museum, to which she has donated
several family mementos: her father's old carved pipe and her
mother's wedding veil and, in a separate case, for all the world to
see, a white cotton garment labeled 'Girlie Fergus' Underdrawers,
handmade, trimmed with lace, circa 1918'. If Mrs Turner knew
the word *irony* she would relish this. Even without knowing the
word irony, she relishes it.

The professor from Massachusetts has won an important international award for his book of poems; translation rights have been
sold to a number of foreign publishers; and recently his picture

appeared in the *New York Times*, along with a lengthy quotation from 'A Day At The Golden Pavilion'. How providential, some will think, that Mrs Turner doesn't read the *New York Times* or attend poetry readings, for it might injure her deeply to know how she appears in certain people's eyes, but then there are so many things she doesn't know.

In the summer as she cuts the grass, to and fro, to and fro, she waves to everyone she sees. She waves to the high-school girls who timidly wave back. She hollers hello to Sally and Roy Sascher and asks them how their garden is coming on. She cannot imagine that anyone would wish her harm. All she's done is live her life. The green grass flies up in the air, a buoyant cloud swirling about her head. Oh, what a sight is Mrs Turner cutting her grass and how, like an ornament, she shines.

JANE URQUHART

Italian Postcard

Whenever she is sick, home from school, Clara the child is allowed to examine her mother's Italian postcards, a large pile of them, which are normally bound by a thick leather band and kept in a bureau drawer. Years later when she touches postcards she will be amazed that her hands are so large. Perhaps she feels that the hands of a child are proportionally correct to rest like book-ends on either side of landscapes. Or maybe it's not that complicated; maybe she just feels that, as an adult, she can't really see these colours, those vistas, and so, in the odd moments when she does, she must necessarily be a child again.

The room she lies in on weekdays, when she has managed to stay home from school, is all hers. She'll probably carry it around with her for the rest of her life. Soft grey wallpaper with sprays of pink apple blossom. Pink dressing-table (under the skirts of which her dolls hide, resting on their little toy beds), cretonne curtains swathed over a window at the foot of the bed she occupies, two or three pink pillows propping her up. Outside the window a small back garden and some winter city or another. It doesn't really matter which.

And then the postcards: turquoise, fuchsia, lime green—improbable colours placed all over the white spread and her little hands picking up one, then another, and her little mind trying to imagine her mother walking through such passionate surroundings.

In time, her mother appears at the side of the bed. Earlier in the morning she has brought the collection of postcards. Now she holds a concoction of mustard and water wrapped in white flannel and starts to undo the little buttons on the little pyjama top.

While the mustard plaster burns into her breastbone Clara continues to look at the postcards. Such flowers, such skies, such suns burning down on such perfect seas. Her mother speaks the names of foreign towns; *Sorrento*, she says, *Capri*, *Fiesole*, *Garda*, *Como*, and then after a thoughtful pause, *You should see Como. But most of all you should see Pompeii.*

Clara always saves Pompeii, however, until the end—until after her mother has removed the agonizing poultice and has left the room—until after she has gone down the stairs and has resumed her orderly activities in the kitchen. Then the child allows the volcano to erupt, to spill molten lava all over the suburban villas, the naughty frescos, the religious mosaics. And all over the inhabitants of the unsuspecting ancient town.

In the postcards Pompeii is represented, horrifyingly, fascinatingly, by the inhabitants themselves, frozen in such attitudes of absolute terror or complete despair that the child learns everything she needs to know from them about heartbreak and disaster: how some will put their arms up in front of their faces to try to ward it off, how others will resign themselves, sadly, to its strength. What she doesn't understand is how such heat can freeze, make permanent, the moment of most intense pain. A scream in stone that once was liquid. What would happen, she wonders, to these figures if the volcano were to erupt again? How permanent are they?

And she wonders about the archaeologists who have removed the stone bodies from the earth and, without disturbing a single gesture, have placed them in glass display cases inside the museum where they seem to float in the air of their own misfortune—clear now, the atmosphere empty of volcanic ash, the glass polished.

These are the only postcards of Pompeii that Clara's mother has. No bright frescos, no recently excavated villas, no mosaics; only these clear cases full of grey statues made from what was once burning flesh.

Twenty-five years later when Clara stands with her husband at the entrance to Hotel Oasie in Assisi she has seen Sorrento, Como, Capri and has avoided Pompeii altogether.

'Why not?' her husband asks.

'Nobody lives there,' she replies.

But people live here, in this Tuscan hill town; the sun has burned ⸂e into their faces. And the colours in the postcards were real after all—they spill out from red walls into the vegetable displays on the street, they flash by on the backs of over-dressed children. Near the desk of the hotel they shout out from travel posters. But in this space there is no sun; halls of cool remote marble, sparse furnishings, and, it would seem, no guests but themselves.

'Dinner,' the man behind the desk informs them, 'between seven and nine in the big salon.'

Then he leads them, through arched halls, to the room.

Clara watches the thick short back of the Italian as she walks behind him, realizing as she does, that it is impossible to imagine muscle tone when it is covered by smooth black cloth. She looks at the back of his squarish head. Cumbersome words such as *Basilica*, *portcullis*, *Etruscan*, and *Vesuvius* rumble disturbingly, and for no apparent reason, through her mind.

Once the door has clicked behind them and the echoing footsteps of the desk clerk have disappeared from the outside hall, her husband examines the two narrow beds with displeasure and shrugs.

'Perhaps we'll find a way,' he says, 'marble floors are cold.' Then looking down, 'Don't think these small rugs will help much.'

Then, before she can reply, they are both distracted by the view outside the windows. Endless olive groves and vineyards and a small cemetery perched halfway up the hill. Later in the evening, after they have eaten pasta and drunk rough, red wine in the enormous empty dining-room, they will see little twinkling lights shine up from this spot, like a handful of stars on the hillside. Until that moment it will never have occurred to either of them that anyone would want to light a tomb at night.

Go and light a tomb at night
Get with child a mandrake root.

Clara is thinking Blake—in Italy of all places, wandering through the empty halls of Hotel Oasie, secretly inspecting rooms. All the same so far: narrow cots, tiny rugs, views of vineyards and the graveyard, olive trees. Plain green walls. These rooms, she thinks, as Blake evaporates from her mind, these rooms could use the services of *Mr Domado's Wallpaper Company*, a company with one employee—the very unhappy *Mr Domado himself*. He papered her room once when she was a sick child and he was sick with longing for his native land. When Italian postcards coincidentally littered her bedspread like fallen leaves, *Ah yes*, said Mr Domado, sadly picking up one village and then another. *Ah yes.*

And he could sing—Italian songs. Arias that sounded as mournful as some of the more lonely villages looked. Long, long sobbing notes trembling in the winter sunshine, while she lay propped on pink pillows and her mother crept around in the kitchen below silently preparing mustard plasters. Mr Domado with tears in his voice, eliminating spray after spray of pink apple blossoms, replacing them with rigid geometric designs, while Clara studied the open mouths of the stone Pompeii figures and wondered whether, at the moment of their death, they were praying out loud. Or whether they were simply screaming.

Screaming, she thinks now as she opens door after door of Hotel Oasie, would be practically a catastrophe in these echoing marble halls. One scream might go on for hours, as her footsteps seem to every time she moves twenty feet or so down to the next door, as the click of the latch seems to every time she has closed whatever door she has been opening. The doors are definitely an addition to the old, old building and appear to be pulled by some new longitudinal force back into the closed position after she releases her fingers from their cold, steel knobs. Until she opens the door labelled *Sala Beatico Angelico* after which no hotel room will ever be the same.

Neither Clara nor her husband speak Italian, so to ask for a complete explanation would be impossible.

'A Baroque church!' she tells him later. 'Not a chapel but a complete church. All the doors are the same, *this* door is the same except for the words on it, and you open it and there, instead of a hotel room, is a complete church.'

'It appears,' he says after several moments of reflection, 'that we have somehow checked into a monastery.'

Sure enough when she takes herself out to the rose garden later in the afternoon to sit in the sun and read *The Little Flowers of Santa Chiara* in preparation for the next day's trip to the Basilica, the hotel clerk greets her, dressed now in a clerical collar. Clara shows no surprise, as if she had known all along that hers was not to be a secular vacation; as if the idea of a retreat had been in her mind when she planned the trip. She shifts the book a little so that the monastic gardener will notice that she is reading about

St Francis' holy female friend. He, however, is busy with roses; his own little flowers, and though he faces her while he works his glance never once meets hers. She is able, therefore, to observe him quite closely—the dark tan of his face over the white of his collar, his hands that move carefully, but easily, through the roses, avoiding thorns. Clara tries, but utterly fails, to imagine the thoughts of a priest working in a rose garden. Are they concerned, as they should be, with GOD, the thorns, perhaps, signifying a crown, the dark red stain of the flower turning in his mind to the blood of Christ? Or does he think only of roses and their health: methods of removing the insect from the leaf, the worm from the centre of the scarlet bud? His face gives her no clue; neither that nor the curve of his back as he stoops to remove yet another vagrant weed from the soft brown earth surrounding the bushes.

Clara turns again to her book, examining the table of contents: *The Circle of Ashes*, *The Face in the Well*, *The Hostage of Heaven*, *The Bread of Angels*, *The Meal in the Woods*, and finally, at the bottom of the list, *The Retinue of Virgins*. St Francis, she discovers, had never wanted to see Chiara. The little stories made this perfectly clear. Sentence after sentence described her aversion. After he had clothed her in sackcloth and cut off all her hair in the dark of the Italian night, after he had set her on the path of poverty and had left her with her sisters at St Damiens, after she had turned into a *hostage of heaven* and had given up eating altogether, Francis withdrew. *Beware of the poison of familiarity with women*, he had told his fellow friars. In a chapter entitled *The Roses*, the book stated that Francis had wanted to place an entire season between himself and Chiara. *We will meet again when the roses bloom*, he had said, standing with his bare feet in the snow. Then God had decided to make the roses bloom, spontaneously, right there, right then, in the middle of winter.

Clara cannot decide, now, what possible difference that would make. As a matter of fact, it looks to her as if God were merely playing a trick on Chiara and Francis. If Francis said they would meet again when the roses bloom, why not have the roses bloom right now? Perhaps then there would be no subsequent meeting since the roses had already bloomed. This would have certainly been a puzzle for Chiara to work on during the dreary winter days that stretched ahead of her in the unheated convent. She could work it over and over in her mind like a rosary. It might have kept her, in some ways, very busy.

Francis, on the other hand, was always very busy. As the book said: *Francis came and went freely from St Mary of the Angels but Chiara found herself like a prisoner at St Damiens*. Francis might have dropped by to see Chiara while he was out rushing around, but he didn't. *On the other hand, Francis stayed well away from St Damiens*, the book continued, *for he did not wish the common people should take scandal from seeing him going in and out*. So basically, it would appear that poor Chiara, poison that she was, rarely spoke to her mentor, the man whose principles she built her life around. At least not until *The Meal in the Woods*.

After she had asked him repeatedly to share a meal with her, Francis finally relented. Speaking once again to his fellow friars (he seemed never to have spoken to Chiara), he argued, *She has been a long time at St Damiens. She will be happy to come out for a little while and to see in the daytime that place to which she first came at night, where her hair was cut from her, and where she was received among us. In the name of Jesus Christ we will picnic in the woods.* Somehow, during the course of this unusual picnic, the woods began to glow as if they were on fire. It is not clear to Clara whether God or Francis was responsible for this miracle. It may have been a collaboration. It is perfectly clear, however, that Chiara had nothing to do with it. Her role was that of appreciator—one that she, no doubt, played very well. And, as usual, she wasn't eating. The chapter ends with this statement: *Finally Chiara and Francis rose from the ground, overjoyed and filled with spiritual nourishment, not having touched as much as a crumb of the food*.

Clara is beginning to feel hungry. Delicious smells are coming from what she now knows is the refectory. The gardener is placing his tools, one by one, in the wheelbarrow. Then, without looking in her direction, he pushes the little vehicle away from her, toward the potting-shed.

'Our hotel clerk,' she informs her husband at dinner, 'is a gardener as well as a priest. I was reading up on my namesake out on the terrace and I saw him in the garden, working away.'

'I discovered the other part of the building,' her husband replies. 'There is a glass door with *Keep Out* written on it in four languages, and then an entire wing where the priests must stay when they open the place to tourists.'

'You didn't peek?' asks Clara, fully aware that, had she discovered it, she might have opened the door.

'No—written rules you know,' and then, 'Have you decided to like your namesake? Do you think you take after her?'

Clara reflects for awhile. 'I think she was a very unhappy woman. She kept on wanting to see Francis and he kept not wanting to see her.'

'Probably just propriety, don't you think? You can't have Saint Francis spending a lot of time hanging around the convent you know, wouldn't look good.'

'Possibly . . . but maybe it was just an excuse. Maybe he really *didn't* want to see her. The poor girl—she was in love with him, I expect. He was probably God to her.'

'Maybe *he* was in love with her. Did that ever occur to you? Maybe that's why he stayed away.' Her husband glances down to the end of the room. 'Look who is coming,' he says. 'Our desk clerk is not only a gardener and a priest, he is also a waiter.'

The next afternoon Clara decides she will not visit the Basilica after all. She would rather read in the rose garden than gaze at frescos.

'Later,' she tells her husband. 'You check it out, tell me about it.'

Postcard views and skies are outside the walls of the hotel as usual, and now the closer, more exaggerated colours of the roses. It is hotter than the previous day so the priest has abandoned his collar. Clara notices that he has a perfect mole situated right in the centre of his throat. A sort of natural stigma, she decides.

The chapter entitled *The Door of the Dead* is fascinating her. She is reading it for the fourth time. It seems that the ancient houses in Assisi often had two doors: a large one through which the family normally came and went, and a smaller one, elevated above the ground, through which the dead were passed, feet first in their coffins. Chiara, on the night she went to meet Francis in the woods, decided to leave the house through the second door. *She wanted to get away secretly*, the book states, *and she was absolutely sure she would meet no-one on the threshold of that door*. With the help of a minor miracle on God's part she was able to slide bolts and move hinges that had been rusted in position for fifteen years. Then she jumped lightly to the ground and ran out of the village. *Never again would she be able to return to her family*, the chapter concludes, *Chiara was dead. Chiara was lost. Chiara had passed over into another life*.

Clara wonders if the priest, who is working directly in front of her, has also passed over into another life, and whether, if this is so, the roses look redder to him than they do to her. Whether he lives a sort of *Through the Looking Glass* existence.

She adjusts the angle of her chair. He is working close enough now that their shadows almost touch. A vague sadness stirs near Clara's heart, stops, then moves again. Restless lava shifting somewhere in the centre of a mountain.

Her husband has decided that they will stay at Hotel Oasie for the remainder of their vacation. He likes it there. He likes Assisi. He is moved by all of it, as much, he says, by the electrified confessionals in the Basilica as by the Giottos. He claims that the former are like the washrooms on a jumbo jet in that they have automatic *occupied* and *vacant* signs that are lighted from behind. He is amazed, he continues, at how easily the Italians have adapted their highly superstitious religion to modern technology—the lighted tombs, the electric candles in front of religious statues, the *occupied* signs. This amuses and pleases him. He will write a sociological paper on it when they return to North America.

She isn't listening to him very carefully because she has fallen in love, just like that, bang, with the gardener, waiter, desk clerk, priest. She has, by now, spent four long afternoons with him in the rose garden and he has never once looked her way. Unless, she speculates, he looks her way when she is absorbed in *The Little Flowers of Santa Chiara*, which is possible. On the third afternoon she made up a little rule for herself that she would not lift her eyes from the book until a chapter was completely finished. In that way she has balanced her activities. Ten minutes of reading followed by ten minutes of studying the priest. This means, of course, that he is never in the same location after she finishes reading, say, *The Door of the Dead* as he was after she finished reading *A Kiss For the Servant*. She is then forced to look around for him, which makes the activity more intriguing. One afternoon, after finishing the chapter called *Infirmity and Suffering*, she looked up and around and discovered that he had disappeared completely, simply slipped away while she was reading. Almost every other time, though, she is able to watch him collect his tools, place them in the wheelbarrow and walk toward the potting-shed. And this makes her grieve a little, as one often does when a lengthy ritual has been appropriately completed.

'Did you know,' she asks her husband angrily at dinner, 'Did you know that he wouldn't even let her come to see him when he was DYING? I mean, isn't that taking it a bit too far? The man was dying and she asked if she could see him and he said no, not until I'm *dead*.'

The priestly waiter serves the pasta. Clara watches his brown left hand approach the table and withdraw. 'Scusi' he says as he places the dish in front of her. She cannot accuse him of never speaking to her. He has said 'Scusi' in her presence now a total of seventeen times and once, when a meal was over, he had looked directly into her eyes and had asked, 'You feeneesh?'

Now she stabs her fork deliberately into the flesh of the ravioli. 'Moreover,' she continues, 'that little book I am reading has next to nothing to do with Chiara; mostly it's about Francis—until he dies, of course—then it's about her dying.' Forgetting to chew, Clara swallows the little piece of pasta whole.

'Well,' says her husband, 'at least Giotto included her in some of the frescos.'

'Hmm,' she replies, decidedly unimpressed.

Clara gazes at the priest and her heart turns soft. He is staring absently into space. Imagining miracles, she decides, waiting out the tenure of the dinner hour so that he can return to his quiet activities. Evening mass, midnight mass. Lighting candles, saying prayers. Does he make them up or follow rituals? Are there beads involved? Does he kneel before male or female saints? Any of this information is important to her. Still, she would never dare enter the church she has discovered at the end of the hall. In fact, with the exception of the Basilica with its electrified confessionals and famous frescos, she has not dared to open the door of any church in town. They are spaces that are closed to her and she knows it.

'Have you ever felt that a church was closed to you?' she asks her husband.

'Of course not,' he answers. 'After all, they are not only religious institutions, they are great public monuments, great works of art. They are open to all of us.'

Clara sighs and turns her eyes, once again, to the priest. The way he is carrying the crockery back to the kitchen, as if it were a collection of religious artifacts he has recently blessed, almost breaks her heart.

It is her fifth afternoon in the rose garden. He is there too, of course, pinning roses onto stakes. 'Crucifying them perhaps,' she thinks vaguely, lovingly.

By now she knows that this man will never EVER respond to her, never EVER speak to her; not in his language or hers—except at meal time when it is absolutely necessary. Because of this, the sadness of this, she loves him even harder. It is this continuous rejection that sets him apart. Rejection without object, without malice, a kind of healing rejection; one that causes a cleansing ache.

The ache washes over her now as she watches him stand back to survey his labours. She loves the way he just stands there looking, completely ignoring her. She is of absolutely no consequence in the story of his life, none whatsoever, and she loves him for this. She has no desire for change; no mediaeval fantasies about being the rose that he fumbles with, the Saint that he prays to. She wants him just as he is, oblivious to her, causing her to ache, causing her to understand the true dimensions of hopelessness, how they are infinite.

She turns to the chapter in the book called *The Papal Bull*. This is an oddly political section and her least favourite. It concerns the legitimization of the various Franciscan orders including Santa Chiara's Poor Sisters—the legitimization of lives of chosen self-denial. At this point Clara is finding it difficult to concentrate on what the Pope had to say, finds it difficult to care whether it was legitimate or not.

She is surprised, when she allows herself to look up, to find the priest's gaze aimed in her direction. She prepares to be embarrassed until she realizes that he is, at last, reading the title of her book.

'She wanted words from him,' Clara tells her husband later. 'Words, you know, spiritual advice. You know what she got instead?'

'What?'

'She got a circle of ashes—a circle of goddamn ashes! The book tries to make this seem profound; the usual, he put a circle of ashes on the convent floor to demonstrate that all humans were merely dust, or some such nonsense. You know what I think it meant? It think it meant that regardless of what Chiara wanted from him, regardless of how badly she might have wanted it, regardless of whether or not she ever swallowed a single morsel of food, or wore hairshirts, or humiliated herself in any number of ways, regardless of what she did, all she was EVER going to get from him was a circle of ashes. I think it meant that she was entirely powerless and he was going to make damn certain that she stayed that way.'

'Quite a theory. I doubt the church would approve.'

'God, how she must have suffered!'

'Well,' he replies, 'wasn't that what she was supposed to do?'

In the middle of her seventh afternoon in the rose garden, after she has finished reading a chapter entitled *The Canticle of the Creatures* (which she practically knows now by heart), and while she is studying the gestures of the priest who has moved from roses to vegetables, Clara decides that her heart is permanently broken. How long, she wonders, has it been this way? And why did it take this priest, this silent man who thinks and prays in a foreign language, to point it out to her. This is not a new disease, she knows suddenly. It's been there for a long, long time; a handicap she has managed to live with somehow, by completely ignoring it. How strange. Not to feel that pain that is always there by never identifying it, never naming it. Now she examines the wound and it burns in the centre of her chest the way her mother's mustard plasters used to, the way molten lava must have in the middle of Vesuvius. Her broken heart has burned inside her for so long she assumed it was normal. Now the pain of it moves into her whole body; past the pulse at her wrists, down the fronts of her thighs, up into her throat. Then it moves from there out into the landscape she can see from the garden, covering all of it, every detail; each grey, green olive leaf, each electric candle in front of each small pathetic tomb, every bird, all of the churches she can never enter, poppies shouting in a distant field, this terrible swath of blue sky overhead, the few pebbles that cover the small area of terrace at her feet. And all the air that moves up and down her throat until she is literally gasping in pain.

Pure eruption. Shards of her broken heart are everywhere, moving through her bloodstream, lacerating her internally on their voyage from the inside out into the landscape, until every sense is raw. She can actually see the sound waves that are moving in front of her. She wonders if she has begun to shout but then gradually, gradually, isolated sound dissolves into meaning as her brain begins its voyage back into the inside of her skull.

'Meesus,' the priest is saying, pointing to her book. 'She is still here, Santa Chiara. You go see her—you go to Chiesa Santa Chiara—you go there and you see her.'

Then he collects his gardening tools, places them in his wheelbarrow and walks purposefully away.

She goes alone, of course, two days later when she feels better and when she knows for sure they will be leaving Assisi the following morning. She is no longer in love with the priest; he has become what he always was, a small brown Italian busy with kitchen, clerical and gardening tools. The heartbreak, however, which preceded him and will continue, is still with her, recognized now and accepted as she stands across the road from the Church of Santa Chiara watching a small cat walk on top of its shadow in the noonday sun.

Inside the door total darkness for a while, followed by a gradual adjustment of the eyes to dark inscrutable paintings and draped altars and the slow movements of two nuns who are walking toward the front of the church. She follows them, unsure now how to make her request and then, suddenly, the request is unnecessary. There, boom, illuminated by the ever present electricity, is the Saint, laid out for all to see in her glass coffin. 'She is, you see,' one of the nuns explains, 'incorruptible. She is here 700 years and she does not decay because she is holy.'

Clara moves closer to see the dead woman's face, now glowing under the harsh twentieth-century light, and there, as she expects, is the pain. Frozen on Chiara's face the terrifying, wonderful pain; permanent, incorruptible, unable to decay. The dead mouth is open, shouting pain silently up to the electricity, past the glass, into the empty cave of the church, out into the landscape, up the street to the Basilica where images of the live Chiara appear, deceitfully serene, in the frescos. It is the heartbreak that is durable, Clara thinks to herself, experiencing the shock of total recognition. Everything else will fade away. No wonder the Saint didn't decay. A flutter of something sharp and cutting in Clara's own bloodstream and then she turns away.

Before she steps out into the street again she buys a postcard from one of the nuns. Santa Chiara in her glass coffin, as permanent as a figure from Pompeii in her unending, incorruptible anguish.

Clara places the card in an inside pocket of her handbag. There it will stay through the long plane ride home while her husband makes jokes about the washrooms resembling Italian confessionals. It will stay there and she will clutch the leather close to her broken heart, clutch the image of the dead woman's mouth. The permanent pain that moves past the postcard booth into the colours of the Italian landscape.

HELEN WEINZWEIG

Causation

The woman hesitated at first to let him in. 'Piano tuner,' Gyorgi Szigeti said, then waited, leaning against the door frame. He waited for her to decide whether he was a musician and therefore eligible to come in the front door, or whether he was a tradesman to be directed to the rear entrance. What she could not have known was that Gyorgi had no intention of using the servants' entrance. He stood before her, proud in his black bowler hat, his long white silk scarf knotted loosely and flowing down over his shiny black leather jacket. 'Piano tuner,' he repeated to the woman, who had not moved. She was transfixed. 'Oh my God,' she said, 'not you, not you!' He did not question her words: by habit he took no notice of the eccentricities of the rich. Slowly, slowly, she widened the doorway.

No one ever had to show him where the piano was. He found it the way a dog searches out a bone. Traversing miles, it seemed, of Oriental carpets to reach the ebony grand piano at the other end of a vast room, he experienced a numbness, a detachment, as if asleep and dreaming: he had a sense of having once before covered the distance. And the short, sturdy woman in a flowered housecoat (he had noticed) who was following him—he knew her, too. But then, he knew a lot of women, some also short and sturdy, and maybe that's all it was: so many women.

'It's my own piano,' she was saying. Her heavy hand clumped across the keys. 'This B keeps getting out of tune,' striking the note five times to let him hear how bad it was.

Gyorgi Szigeti almost fell to his knees. He was in the presence of a Bechstein grand piano.

She was still talking. 'Everything you see in here, all the furniture in the house, was chosen by my ex-husband. He lets me keep my piano only because he is a music lover.'

Gyorgi removed his black leather jacket, draping it on the back of a gilded chair with curved legs. The bowler hat and silk scarf he arranged carefully on the seat. He ran his fingers over the piano keys. The sound was as brilliant as he remembered a Bechstein to be; the bass was resonant and the top notes vibrant. This was unexpected: in these wealthy homes the pianos were regarded as furniture and tuned only when an anticipated house guest was some sort of performer.

'I'm a singer. A concert artist. An opera star,' she announced. 'That is, I used to be an opera star.'

While Gyorgi worked, she sat on the piano bench, which he had moved aside. She hummed each note in unison with his repeated plunking as he tightened strings. She had perfect pitch. It spurred him on, this breathless attention of hers; then the two of them listening, listening together, both now intent on the climactic moments when he brought each white whole note and each black half note to perfection. He felt like the Creator of All Sound. When he tightened a string, he had a way of tightening his mouth, twisting the left corner upward into his cheek, which resulted in a threatening grimace. Once the ideal sound was achieved, his mouth loosened.

She rose to leave. 'Would you like some coffee?'

Gyorgi looks around, then re-enters the room in his mind, retraces his steps in imagination; but this time, instead of seeing her figure stride out the doorway, as it is doing at this very moment, he sees her laid out in a satin-lined coffin, in the same flowered housecoat; and instead of her sluttish make-up, the face in death is delicately tinted as if in the blush of youth. The mortician's skill has fixed the happiness he, Gyorgi, gave her. After the funeral he stays on in the old house, sleeping in one of the spare rooms, surprised at his delicacy, even in fantasy, in not using the bedroom where he had made her ecstatic. The letter from the lawyers comes, addressed to Gyorgi Szigeti, to this house. She has left him everything. Everything, including the beloved Bechstein, is his. Just in time, before her return interrupts his fateful vision, he recalls with a sudden clarity the source of his images: an account in this morning's newspaper: rich elderly widow . . . a young man of thirty-three . . . they married . . . she died . . . left him everything she owned . . . great wealth . . . her daughters suing . . . old mother was crazy . . . 'They're crazy,' the new heir had protested to the judge, 'she was more fascinating, more of a woman, than those two dried-up broads will ever be if they live to be a hundred.'

Over coffee, perhaps because he had already lived out the scene in his mind, Gyorgi leaned forward and said in a voice deep with sincerity:

'You are still a beautiful woman. You have so much to give . . .'

She eyed him silently. She was about fifty-five, but in her clear, light eyes, raised to meet his directly, age had been postponed. It was a matter of pride with him that in his persuasions Gyorgi rarely lied. In every woman he found qualities he could honestly admire. He went on, emboldened:

'Your eyes—they are the eyes of a girl.'

She denied nothing: that was all that mattered.

'These Bechsteins,' he ventured, 'do not take kindly to the extreme cold and intense heat of our climate. The wood . . . changes of temperature . . .' He brought out a small notebook from his back pocket. He could come back next week. To see if the tuning held.

Uppermost in her mind is the fact that his wide, curved mouth is at odds with his small, deep-set, dark eyes, suggesting to her an easygoing cruelty.

At his ring the following week she flung open the door. Her face was heavier than before with rouge and lipstick, her brows blacker, her lids greener. Gyorgi believed that if he ate enough of the stuff women put on their faces he would get cancer. In such cases he would put his lips to the bare hollows of her throat.

Today she ignored his pretence of tuning the perfectly tuned instrument. She didn't listen; she chattered.

'Once I was Violetta with the San Francisco Opera Company. Oswald, my former husband, loved *Traviata*. He loved me. He offered me the world if I would give up the stage and sing for him alone: wealth, babies, a fire in the hearth on Sunday nights. Oh, he knows his operas . . . I worked hard, practised every day. In the evening, with the two babies asleep in the nursery, I sang for him. I dressed for the part. The costumes accumulated: Cio-Cio San, Carmen, Tosca, Mignon.

'The idyll lasted almost five years. One morning I awoke to find him standing at the foot of the bed. The room was still dark so that I could not quite see his face, just the outline of his figure, fully dressed. He had been waiting, I sensed, for me to awaken. I sat up and then he spoke, slowly and distinctly:

' ''You are not the great artist I thought you were. You cannot place your voice, and when it comes out from behind your big nose, the glorious music falls to the floor like a bag of cement. You are ridiculous in the clothes of the great heroines: you have the passion of a disposable lighter. You have deceived me.'' With that he left and never returned.'

'Did he leave you for another woman?' Gyorgi asked, for that is what he knew of the way of the world.

'No, no, he wouldn't do that. He is a very respectable man.'

'Did he marry again?'

'Ha! The only woman he'd consider would have to be a virgin who chose marriage to Oswald instead of entering a nunnery.' She gave him a sly smile. 'You know what? I think Oswald was jealous of my music. When I played the role of Mimi or Aïda or Desdemona, I became the woman I was portraying. I didn't mean to, but I escaped him each time—*that's* what he couldn't stand.'

Gyorgi tilted his head in a pretence of interest. He had no idea what she was talking about, but he realized that she was determined to reveal herself to him. It was as if women had to expose themselves—their defeats, their triumphs, their hopes and beliefs—before they undressed. In his opinion, a nude man in a raincoat was more honest. Gyorgi listened to women for their 'tone' quality, the same way he listened when he was tuning a piano. He noticed that her forehead glistened with perspiration.

'I can't pay you today,' she said. 'Oswald has gone to India to see his guru. He left me without a cent. Again.'

'It's all right,' he said gently, 'you can pay me any time.'

Even after she had paid him, Gyorgi took to dropping in, making his visits sporadic, so that they would seem compulsive, as if he couldn't resist seeing her. She was always unprepared, and would run to comb her hair and put on fresh lipstick. Once he stopped her, saying he liked her the way she was. Above all, he would want her to be perfectly natural with him. She was so moved by these sentiments, she wanted to do something for him in return.

'Would you like to hear Cio-Cio San's farewell aria? No? I see. But you obviously know everything about pianos.'

'I was an apprentice for five years in the Bechstein factory in Berlin.'

'What else can you do?'

'I can build a bomb shelter.'

'Good. Then you can take care of this house. What do you say—live here and look after things. Oh, you will go out to your work as you always have, but instead of a small room in a smelly boardinghouse—ah, I thought so!—you can stay here. Pick any of the five spare rooms. What do you say?'

Gyorgi couldn't speak. He put his hands on his lap lest she see how they shook. A mansion, a Bechstein—all within the space of a few weeks. He hung his head and assumed the obsequious manner of his youth.

Then he went through the house, taking the stairs two at a time. The rooms were full of the kind of masterpieces he had seen only behind thick silken cords in museums. Everything was old and massive or old and fragile; everything was forceful with value. She ran after him, unable to keep up, observing that he moved with an animal grace, as if he had lived all his life out of doors.

'I can't understand why a man would want to leave you. It's a wonderful house,' he said.

'Oswald doesn't care about material things—furniture, cars, clothes—he has no interest in them. He wants to touch the infinite, discover the ineffable; he is on a journey of the spirit, he is concerned only with his immortal soul.'

'So?' said Gyorgi. 'So?' he repeated. 'He has never had to work hard in order to eat.'

'You must know that I still love him.'

Suddenly she was crying, crying for no reason that he could see.

He waved an arm into the air, around and around. 'You have everything; you have it all!'

'Nothing! Nothing, I tell you. There is only the music, notes on a page, enduring, eternal, nothing else exists.' Then, in afterthought, her voice distant, she added, 'You are the exception.'

He chose the sixth bedroom. Hers. Awaiting her in the wide bed, he called out, 'And wash that damned crap off your face.'

When she came back into the room, she grasped the post at the foot of the huge bed, weaving slightly as if drunk, and intoned:

'I adore you, you are low-born, you have no character, you are inevitable. Ours will be an affair of terrible limits. Your insults are without principle. Whatever grief you will cause will come naturally and I shall recover as one does after slipping on ice. Most important, though, Oswald will no longer be able to draw blood with his blunt knives. I shall continue to go to him every week for money. But it will be for you. That will make it easy. No. More than that. I shall *enjoy* the humiliation. I will answer his interrogation: ''Why is the butcher's bill so high?'' ''Because I have a tall, strong man to feed,'' I will sit in the leather chair in his office while he counts out the ten-dollar bills, slowly, sliding them halfway across the desk. I will lean forward and scoop them up and thank him. Oswald will unbutton his vest and look across at me like a judge with a three-time loser and condemn me, as he always does, with good advice. But I won't care. He has lost his power: tonight I hand it over to you.'

During the prolonged love-making that follows, she opens her eyes a few times. Once she sees his mouth tighten and a corner go up into his cheek into an ugly grimace.

Gyorgi moved in. It was then that he was faced with what he had missed that first time because his head had been bursting with the delirium of his good fortune. There was everywhere a fury of disorder, as if a bomb had gone off in each room separately. The halls had boxes and overshoes strewn about. There was dirt on every surface; old dust that had hardened; mouse droppings in the kitchen and cockroaches in the sinks. She shrugged off his dismay. 'Oswald won't pay for a cleaning woman.'

Gyorgi loved control and completeness. He set about to restore order, spending every weekend sweeping, scrubbing, repairing, room by room, starting with the bedroom. The kitchen alone took a month. The cellar, he figured, could occupy him as long as she lived.

There was no design to her life. Asleep when he left, off in a world of song when he got home; she could not remember what, if anything, she had accomplished, nor what had transpired during the day. 'Some phone calls. Nothing much. How was *your* day?' And showered him with kisses. One of the phone calls, he surmised, was for the frozen chicken pie and canned pea soup that he was eating for dinner. And he, who required a daily pattern to blanket his years, felt a chill of apprehension.

'Now, my handsome Magyar,' she crooned, 'I'll sing for you and you alone. I learned some Hungarian folk songs set by Kodály.'

'I told you a dozen times, I hate Hungarian anything. Maybe there's a soccer game on TV.'

'Don't you ever tire of watching grown men kick a ball?'

'You have the memory of an imbecile: I told you: I was a professional soccer player. I toured Germany.'

Each day Gyorgi went out on his calls. He had given up his black leather jacket and now wore a navy blue blazer with a crest embroidered in red and white on the upper left pocket. He refused to part with his bowler hat and long white scarf. He no longer said, 'Piano tuner' at the front door. Instead, he presented, wordlessly, his business card with his name and elegant new address and *Pianos Tuned to Perfection* embossed in shiny black script. As the days got shorter, he came home earlier and earlier. Some cold days he did not go out at all. He would float about the house, content to hammer, force windows open, stop taps from dripping. She would follow him around like the small daughter he once had. While he worked, she would sit on the floor, always in the flowered housecoat, telling him stories about people she knew.

'You're making it up,' he sometimes accused her. 'No, no,' she protested, 'that's what he really did.' Or, 'She was desperate. A woman in that state will say anything.' His disbelief at times bordered on wonder: did people of wealth and substance really carry on crazy like that? Keeping his eyes on his work, never turning his head, pretending a lofty indifference, he would probe with ruttish questions: what had taken place with her and Oswald in bed; what had she done with other men; how many lovers; in what combinations. And she, without a second thought, would lay open intimacies as one spreads open an umbrella in the rain. And always she hugged her knees and chortled deep in her throat, 'But you, my darling, are the best, you are the champ.' On those days a camaraderie was struck between them and he felt himself to be her equal in the sense that she was no better than he. More than that: he felt himself elevated, and ceased to regret, once and for all, that he was so unschooled that she had to read to him the instructions on a can of varnish.

Every night he made love to her. He treated the whole business as his part of the bargain. In bed his movements were as easy and graceful as when he painted a wall or repaired a broken drainpipe. He was precise; he was unhurried. Afterwards, Gyorgi would turn over as if fatigued, although his exultation was boundless. He did this rather than listen to her. 'You talk too much,' he would say, 'people screw up by talking too much.'

Once she frightened him in the middle of the night by shaking him awake. The bedside lamp was on. She was sitting bolt upright.

'Quickly,' she said in an urgent voice, 'don't think, tell me, quickly, what is life?'

'Life,' he said obediently, 'is. Life is. That's all. You're either alive or dead.'

'Wrong!' she said sharply. 'Life is an imposition. Oswald refuses to admit it. He wants life to be raw, with the bones showing. Today he presented me with a new account book, with more spaces for more entries. He threatened me again: unless I am more exact about the money I spend, he will cut off my alimony. He *imposes* himself on my life.'

Gyorgi condescended. 'What are you complaining about? A short ride in the Mercedes and you're living fat for another week. Perfect octaves don't buy houses like this.'

'You comprehend nothing.' She turned from him. 'You know nothing of the malice that masquerades as virtue. You are young: you still make plans.'

He stared at the long, heavy drapes.

'After the war we were thrown out of Hungary and shipped in boxcars to Germany. We lived behind barbed wire, then in barracks, then in a shack somewhere outside Frankfurt. All night long we heard the screams of the tortured. My brothers and sisters and I jumped out of bed when we heard the cries. We took turns standing on a chair at the small, high window. We could see nothing. Our parents never woke up.'

She studied him: there was no humility in him. She laid her head on his chest and a hand on his shoulder. Gyorgi yawned and lay back with his hands under his head.

'Fate,' she whispered, 'weaves its mysteries in the dark; that is why we do not know our destiny in the light of day.'

'That's true,' he agreed, understanding nothing. He had no sense of the abstract, but he recognized, if not destiny, certainly an opportunity. 'You have a beautiful house. I'm surprised you never married again.'

'Oswald wouldn't like it. Besides, if I married I wouldn't have this beautiful house.'

Gyorgi, startled, heard only the first part: 'Oswald wouldn't like it.' What did Oswald have to do with her desire to marry again? His own life had been a series of divorcements so immutable that he never again saw his parents, his brothers and sisters, two wives, countless lovers, as well as a number of unreasonable employers.

If his decision to part, made simply and honestly, was challenged, he used his soccer-field fists, elbows, knees, or boots to make his meaning clear.

'We are lovers now,' he pursued, 'let us be as if married. I will care for you as my father did for my mother; you will care for me as my mother did my father.'

'But you are already here, in my house, in my bed . . .'

Lack of sleep made Gyorgi irritable. She was missing the point.

'From now on,' he rasped, 'you will do a woman's work.'

'Oh, oh,' she moaned, 'more impositions . . .'

'We must speak of necessities,' he went on inexorably. 'Food is a necessity. Respect is a necessity. It is necessary to respect the place you eat and sleep in. The way you live now, you turn roses into shit. Starting tomorrow, you will keep the house clean, wash the clothes, cook the meals. I will take out the garbage, attend the mousetraps, spray the roach powder.'

'My music . . .'

'*Deine Stimme ist zum Kotzen,*' he said as day dawned, 'you have the voice of a crow.'

'Yes, yes,' she said, falling in with his thought, 'I will buy a loom and learn to weave.'

'Don't be stupid. You're too clumsy.'

She flung her faith into the new day. Laughing now and clapping her hands she exclaimed:

'You noticed! Oh, how I do love you!'

She no longer rouges her lips and cheeks nor colours her eyelids. Gyorgi has convinced her of his preference for an unadorned face. This he has done by holding her head down in the bathroom sink filled with water. Her giggles spluttered, she choked, she lost consciousness. She has learned that he means what he says. She thinks he has helped her begin a new life. She telephones everyone she knows to tell them that she gets up in the morning and that she bakes bread.

Just before Christmas there was a party. Gyorgi was surprised, considering her indolence, that she had so many friends. Well, maybe he could understand: she was guileless; she harboured no ill will. He was sent to the convenience store on Summerhill Avenue for peanuts and chips and mixes. 'Not to worry,' she assured him, 'everyone brings a bottle. All we need are enough clean glasses.' He went back and bought five dozen plastic glasses.

Gyorgi dressed for the evening. He wore a white shirt and a patterned silk tie and real gold cuff links—gifts of grateful women. He looked distinguished, almost, in a suit. The synthetic brown cloth hung on his frame like an admiral's uniform. She introduced him: 'Isn't he gorgeous!' He walked behind her and watched gravely while she went about kissing men and 'adoring' them. In his turn he was careful not to flirt with women. He could take no chances: women mistook his compliments for confessions.

He assumed the dignity of the foreman he remembered in the Bechstein factory, hands behind his back, observing everyone, recording, alert to what might be expected of him. He mixed drinks, removed coats, and carried them upstairs; clipped pairs of galoshes and boots together with clothespins. After a while he realized that the guests made no distinction between him and themselves. An envoy from India invited him to a cricket match in Edwards Gardens next summer; Gyorgi invited him in return to a soccer match next summer, also in Edwards Gardens. A pretty psychiatrist wept on his breast in revealing an unhappy marriage; he told her of his own two divorces. A stockbroker took him aside, confided that metals were going to be big, and gave him a business card. Gyorgi went upstairs and got his business card, which he gave to the stockbroker. Gyorgi was overcome by a sophistication he had never known before. In his new expansiveness he slid into discussions.

'Hitler never wanted war,' he said with the authority of one who also has an inside track to matters of importance. 'He waited outside Poland for word from Chamberlain, who double-crossed him and declared war on Germany. The Allies have falsified history. Hitler could have invaded Britain but ordered the generals to hold off, always hoping for peace. The Holocaust was a lie, spread by Jewish international bankers.'

She, meanwhile, had been circling. In the silence that followed his revelations she linked her arm through his and pulled him away just when he was about to heap fact upon startling fact. Tomorrow (he intends) he will tell her: 'It is not respectful for a woman to interrupt a man when he is speaking. You must never do that again.'

Instead, it was she who faced him when everyone had gone. She was calm; there was a hardness about her as she stood looking up at him without a flicker or a twinge. 'You must never, never again reveal your fascism. I will not permit racist talk in my house.'

When the spring sun began to stream through the shiny windows and the lawn gave off a yielding odour, Gyorgi, too, softened. He permitted her to sing for him in the evening, to wear costumes and a little make-up. She accompanied herself at the Bechstein, the rings on both hands flashing under the crystal lights. He listened to her stories of the operas, stories of terror and love and irony and death. He listened and planned. There would be the garden to attend to, storms to be taken down, screens to be installed, diningroom chairs to be repaired. Days of work; music and parties; nights of love. The picture of an old woman dying and leaving him her big house faded, then disappeared altogether.

This night she was dressed as Mimi, looking quite appealing, he thought, in a pink bonnet tied with satin ribbons under her chin. She looked girlish and demure. He even recognized the song in which Mimi asks for a muff to warm her poor, cold hands. Suddenly she broke off, rose abruptly from the piano, turned off the lights, lit a candle, and waving it high overhead, announced:

'I want to die slowly like Mimi.' She placed the candle on the table at the side of his chair and sank at his feet. 'Do you still want to marry me?'

'Marry me . . . ?' Gyorgi repeated, and his voice broke. He saw himself answering the ring at the front door, raising his eyebrows, and, if necessary, directing the caller to the servants' entrance. Forgiveness flowed over him. In his mind he sent money to his mother and father to come for a visit to see what he had made of himself. Then would come his brothers and sisters, each in turn. He drew her up on his lap. He removed Mimi's bonnet and stroked her head.

She, dreaming: 'I feel like Gretel,' cradling into him, 'we will be like Hansel and Gretel, alone in the forest. We will learn to live in innocence, like peasants, gathering nuts and berries, protected from evil by our happiness.'

'You people,' he said, shaking his head, 'I love the way you people want to play poor, with your budgets and your diets, with your gurus and your torn jeans.' Suddenly he became angry. 'It is all one big lie: you people couldn't survive a day's hunger.'

'I'm not pretending. When I marry, Oswald cuts off my alimony. This is his house, lock, stock, and four-poster. We will not be allowed to stay here.' Her teeth were clamped together. 'Oswald would never let us live in his house.'

Gyorgi felt evicted, dislodged from a place in his head. Somehow he did not find it odd that he should be striking out at her. But she was off his lap and out of range with a swiftness that surprised him: she must have expected something like this.

'You tricked me!' he shouted. 'The work . . . the hours . . . I cleaned up your bloody mess . . . it was to have been for me, for me, damn you . . . all this time I was busting my ass for him . . . for *his* house . . .'

In his fury he lunged at her. She ran from him and he after her with his fists extended. His anger also brought confusion: images of her friends, lawyers and judges and others in high places before whom he was powerless: he could smell the acid of a jail cell. He heard a crash. He stopped in his tracks as if shot and he heard her laugh. She was standing with her back to the Bechstein, her rump on the keys, her arms flung out and back in the posture of protection. He was astounded that she knew so little about him after all these days and nights that she could think him capable of harming a Bechstein. He banged his knuckles against each other and did not touch her. He opened his fingers and let his arms hang.

'What will become of you?' she taunted. 'You have been spoiled, spoiled by mahogany and fine linen and oil paintings on the walls. You are unfit now for rented rooms and tired waitresses and the hopes of check-out girls.'

So. They had come to the end of the game. It made him sad: he had liked her: he could have been satisfied. Then, doglike, shaking the discovery off himself, he withdrew, walking backwards. Gyorgi kept going, backwards, stepping over the thick carpets for the last time.

Where she is standing, in her shabby Mimi gown, arms still extended against her beloved piano, dry-eyed, ears strained toward the sounds of Gyorgi's departure, she knows already she will soon sit across the desk from fair, florid Oswald. She hears already his instructions: no calls. Hears Oswald's voice without a rise in it saying: 'What happened this time? Hmm. You got off easy. Give me the account.' She knows, too, that Oswald will lace his pale fingers across his chest and quote for the hundredth time: ' ''Even among galley slaves there were ten percent volunteers.'' For God's sake, when will you stop inviting your own destruction.' She sees already her hungry hand as it moves across the desk. She will take the money to keep her safe for yet another little while.

ADELE WISEMAN

On Wings of Tongue

The winter my father went to Vancouver to look for a job Joe and I were still too young to go to school. We stayed home and my mother found things for us to do after Belle and Arty left the house. In those days the house was full of roomers. You'd be surprised at how many tenants can be crowded into a five room bungalow, particularly if the landlady and her four children are flexible about shifting around to accommodate the guests. For Mrs Lemon alone we had moved our belongings in turn to every room in the house. Every time my mother gave in and said, 'All right, you can come,' we tried to clear out a room other than the one that she had occupied last time, because my mother wanted it to be a fresh start each time. She did not want to remind Mrs Lemon that last time she had moved out because we were piping poison gas into her room.

Joe was still practically a baby. He missed my father terribly. Everybody said so, and I could prove it any time. All I had to say was, 'Where's Daddy? Daddy's gone away.' Fat tears would glaze his trusting eyes; his belly would heave into some mysterious preparatory discipline, and from his mouth would burst the fog-horn bass bellow that was the pride of our house. You couldn't bear to listen for long. Remorsefully, I would yell into his weeping, 'He's coming! He's coming home!' Joe would hesitate uncertainly, the sobs clucking and gurgling. I completed the cure. 'What'll he bring? What'll he bring me?' It was a pleasure to see the joy spread over his good-natured face. 'What'll he bring Joe?'

'Me! Me!' chuckled Joe. I played nicely with him for a while after that.

Every morning I took a trip. Sometimes I took Joe. We had our route laid out. To a certain listing, brown-shingled house down the street we went, labouring through unshovelled snow. Up icy front steps we climbed on all fours. Finally we stood rattling the doorknob and banging with our fists on the door. If no one came to the door I would stand back and let Joe holler into the sparkling air. That was when it was good to have him with me. 'Mrs Fi . . . fer!' His powerful roar shattered the air, scattering the billion tiny crystals that darted thick and glittering in the daylight and sending them blinking to hide in the snow. That brought Mrs Fifer running.

Joe got his voice from an uncle on my father's side. That uncle was born with church bells in his chest. An aesthetic priest had gone mad over his voice and had pressed him into the service of the church choir, because there was no one in all Russia who could intone like he could, 'Christ is risen!' Through three successive pogroms his voice had been the salvation of his entire family, and of everyone else who'd had the sense to seek refuge in his house. For when the parishioners ran amok they left his house religiously alone. 'They respect me,' he used to say, with not a little pride.

We all of us in our house had little characteristics that were passed on to us from relatives, some of whom we had never known, so that we grew up with the feeling that we were part of a much larger family than we actually had. They told me that I took after my aunt Yenta, my mother's sister, who lived only a few blocks away. It was because I talked too much. Yenta herself was always the first, though, to accuse me of spreading family secrets. Nobody ever told me why they weren't secrets until I talked about them. They were just things everybody in the house discussed. But the minute they found out I'd told Mrs Fifer they became secrets.

Mrs Fifer was an old lady. She and her husband lived in one of the ground-floor apartments in the ramshackle house right next door to the apartment of my aunt Yenta's best friend, Dvosieh Krotz. She was always wonderfully pleased to see me, and Joe too, though he wasn't much to talk to yet. She loosed our clothing, unwound our scarves, and gave us cookies from a shredded-wheat box.

As we ate Mrs Fifer would ask me all kinds of questions, and I would answer her while my index finger kept the turning crumbs poked back safely in my mouth. Mrs Fifer liked talking to me. She used to tell my mother what a nice little girl I was to come and visit, and how polite I was to spend time talking to an old lady. My mother always smiled in an apprehensive kind of way.

They were not only family things Mrs Fifer asked about, with her intensely interested, kind old face bent forward to hear what I said. She took an interest in our roomers too, what they said, what they did, what my mother thought of them, did they pay their rent on time, which ones were on relief, did any of them have secret jobs the relief didn't know about, was it true this one had fought with that one over a pot on the stove, and so on. I loved to listen to the talk in our house, so I was particularly good at correcting Mrs Fifer when she said, for instance, 'And did your Daddy say so and so?'

'No, he said such and such,' I would reply, proud to be able to set an adult straight.

How did my auntie always know what I'd been saying to Mrs Fifer? I could tell by her preliminary stamping on the ice outside and by the way she slammed into our house, rattling the frosted windows, how serious her visit was going to be in its consequences for me. She would always call out before she was fully over the threshold, 'I'm not staying. Don't make tea.' She kicked off my uncle's old galoshes and came up the five hall steps, bringing the chill of the outdoors into the room with her. Joe, who sat with his flannel kimono loose, shuddered up and down his rolls of baby fat, accompanying his shudders with resonant, self-comforting growls.

'What?' cried my aunt, readily indignant, 'is the child doing naked?'

'Don't come near him, auntie,' I said, 'Mama's fixing his combinations. We got the other ones wet outside.'

'You,' said my aunt, 'Leubitchka with the active lips, does Mrs Fifer know that too already? It hurts me for you Rivka,' she turned to my mother. 'This child has a faceful of mouth, a mouthful of tongue, a tongueful of every little thing that goes on in this house, so Mrs Fifer can run and spread it like fire all over the prairie.'

'Mrs Fifer's sick,' I said, 'in an armchair, covered over. I was there with Joe.'

'Not too sick to ask questions,' said my aunt bitterly. 'It hurts me, Rivka. . . .'

'It hurts me,' like 'I'm not staying, don't make tea,' was one of those baffling statements that Yenta made. She always stayed. She always drank tea. And she never told you where she hurt. She always changed the subject in mid-sentence. 'It hurts me your name should be dragged through the mud.'

There was no mud any more. 'Through the snow.' I offered.
'What?' said my aunt.

'Nothing,' I said. Maybe she meant 'It hurts me your name
should be dug to the mud.' But why did it hurt? And how did a
name get dragged or dug? Anyway, with her dark, flashing eyes
and glowing skin, she never looked as though anything was
hurting her.

'It's not Mrs Fifer spreads the stories,' said my mother quietly.

'Don't be foolish,' said my aunt heatedly. 'They fly by themselves, all over town.' She looked at me. 'On wings of tongue
they fly.'

I laughed. I liked the way my aunt talked. She laughed too. In
spite of the things she called me we got along, and it sounded as
though it might go easy with me and Mrs Fifer today, though you
never could tell. They laughed and laughed and suddenly they
jumped you.

'Mama says Mrs Fifer doesn't tell anything,' I said, before I could
stop myself.

'Oh she doesn't?' said my aunt. 'So if your mother says she
doesn't then she doesn't. Should I argue? When your mother gets
stubborn I might as well talk to the walls.' My aunt stopped talking.

My mother, smiling, looked up from her stitching. 'How's your
friend Dvosieh?'

My aunt ignored the question and addressed me directly. 'Why
do you talk so much? Where do you get your tongue? Why do
you tell her everything?'

'She asks me,' I faltered. 'I take after you,' I added quickly.

'Don't be disrespectful,' said my mother.

'But you say so,' I said.

'It's not what you say but when,' explained my aunt, 'that makes
respect. Is it true then?' she continued, 'what she told Mrs Fifer?
Are you taking Mrs Lemon in again? As if you haven't got enough
to worry about. Don't do it Rivka. What do you need her for? Tell
her no for a change. Let her find somewhere else.'

'She's here already,' said my mother.

'In the house?' my aunt's voice disappeared suddenly in her
lips.

'No, she had to report to the relief,' said my mother. 'But she
moved in this morning.'

My aunt frowned. Her eyes seemed to light on me.

'That's what I told Mrs Fifer,' I said.

My aunt shook her head. 'She's getting worse, not better. One day she's fine, talks like anybody else; the next day suddenly, out of nowhere, an accusation you can't make sense of; then locks herself in her room, not a word; then starts to run around to the neighbours. Did you hear what happened? Yesterday she went to her husband's people again and made a scandal. She said they're keeping her husband locked up a prisoner in the TB hospital. She said they're paying the government to put germs in his X-rays to kill him. They wouldn't let her into the house so she went shouting up and down their fancy street.'

'It must be very embarrassing for them,' my mother said. 'The rich are so sensitive.'

'It hurts me for them,' said my aunt in a surprisingly satisfied voice for one in pain. 'They didn't even offer her a glass of tea, not a bite. They tried to give her money to go away, five dollars to ease her pain. She threw it at them. And they from behind closed doors, afraid to let her in, a human being like themselves. She didn't have a mouthful of saliva to chew on all day. She walked from their place to the Hudson's Bay Company in the snow, and fainted twice, once in the notions and the second time when they took her to the restroom. So strangers called an ambulance and took her to the hospital. It's all over town.'

'I know,' said my mother. 'An ambulance brought her this morning.'

My aunt laughed. 'She certainly gets free public transportation. It's always ambulances and police cars.' My aunt could never overcome the suspicion that it was somehow useful to Mrs Lemon to be sick. In spite of her hard talk Yenta had taken Mrs Lemon into her own house three disastrous times already. Things always started off well enough, with my aunt proud of how well she could handle a problem that had once again vanquished my mother, and Mrs Lemon temporarily tranquil because she had once again fought off some obscure threat. Then my auntie's crony, Dvosieh Krotz, would come over to sit in and give advice, the same crony who lived behind the wall of Mrs Fifer's flat.

Dvosieh advised friendship and reason, and the sane discussion of past delusions in the calm of present clarity. My aunt showed her friendship through the simple means of frequent reiteration. 'I say to her,' she would explain to my mother, 'You see, I'm your friend, Mrs Krotz is your friend. We're all your friends.' And Yenta was not one to be stingy with her sympathy. 'Your poor husband, where is this "san"? Up north? What's up north? The Eskimos!

Why would they put a TB san up north? So they can cure him of consumption and kill him with pneumonia?'

Under the stress of reason, advice and friendship, Mrs Lemon's suspicions were rapidly forced, like monstrous bulbs, in her mind's darkness. By some inspired stroke of malignancy her fits always crystallized around Yenta's most sensitive spot. My aunt is a wonderful cook and a proud one, justly famed in our neighbour-hood. Mrs Lemon always ended up by accusing her of poisoning her food. My aunt could not resist taking it personally. She would become incensed and run among the neighbours herself. When my mother tried to reason with her she grew even more irate, 'See here Rivka, listen here. You say it's madness, so let it be an equal madness for everybody. Has she ever told you you poison her food? No!'

'But I've gassed her and drugged her and I whisper in her room at night,' my mother defended herself.

'That doesn't make any difference. Three times she's lived in my house and three times I've poisoned her. It's too much. If at least once I'd gassed her I wouldn't feel so much she was delib-erately needling me. She means something by it.'

'She's sick,' sighed my mother.

'You always find something good to say for everybody,' sniffed Yenta.

This time, however, my aunt had a more serious threat to disclose against Mrs Lemon than her own erratic ire. After this last scan-dal in the south end the in-laws had sworn, in front of witnesses, that if it happened once more, if once more she made trouble, they would have her put away.

'They wouldn't,' said my mother after a silence. 'She's harm-less.'

'Oh yes they would,' said my aunt. 'They're out of all patience. Once more and they'll put her away for good. They don't like scandals on the south side.'

'You make money you lose patience,' said my mother.

'Where will they put her away?' I asked.

My mother and aunt looked at each other. 'Nowhere,' said my mother hastily.

'Mrs Fifer has her radio on,' said my aunt, pursing her lips.

'Mrs Fifer hasn't got a radio,' I was happy to contribute.

My mother sighed. 'Just don't repeat everything we've said to Mrs Lemon.'

'All right,' I said. 'I like Mrs Lemon,' I added. 'Joe and I don't want them to put her away. Nor Belle nor Arty neither.'

'Just don't talk,' said Yenta quickly, 'and they won't.'

'She's like you, Yenta,' my mother remarked.

'Like me? How like me? I'm no child. A child shouldn't sell your teeth every time you open your mouth.'

This was not the first time I had heard that 'they' could do something dreadful to Mrs Lemon. No wonder she had fits. I could not separate the idea of Mrs Lemon's being 'put away for good' from the memory of the time our dog Rhubarb had to be put away, and the man had come with a closed wagon with a grilled door in back to take her away, and she had stood still behind the grille, and had left us all standing and watching and stained forever with her mute, despairing eyes. Just let them try to come and get Mrs Lemon.

Mrs Lemon played with us, not the way most adults do, always with the end of the game in sight, as though telling themselves approvingly over their impatience, 'now we are playing with the children for a little while.' Rather, she let us play with her. Quietly she sat or stood or turned as we directed her, never imitating us and never rushing us through her time. We usually played in the kitchen those winter afternoons. Sometimes we played in her room, but my mother didn't like that. She said that if Mrs Lemon saw that we kept strictly away from her room there would be less chance of upsetting her. So it was mostly in the kitchen that we had our games, the warm white kitchen with its frost-fuzzed windows, its big grey electric stove, its knife-scarred wooden table covered by a knife-scarred printed oilcloth, and its wooden rung chairs, behind which Mrs Lemon allowed herself to be barricaded while Joe and I pretended we had captured her and had her in our power. She stood quietly, occasionally saying something nice in reply to my mother, like 'No, they're not bothering me.'

I liked the way Mrs Lemon looked. She made me think. She didn't look like a lemon. She was thin and brown. Her hair was black and rolled round and round at the back of her head. Her eyes were big and bugged out a little, with dark brown middles and yellowish white parts. And she was extra brown all around the eyes.

In spite of my mother's instructions Joe and I were not strangers in Mrs Lemon's room. We knew her few belongings well, especially the raddled orange fur collar with the fox's head and its loosely snapping jaw. On her bureau sat a little brown old-country picture of her mother, her father, and two sturdy boys, with a little, big-eyed girl between them I knew was Mrs Lemon long ago. I always wanted to ask her which one was the brother who had dropped dead when they were burying her father; right into the grave he dropped. I knew all about what a sad life she had had that made her go funny sometimes. But I never did. There was another picture, in a small frame, of Mr Lemon. He wore a white collar and looked bristly, and I said like my mother did when she mentioned him sometimes, 'He'll get well soon,' in the same confident voice that pleased Mrs Lemon. The candy was in an almost empty top right-hand drawer, in a box with a gypsy on it.

Sometimes she would say, 'Do you want to take a walk with me?' And my mother would say, 'Mrs Lemon, you shouldn't, they're too wild.' And she would beg and make promises along with us until my mother said, 'All right, but you mustn't buy them anything.' And Mrs Lemon wouldn't say anything and my mother would bite her lip, for fear she had hurt Mrs Lemon's feelings by implying she couldn't afford to spend her relief tickets on us.

They would truss us up and we would move stiffly off between the snowbanks. I slithered around on Arty's old moccasins and screamed into Joe, knocking him over like a kewpie doll, sideways, into the piled-up snow, where he lay, one arm standing straight out, the other buried. His cries shattered the still, needle-charged air. Mrs Lemon dug him out, soothed him, called him 'little snowman', and I magnanimously let him push me back, which he did, chuckling his deep bass chuckle. I flung myself, screaming into the bank, and waited for a panting Mrs Lemon to right me before I flung myself on Joe again. We were snow-plastered and steaming through every layer by the time we reached the corner grocery. Inside it was hot and dingy and glamorous. We consulted with Mrs Lemon for a long time and then she bought us each a string of pink and white crystallized sugar and a flat square package of bubble gum with a hockey picture in it that Arty would be nice for.

'I'm not giving Arty my hockey picture,' I suggested to Joe. Joe gripped his with his mitt against his chest and shook his head fiercely, eyes shining, cheeks fiery, nose running. But I knew very well he would rush, the minute Arty made his noisy, dishevelled entrance from school, with his hockey picture extended, for the immediate gratification of a big brother's thanks. Arty wouldn't win mine so easily. I knew the subtler pleasures of the drawn-out wooing and the gradual surrender 'I have one too, Arty, see? No you can't. What'll you give me? Can I play in your igloo?'

So the winter passed. One day, late in February, my mother was sitting alone in the kitchen, sewing and humming to herself. Mrs Lemon slipped in so quietly my mother didn't even hear her, till the hissing whisper started her out of her chair. 'Do you think I don't know why you're singing? But you won't get me that easily.' My mother got up and made some tea, which they drank in utter silence. After that, Mrs Lemon stopped talking almost entirely. Sometimes she sat in the kitchen without speaking for hours at a time, while my mother did her work, occasionally throwing her an anxious glance. At other times Mrs Lemon stayed in her room. My mother warned us to leave her alone, then, and I heard her tell my sister that maybe if we just kept still too it would blow over.

One day she left the house very early. She spent the whole day wandering among the neighbours and talking to people about her suspicions. My mother knew what she was doing, as she had often received such confidences when Mrs Lemon was living elsewhere. 'Maybe she'll just talk it out of her system,' she told my aunt, who had come rushing over with the news.

'No.' My aunt was triumphantly certain. 'There'll be trouble.'

Mrs Lemon returned home that evening, thoroughly chilled, blue tints frozen into her swarthy skin, and for the next few days she lay coughing in bed. My mother tended to her, talking gently and soothingly, and pretended she didn't notice that she got no answer.

'Maybe the fever will burn it away,' said my mother hopefully.

'No,' said my aunt, 'I tell you Rivka, you won't avoid a scandal. And this time. . . .'

'I'll try to keep her in the house till it blows over,' said my mother.

The coughing ceased and my mother listened anxiously to the silence. She sighed more frequently as she listened, and raised her hand often from her sewing to run it through her softly waving black hair.

Then one day Mrs Lemon, who must have been waiting behind her door for a long time, took advantage of a moment when my mother had gone into her bedroom to slip out of her room, through the kitchen, down the hall steps and out the side door. Joe and I were playing on the kitchen floor and we called out to her, but she didn't seem to hear our pleased hellos; she was all dug down into her coat. Only the fox winked and snapped at us from her back as she bounded down the steps.

My mother ran out of our bedroom, but too late she scratched at the ice of the window. 'What was she wearing? Was she dressed warmly?'

'Her winter coat and her live fox,' I said. My mother still looked worried. She looked more worried as the day wore on. She talked to my sister in a low voice when Belle and Arty got home from school, and my sister looked worried too. I hung around them and looked worried too, and asked questions that touched on raw worry and was hushed up.

We were eating supper when Mrs Lemon returned. She rushed up the stairs and through the kitchen to her room, still hunched in her coat, and I called after her, but again there was no reply, and my mother shushed me up.

We were still around the table when my aunt came stamping in. She came up the stairs with her coat still buttoned and a very excited expression on her face. 'Is she in?' she nodded in the direction of Mrs Lemon's room, and formed the words through almost silent lips.

My mother nodded.

'You'll have visitors tomorrow,' said Yenta softly, and nodded toward Mrs Lemon's room again. 'Didn't I warn you?' My aunt undid her coat but remained planted in my uncle's old galoshes in the kitchen doorway. 'She went there again, threw herself down into the snow on their lawn, made a big outline, it's still there, for all the neighbours to see, made a scene. . . .' 'She'll catch cold again,' murmured my mother.

'She'll be well taken care of,' said my aunt grimly. She paused and looked anxiously toward Mrs Lemon's room and we all listened with her. 'So . . . that's it. Maybe it's better this way Rivka, though . . . you know . . . somehow . . . it hurts me . . .'

'It hurts me too,' said my mother softly, staring down at Joe's plate. 'It hurts me too.'

The next morning I fought against going out of the house, though a part of me wanted to go and talk to Mrs Fifer. I felt funny-bad all over, and I could tell that my mother felt badly too, though she insisted on sending us out for our fresh air until she realized that there was a blizzard blowing up. I whined about after her all morning, and Joe growled after me. It was out of his range to whine.

By early afternoon the snow was whipping past the windows

and piling up against the fences and walls and making spooky sounds all around the house. We had to turn the lights on. Mama began to worry about the children who were at school. I told her not to worry about any little blizzard bothering Arty and Belle.

Suddenly, Mrs Lemon made her appearance in the kitchen. She looked around quickly and without saying anything went to stand at the kitchen window, looking out to where you could see nothing but swirling snow. My mother was looking at her.

'Joe,' I jumped up. 'Let's capture Mrs Lemon!' Delighted, Joe slid off his chair and began to push it toward her, while I began to push my own. 'You're our prisoner!' I shouted out, and rushed to pull another chair to her side. 'Prisoner!' repeated Joe in organ tones.

'Children!' said my mother.

Mrs Lemon had turned from the window and stood looking at us from behind the chairs.

'Children,' said my mother again. 'Come here!' She had risen.

I looked from her to Mrs Lemon. 'She'll be our prisoner,' I cried. 'Then they can't put her away!'

'Leuba!' cried my mother, in a terrible voice.

I started to cry. 'We don't want them to send Mrs Lemon away!'

At the word 'away', Joe cut loose like a trained bullfrog. 'Gone away!' he bellowed, eyes closed, mouth enormous, comprehending in its quivering pink cavern the whole reverberating enormity of deprival. Unable to compete with his mighty gust of expression I contented myself with short, breathy, gasping whimpers and siren whines.

'Children!' my mother implored, 'children!' We pitched on fervently. 'Away!' I prompted as Joe paused for breath. Instantly he exhaled his heartbreak in a fresh gust of shattering sound.

'Children!' my mother's hands were at her ears. 'Children! Children!'

'Children,' said Mrs Lemon suddenly, from behind her barricade. 'Children,' she said in a dazed voice.

I stopped in mid-note, amazed at the first sound I had heard Mrs Lemon utter in days. Joe, unaware of all else but his art, bellowed on. Confused, I forgot how to turn him off. 'Joe,' I yelled. He redoubled his efforts. His face had turned a fierce red that extended all down his neck. My mother, alarmed, started to pat him lightly on the back, murmuring, 'Yosele, what's the matter? Yosele.'

'Shut up!' I yelled, right into Joe's open mouth, so suddenly that he made a gulp and clicking sound and a little 'whirrr', as though his spring had snapped, and he remained voiceless, staring at me with the big, wounded, swimming eyes of one utterly betrayed.

'Leuba!' cried Mrs Lemon, and for the first time ever, other than to help me across the street or to put on my overthings, she laid her hand on me. She had me gently by the shoulder and her voice was dazed and shocked and urgent. 'Never say that to your brother. Never, never say that to your brother.'

I had an awful feeling inside of me, as though I had swallowed a big stone. I started to cry, this time soft, painful tears that wouldn't make a noise but only little groans inside of me. 'I only meant,' I said to Joe, who was also streaming big, sighing tears, 'I only meant, Daddy's coming, honest Joe, he's coming soon,' I bawled. My mother held and rocked us both.

'They miss their father,' said Mrs Lemon. 'Poor children, they miss their father.'

By the time my aunt arrived, all puffy and snowed over, Mrs Lemon was sitting with Joe on her lap, playing tickle with him and receiving raucous response. No blizzard has ever prevented my aunt from just dropping by at the crucial moment of a crisis, and from sitting with her lips all pursed up and her eyes fixed on one or other of us, with an accusing or anticipatory stare. Only this time she quickly became aware that something was amiss. Yenta's glance shot questioningly back and forth from my mother to Mrs Lemon. What had happened? My aunt looked almost indignant. Had Mrs Lemon gone crazy all of a sudden?

'It's a nice blizzard,' said my mother, looking at her. 'If only people who have far to go would have the sense to stay home.'

'Troublemakers should always stay home,' said my aunt, and smiled at Mrs Lemon in the friendliest way.

Suddenly, three more people were huffing and puffing up the stairs into the kitchen, all in enormous, snowed-over coats, all standing and making cold noises and throwing chills around while my mother and aunt helped them off with their overthings, all apologizing because they were dripping on the kitchen floor, as the hall was too small to hold them. Mrs Lemon went and got a chair from her room and my aunt brought another from our room and my mother took her sewing off another chair and pretty soon they were all sitting and blowing on their knuckles and talking about how cold it was and my mother had a fresh kettle on.

Joe had offered himself genially back to Mrs Lemon's arms, and he now sat at princely ease, staring at the visitors from astride her knee. Mrs Lemon started to demonstrate my brother's extraordinary vocal endowments to the newcomers by tickling his belly. The strangers were struck dumb with admiration.

Then the men started to explain how hard it was to drive in a snowstorm, and how they had started out long ago and had stalled twice along the way. The heavy woman who had come with them sat gingerly on her seat and looked all around and finally up and down over her black beads at my aunt, who wore my uncle's old red woollen socks over her shoes, and pulled right up under her skirt, because my uncle is a tall man, with her bloomers tucked into them. They had big yellow and blue darns on them, beautifully sewn, because my aunt is a perfectionist. The lady coughed as she looked, and my aunt spread her knees further apart to give herself purchase, leaned slightly forward, straight of back, folded her arms across her chest, and stared back, with pursed lips and a coldly ironic eye. My aunt is a handsome woman, with a haughty face and thick, straight black hair. She was not going to be stared down on account of her socks.

One of the men, smallish, with a glistening stone in his tie that looked as though it would melt any minute, leaned from his chair and whispered, hesitantly but loudly enough for me to hear, to the beaded lady, 'Er . . . which one?' The beaded lady then introduced Mrs Lemon as her sister-in-law, and all kinds of cross-introductions were made. I stared at her. This was the enemy, on whose lawns the scandals were enacted, and who never even offered a glass of tea, though my mother even now was pouring hers.

I cannot remember in detail exactly what was said during the next little while, but I do remember that I behaved very badly. The kitchen gradually filled and filled and stretched outward with sound, much of it coming from my lips. Numerous faces all turned toward me, with varying expressions of amazement, distaste, disapproval, despair, as I talked, interrupted, contradicted and mimicked. The rich lady coughed at the smoke from the cigarettes the men had lit, which was mingling with the steam from the kettle to fog up the room. She took noisier and noisier breaths. My aunt told her very kindly that she hoped her brother's ailment didn't run in the family, which made her cough so hard her beads rattled. I started to cough too, and my brother Joe chuckled approvingly at me, adding a stentorian spur to my antics. He thought it was a fine game. My mother pleaded with me in a shocked voice to be quiet, please. I couldn't. I no longer knew how.

Then my aunt and the rich relative got into what seemed to me a traitorously amiable conversation about what an unmanageably talkative child I was, and my aunt told her how I couldn't keep family secrets, and I remember being fiercely hurt that she should sell a family secret of such magnitude to an enemy, and in front of strangers.

Finally, my mother ordered me out of the room and I stood there bawling and insisted that I wouldn't go unless Mrs Lemon came with me. By this time she was the only true ally I had left in the world and I could not leave her to treachery. My last-ditch tantrum was interrupted by loud noises at the door. My brother Arty and my sister Belle were outside quarrelling about who would get into the house first, Belle, with both arms book-laden, with snowpants under her thick coat, besparkled and dishevelled, and chubby Arty, in breeches and high boots and fur-lined jacket, banging his hockey stick against the wall of the house and lashing icicles from the eaves as he argued. There wasn't room for both to squeeze in at once, so meanwhile they held the door open and the blast whipped up blue around the fogged-up kitchen, and everybody shivered.

'I don't care if you are a lady,' challenged Arty, who had wedged his hockey stick in front of Belle so that it suddenly appeared in the kitchen doorway with an ancient pair of razor-sharp skates hanging from knotted yellow laces over its edge.

'Belle! Arty!' boomed Joe joyously, as the skates narrowly grazed his skull. The three strangers exchanged glances as the stick and swinging skates advanced into the kitchen, the blades blinking ferociously and slashing indiscriminately through the air.

'Arty!' cried my mother aghast. 'Belle, shut the door for goodness' sake! We have guests!' she added hopefully.

'I can't,' wailed my sister. 'He won't let me in.'

'Arty, take your skates away!' cried my mother, as the wind howled around the kitchen.

The guests broke for the bedroom. They found their coats. There was confusion in the kitchen for the next few moments, with Belle and Arty getting out of their wet clothes and the guests trying to

get into theirs, and everybody exchanging polite 'good-byes' and
'come agains' and the beaded lady saying something about 'in
good hands', and the small man with the pin saying something
about 'family atmosphere', as he nodded his way vigorously to
the hall. Then they left. Soon afterwards my aunt left, having
just remembered she had a word to say to her friend Dvosieh
down the street. Mrs Lemon said she was tired, suddenly, she
didn't know why, and retired to the quiet of her room.

'What happened?' asked my sister.

'She feels better,' said my mother.

Joe deserted us to go and look at Arty's sled with him in the
cellar. Belle and my mother started doing the dishes. My mother
said she was afraid supper might be a little late tonight. Everything
was flat and quiet suddenly. I picked up the crumbs on the table.
'What can I do?' I asked. My mother came to the table and stood
looking down at me. She looked lovely, with her long, fine nose,
her delicate skin all pink, her deep-set eyes shining golden brown.
'Aren't you tired?' she asked, as though she really thought I might
be, so early.

'No. Can I help you?'

'You know,' said my mother, 'the way you behaved . . .' Suddenly, unaccountably, she grabbed me up, so violently that my
curls bounced over my eyes. 'You've helped enough,' she said
into my ear, and it felt, from the way her stomach was shaking
and from the muffled sounds she was making in my hair, as though
she was laughing.

Notes

CLAUDETTE CHARBONNEAU-TISSOT was born in Montreal in 1947. She has published a number of works of fiction, including *Contes pour hydrocéphales adultes* (1975), *La Contrainte* (1976), *La Chaise au fond de l'oeil* (1979), and *L'Assembleur* (1985).

MARIAN ENGEL was born in Toronto in 1933. She published seven novels, most notably *The Honeyman Festival* (1970) and *Bear* (1976), which won the Governor General's Award; a collection of short stories, *Inside the Easter Egg* (1975); and fiction for children. She died in 1985. *The Tattooed Woman* (stories) was published posthumously in 1985.

MARGARET GIBSON was born in Toronto in 1948. Collections of her short stories include *The Butterfly Ward* (1976) and *Considering her Condition* (1978). She has suffered from mental illness and was hospitalized for the first time at the age of fifteen, an experience that became the basis for her story 'The Butterfly Ward'.

PHYLLIS GOTLIEB was born in Toronto in 1926. She has published poetry including *Within the Zodiac* (1964) and *Doctor Umlaut's Earthly Kingdom* (1974); verse-dramas; and numerous science-fiction novels, including *O Master Caliban!* (1976) and *Emperor, Swords, Pentacles* (1982). Among her collections of stories are *A Judgement of Dragons* (1980) and *Son of the Morning and Other Stories* (1983).

KATHERINE GOVIER was born in Edmonton in 1948. She has published two novels, *Random Descent* (1979) and *Going Through the Motions* (1982). Her recent collection of stories *Fables of Brunswick Avenue* (1985) was widely acclaimed. She has also published journalism in Canada, the U.S., and England.

ELISABETH HARVOR was born in Saint John, New Brunswick, in 1936. Her first collection of stories, *Woman and Children*, was published in 1973. Her stories have appeared in *The New Yorker*, *Toronto Life*, *Saturday Night*, *Hudson Review*, and in the Norwegian anthology *Canada Forteller* (1985).

JANETTE TURNER HOSPITAL was born in Melbourne, Australia, in 1942 and now lives in Kingston, Ontario. She won the Seal Books First Novel Competition in 1982 for *The Ivory Swing* and has since published two novels, *The Tiger in the Tiger Pit* (1983) and *Borderline* (1985).

ISABEL HUGGAN was born in Kitchener, Ontario, in 1943 and now lives in Ottawa. She has published two collections of stories, *First Impressions* (1980) and *The Elizabeth Stories* (1984).

JANICE KULYK KEEFER was born in Toronto in 1953. She now lives in Annapolis Royal, Nova Scotia. Her works include a collection of stories, *The Paris-Napoli Express* (1986) and a book of poetry, *White of the Lesser Angels* (1986).

BHARATI MUKHERJEE was born in Calcutta in 1940. Her works include two novels, *The Tiger's Daughter* (1972) and *Wife* (1975), and *Darkness* (1985), a collection of stories. With Clark Blaise she has published two works of non-fiction: *Days and Nights in Calcutta* (1977) and *The Sorrow and the Terror: The Haunting Legacy of the Air India Disaster* (1987).

MADELEINE OUELLETTE-MICHALSKA was born in 1934 in Rivière du Loup, Quebec. She has published poetry, literary criticism, and journalism. Her novels include *Le Jeu des saisons* (1970), and *La Maison Trestler, ou le huitième jour d'Amerique* (1984). Her collection of essays *L'Échappée des discours de l'oeil* (1981) won a Governor General's Award. She received the Prix Molson in 1982.

MONIQUE PROULX was born in Quebec City in 1952. She has written radio and television plays, as well as film scripts and plays for theatre. She is best known for her short fiction. Her collection *Sans coeur et sans reproche* (1983) received Le Grand Prix Littéraire du Journal de Montreal.

ROBYN SARAH was born in New York in 1949 and grew up in Montreal. She is the author of three books of poetry, *Shadow-play* (1978), *The Space Between Sleeping and Waking* (1981) and *Anyone Skating on that Middle Ground* (1984). Her stories have appeared in *The Antigonish Review*, *The Malahat Review*, *Queen's Quarterly*, and *Canadian Fiction Magazine*.

CAROL SHIELDS was born in Oak Park, Illinois, in 1935. She married and moved to Canada and now teaches at the University of Manitoba. She has published several volumes of poetry, but is best known for her fiction, including *Small Ceremonies* (1976), *The Box Garden* (1977), *A Fairly Conventional Woman* (1982), and *Various Miracles* (1985).

JANE URQUHART was born in Geraldton, Ontario in 1949, and now lives in Wellesley, Ontario. She has published several books of poetry, including *False Shuffles* (1982) and *The Little Flowers of Madame de Montespan* (1983); and a novel, *The Whirlpool* (1986).

HELEN WEINZWEIG was born in Poland in 1915 and came to Toronto at the age of nine. She published her first novel, *Passing Ceremony*, in 1973 and has since published a second, *Basic Black with Pearls* (1980) as well as short stories in *Jewish Dialogue*, *The Tamarack Review*, *Saturday Night*, *Toronto Life*, *The Canadian Forum*, and other magazines.

ADELE WISEMAN was born in Winnipeg in 1928. Her first novel, *The Sacrifice* (1956), won a Governor General's Award. She has since published a second novel, *Crackpot* (1974); *Old Woman at Play* (1978); and plays, including *Testimonial Dinner* (1978). A collection of her essays is soon to be published by Oxford University Press.